MW00442012

Roads to Gettysburg

Lee's Invasion of the North, 1863

By
Bradley M. Gottfried

WHITE MANE BOOKS
SHIPPENSBURG, PENNSYLVANIA

This White Mane Books publication
was printed by
Beidel Printing House, Inc.
63 West Burd Street
Shippensburg, PA 17257-0708 USA

The acid-free paper used in this book meets the guidelines for permanence and durability of the Committee on Production Guidelines for Book Longevity of the Council on Library Resources.

For a complete list of available publications
please write
White Mane Books
Division of White Mane Publishing Company, Inc.
P.O. Box 708
Shippensburg, PA 17257-0708 USA

Library of Congress Cataloging-in-Publication Data

Gottfried, Bradley M.
    Roads to Gettysburg : Lee's invasion of the North, 1863 / by Bradley M. Gottfried.
        p. cm.
    Includes bibliographical references and index.
    ISBN 1-57249-284-8 (alk. paper)
    1. Gettysburg Campaign, 1863. 2. United States. Army--History--Civil War, 1861-1865. 3. Confederate States of America. Army--History. I. Title.

E475.51 .G68 2001
973.7'349--dc21

                                                                    2001045632

To Adele, Mara, and Emily

Contents

Illustrations

Maps

Foreword

The Gettysburg campaign can be divided into three components: the march to the battlefield, the battle, and the retreat to Virginia. For obvious reasons, the battle has overshadowed the other two components. This is unfortunate, for the men performed superbly in reaching the battlefield. Marches of 20, and even 25 miles a day, in hot, dry weather, with little water, were fairly common. While the men may have grumbled, most did their best to keep up with their units.

This book covers the first phase of the battle—from the time that the two armies left the area around Fredericksburg, Virginia, until they reached the battlefield. Most of the emphasis is placed on the infantry, with lesser attention paid to the cavalry. Wherever possible, I have tried to tell the story through the eyes and pen of the participants.

A number of people made this book possible. Harold Collier of White Mane believed in the project and was always supportive. Alexis Handerahan, the associate editor at White Mane, also patiently worked with me to whip the manuscript into shape. The staff of the Gettysburg Military Park Library, particularly John Heiser and Scott Hartwig, were most helpful, as were the staff of the U.S. Army Military History Institute in Carlisle. Last, but certainly not least, I would like to thank my wife, Adele, for her patience as I juggled many activities.

Background

CONFEDERATE

When Robert E. Lee decided to invade the North is not known but may have been as early as the late winter of 1862–63. Thomas J. "Stonewall" Jackson's mapmaker, Jedediah Hotchkiss, was ordered to prepare a map on February 23, 1863, that included the Cumberland Valley, up through Harrisburg, and then east to Philadelphia. In a letter dated April 9, 1863, Lee told Secretary of War James A. Seddon that the best way to relieve pressure in the West was another invasion of Maryland. Two days later, Lee requested that a 550-foot pontoon bridge be delivered to Orange Court House.[1]

After Lee's smashing victory at Chancellorsville over General Joseph Hooker's Army of the Potomac, he was summoned to Richmond for a four-day session with President Jefferson Davis and his cabinet. A variety of military options were discussed, and Lee recommended an invasion of the North. Only Postmaster General John Reagan disagreed. Lee was subsequently permitted to undertake the invasion.[2]

The issue of supplies was also on Lee's mind, as food was particularly scarce during the winter of 1862–1863. The situation was so severe that each man received a daily ration of only 1,800 calories. Each regiment was ordered to send out daily details to collect edible weeds in place of vegetables. The Confederate commissary general, Lucius Northrop, was unsympathetic to Lee's

1

plight and purportedly said, "If General Lee wants rations let him get them from Pennsylvania."[3] By taking the war into Pennsylvania, Lee's troops could draw on the bounty of the land, while relieving Virginia of the burden, particularly during the harvest season.[4]

In late July, Lee reported that at least one rationale for the invasion was to draw Hooker from his strong position opposite Fredericksburg. He knew that it was just a matter of time before Hooker recuperated from his stunning defeat at Chancellorsville and mounted another move toward Richmond. Lee's favorite mode of operation was "the best defense is an active offense." An invasion would put Hooker on the defensive, and avoid another drive on Richmond. At the same time, Lee hoped to remove General Robert Milroy's troops from the Shenandoah Valley, who were destroying large quantities of food and personal property. Lee also believed that an incursion into Pennsylvania would draw Federal troops from other theaters of the war, such as the vital port of Vicksburg, Mississippi, which was now under siege by Ulysses S. Grant's army.[5]

The citizens of the North were getting tired of war, and a victory in Maryland or Pennsylvania would perhaps cause them to demand peace. Discussions about foreign recognition were also back on track—a decisive victory on Union soil could potentially swing the pendulum.[6]

The Confederate army's morale was never higher. The Army of Northern Virginia had rarely been bested, and had achieved smashing victories on battlefield after battlefield. No one believed more in the army than Lee himself. A fortnight before the start of the campaign he wrote, "the country cannot overestimate its [the army's] worth. There never were such men in any army before & never can be again. If properly led they will go anywhere & never fail at the work before them."[7]

In anticipation of the upcoming invasion, General Lee spent an inordinate amount of time trying to scrounge additional troops from other areas. From Samuel Jones's Department of Southeastern Virginia came three infantry regiments and Albert Jenkins's cavalry brigade. John Imboden's cavalry brigade, which was operating in northwestern Virginia, was also added to the army. Lee met with his three corps commanders on June 1 to review the first phases of the invasion. As he looked at them, he must have felt a pang of trepidation. Only one, James Longstreet (First Corps), was tested and found to be effective in handling large bodies of men. General Richard Ewell (Second Corps) had recently returned to the army after losing a leg during the Second Manassas campaign. Finally, there was General Ambrose P. Hill, commander of the newly created Third Corps. Small and sickly, he was aggressive in battle. Questions hovered around the possible lack of aggressiveness of Ewell and the overaggressiveness of Hill. Lee explained to his lieutenants that the first objective was Culpeper Court House. After concentrating his forces there, the army's future movements would be determined by Hooker's activities.[8]

Of great concern to President Davis were the 32,000 men in General John Dix's Department of Virginia. Scattered south and east of the capital, these troops posed a real threat. Indeed, a raid to West Point, about 35 miles from Richmond, occurred during the latter part of May. If anything could stop the invasion, it would be an aggressive campaign by these Federal troops against Richmond.[9]

Climbing to the heights of Telegraph Hill on June 2, Lee and his three corps commanders carefully observed the Federal army below, at Falmouth. He carefully watched for any signs suggesting a future movement on Richmond. Seeing none, Lee decided to begin the invasion the next day.[10]

UNION

The Federal Army of the Potomac was in disarray after its disastrous defeat at the battle of Chancellorsville in early May. Prior army commanders were removed after their defeats, but Hooker was not.[11] One reason is disclosed by Secretary of the Navy Gideon Welles's diary: "The President has a personal liking for Hooker and clings to him when others give way."[12] Hooker was also politically connected, which made his removal all the more hazardous. Hooker's officers did not share this point of view and were ready for a change.[13]

Hooker was content to lick his wounds around Falmouth, Virginia. He had taken over a demoralized army after the Fredericksburg campaign and rebuilt it into a first-rate force. Now the army's morale was again exceptionally low. Not only had it been bested at Chancellorsville, the army had lost about 32 percent of its men through losses at that battle and expiration of terms of enlistment. In this defensive mode, Hooker kept a close watch on Lee's army. Cavalry typically gleans this type of information. However, the army's cavalry commander, General Alfred Pleasonton, was more interested in fighting the enemy soldiers than seeking their location. When he did collect intelligence, he often misinterpreted its meaning.[14]

The disposition of the Army of the Potomac around Falmouth was: I Corps near White Oak Church; II Corps near Falmouth; III

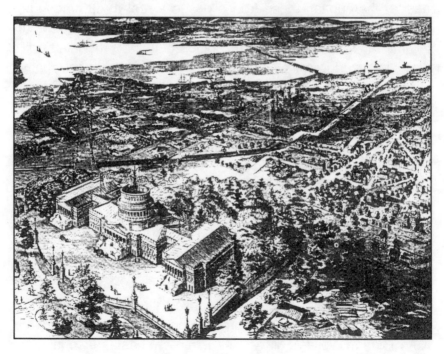

Wartime Washington

Battles and Leaders of the Civil War

Corps at Boscobel (near Falmouth); V Corps near Banks' and United States Fords on the Rappahannock River; VI Corps near White Oak Church; XI Corps near Brooke's Station on the Aquia Creek Railroad; XII Corps near Stafford Court House and Aquia Landing. Two cavalry divisions were camped near Warrenton Junction and a third was near Brooke's Station.[15]

Hooker's Army of the Potomac was not the only sizable force in Virginia. General Samuel Heintzelman commanded the defenses of Washington, which included a small, but mobile cavalry division under General Julius Stahl stationed at Fairfax Court House. The Middle Military Department under General Robert Schenck was headquartered in Baltimore. It included the Harper's Ferry garrison and a division under General Robert Milroy at Winchester. To the south, General John Dix commanded the Department of Virginia, whose troops were scattered along the Virginia coastline in such places as Fortress Monroe, Norfolk, Suffolk, and Yorktown.[16]

The Federal authorities had been sensitized to the danger of a full-scale invasion because of a raid by General William Jones and John Imboden through West Virginia that began on April 21. During the next month, these troopers damaged the Baltimore and Ohio Railroad, captured livestock, and came within 50 miles of the Wheeling-Pittsburgh industrial and mining complex, causing quite a stir among the local authorities.[17]

June 3, 1863

The invasion officially began when Lafayette McLaws's division broke camp and began its dusty march to Culpeper Court House. Lee's other units remained in their camps. All but Hill's Third Corps made preparations to begin their march.[1]

First Corps

The men of McLaws's and John B. Hood's divisions had been ordered to prepare three-days' rations and prepare to move out. This came as no surprise, as they had been told since May 28 to begin preparations. McLaws's men began their march on the night of June 3, first marching south to Spotsylvania, to avoid the prying eyes of the Federal observation balloons. The division halted for the night not far from the Chancellorsville battlefield, and had the distinction of being the first to begin the invasion. Robert Moore of the 17th Mississippi (William Barksdale's brigade) estimated that the men marched seven miles that night. Hood's men remained in camp near Verdiersville, which was closer to Culpeper Court House.[2]

June 3 found George E. Pickett's division far to the south. It had participated in the Suffolk campaign with Hood's division, and now was in camp near Hanover Court House, north of Richmond. Reports of a large body of Union troops caused the division to break camp and march toward Tappahannock. The report proved false, and the men returned to their camp on June 7.[3]

Second Corps

In camp near Hamilton Crossing along the Rappahannock River, Ewell's men were ordered to prepare two-days' rations and be ready to march at a moment's notice. The men did not know their destinations, and rumors were rampant.[4]

Third Corps

Hill's Third Corps remained in its camps near Fredericksburg.

June 4

CONFEDERATE

While McLaws's division continued its march to Culpeper Court House, Hood's division of the same corps, and Robert E. Rodes's division (Second Corps) broke camp and also marched in that direction under the cover of early morning darkness. Lee undertook a number of critical "housekeeping" activities. For example, returning convalescents from Ewell's Second Corps and from Hood's and McLaws's divisions (First Corps) were to be sent directly to Culpeper Court House instead of Fredericksburg.[1]

First Corps

Hood's men grumbled when awoken at 3:00 a.m. It seemed as though they had just gone to sleep at 11:00 p.m. the night before, after cooking their rations. The march toward Culpeper Court House began at sunrise, when the men splashed across Raccoon Ford. Water was scarce and the weather hot and dusty. To make matters worse, the road to Culpeper Court House was hilly. Given these conditions, the men were permitted to frequently halt, so the division did not reach its destination until 1:00 p.m.[2]

McLaws's division began its march at about 5:00 a.m. The route took the men through the bloody Chancellorsville battleground. Unburied soldiers could still be seen from the battle that erupted a month ago. McLaws's men ended their march in the late afternoon near Raccoon Ford on the Rapidan River.

They were comforted to know that somewhere up ahead was Hood's tough division.[3]

Second Corps

While Edward Johnson's and Jubal Early's divisions remained in camp, Rodes's division was up at 2:00 a.m., and on the road an hour later. The men marched 14 miles before finally halting for the night one mile beyond Spotsylvania Court House, at about 3:30 p.m. Samuel Pickens of the 5th Alabama (Edward O'Neal's brigade) recorded in his diary, "it was a very warm day & we were in a cloud of dust most of the time...my eyes, mouth, face & hair were covered with dust."[4]

Third Corps

Lee's initial invasion plan had two corps slipping away from their positions in front of the Army of the Potomac, leaving only General Hill's Third Corps to face the enemy. Hill's orders were to "deceive the enemy, and keep him in ignorance of any change in the disposition of the army." If attacked, Hill was permitted to call up General Pickett's division and General James Pettigrew's brigade from Hanover Junction to the south.[5]

UNION

General Joseph Hooker alerted Secretary of War Edwin Stanton that several enemy camps on the army's right had disappeared during the night. Federal observation balloons near Salem Church could also see clouds of dust in the distance. This was troubling news for the army's commander. John Buford's cavalry division was sent to reconnoiter.[6]

Hooker ordered General George Meade's V Corps to march to vital Banks' Ford over the Rappahannock River. The other corps' orders for the day were to "have reveille at daylight; your command at arms for half an hour after, your batteries harnessed, and everything in readiness for any movement that may be ordered."[7]

Down the peninsula below Richmond, General John Dix wired General Hooker that he was about ready to venture north toward

Williamsburg. He admitted to Hooker, "my force is small, and you must not count on anything more than a diversion." If this caused Hooker some concern, it should have, as it was the first indication of Dix's timidity in moving on Richmond.[8]

I Corps

Orders arrived at 3:00 a.m. for Abner Doubleday's division to prepare for a march. The tents were struck and the men were ready to march by 8:00 a.m. The hours rolled by. The soldiers were then ordered to march to the parade grounds, where they stacked arms. Then they marched to the commissary and drew rations. Their marching orders were countermanded, so they returned to their former camps and threw up their tents. William Perry of the 150th Pennsylvania (Charles Stone's brigade) noted that "all are in good spirits, ready and almost anxious to move."[9]

V Corps

Beginning at 3:00 a.m., General George Meade's Corps marched from Stoneman's Switch to Banks' Ford to guard this vital Rappahannock River crossing.[10]

XI Corps

The men were up at 2:00 a.m. and told to be ready to march in an hour. The column was finally on the road at 4:30 a.m., but marched less than a quarter of a mile to some breastworks. The men remained there for half an hour, then marched back to their camps. Word had it that the officers were trying to see how fast the soldiers could deploy in the event of an attack.[11]

June 5

CONFEDERATE

The concentration toward Culpeper Court House continued. Hood's division reached its destination, while McLaws's division remained in camp south of Verdiersville. With the breaking of camp by Johnson's division at Fredericksburg, all of Ewell's Second Corps were on the road to Culpeper Court House. Left behind was General A. P. Hill's Third Corps, which closely observed the enemy near Fredericksburg. This was quite a gamble on Lee's part. By placing a corps of merely 22,000 men in the path of General Joseph Hooker's large Federal army, Lee risked losing Richmond, should the enemy decide to sweep south toward the capital. Lee probably realized that such a movement would lay open a path to Washington, resulting in a swapping of captured capitals.[1]

Suddenly, the Federal troops on the north side of the river became active. Surgeon L. Guild noted in his report that "the enemy made considerable demonstration opposite Fredericksburg, brought down their pontoon train with great flourish, and in the afternoon of yesterday [June 5], under the protection of eighteen or twenty pieces of artillery, crossed over quite a force, capturing about 50 of our men in the rifle-pits." Lee noted that the enemy's movement was "so devoid of concealment, that I supposed the intention was to ascertain what forces occupied the position at Fredericksburg, or to fix our attention upon that place while they should accomplish some other object." Lee later believed that it

11

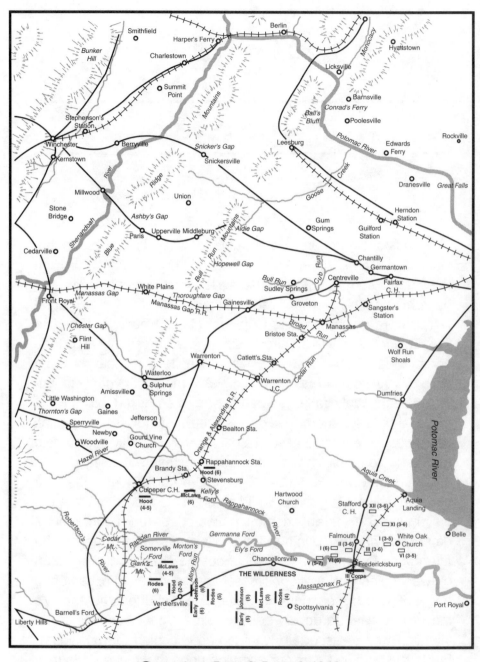

Operations June 3–June 6, 1863
(Dates in June in parentheses)

was merely a reconnaissance in force, as the enemy had seen his five divisions marching toward Culpeper Court House. He did not know this at the time, so he was forced to halt his five divisions in their tracks, and ordered A. P. Hill's Corps's mobilization toward the river.[2]

Of equal concern to Lee was the activity of Federal troops south of Richmond, suggesting another raid on the capital. As Lee closely watched the situation, troops from other commands were rushed to the area. The prospect of losing Pickett's division (First Corps) and Pettigrew's brigade (Henry Heth's division, Third Corps), should they be needed to defend Richmond, was a real one.[3]

On a lighter note, General James Ewell Brown "Jeb" Stuart decided to host a grand review of his 9,500-man cavalry division at Brandy Station. Trainloads of civilians, including President Jefferson Davis and most of his cabinet, arrived to watch the gala event, as did Hood's 8,000-man infantry division. Lee missed the grand affair because he was back at Fredericksburg watching the enemy's movements.[4]

First Corps

While McLaws's division remained in camp all day, Hood's men were on the road by 8:00 a.m. Marching through Culpeper Court House, they continued several miles beyond it to the hamlet of Brandy Station. Here they had the privilege of witnessing Stuart's cavalry grand review. R. T. Cole of the 4th Alabama (Evander Law's brigade) called it the "grandest and most spectacular display." Most of the men were as interested in the pretty women in the audience as they were with the main "show." The division then retraced its steps to Culpeper Court House, where it went into camp.[5]

Second Corps

Rodes's men were on the road again by 6:00 a.m. They were pleased that the heavy dew had settled the dust. Unfortunately, the roads dried out as the sun rose, and the dust reappeared. The 20-mile march finally ended at about 5:00 p.m. near Verdiersville. Samuel Pickens, a hardened veteran of O'Neal's brigade, noted that "I never was so tempted to fall out of ranks for I was almost as badly used up....my legs pained all over & my feet were getting rubbed and sore."[6]

Early's and Johnson's divisions broke camp shortly after midnight, with the former in the lead. Following Stonewall Jackson's custom, General Ewell marched the men 50 minutes, then gave the men a 10-minute rest, before starting the process again. Crossing fields, the men reached Spotsylvania Court House at sunrise. After a two-hour rest, the two divisions were back on the road at 9:00 a.m. The column finally halted for the night near Verdiersville at about 2:30 p.m. Many of the men immediately relieved themselves of their layers of dust by jumping into Catharpin Creek.[7]

Third Corps

Federal artillery opened a furious fire almost as soon as Ewell's Second Corps left. Before long, Federal infantry forced their way across the river. Hill formed his men into a column at 10:00 p.m. and marched them from their camps near Moss Neck to Hamilton Crossing, arriving there the next day (June 6).[8]

UNION

Orders reached the commanders of the II, XI, and XII Corps at about 9:00 a.m. to have their commands ready to move out at short notice with three-days' rations. All leaves of absence were revoked.[9]

General Hooker sent a telegram to President Abraham Lincoln at 11:30 a.m., informing him that the enemy had abandoned several camps on his left flank near Hamilton's Crossing. Hooker was concerned about this situation, as he did not know whether the enemy was changing camps, or was on the move. Reports from deserters caused Hooker to believe that Lee was about to repeat the movements of the prior year, when he first swept around the Federal army's right flank, and then headed for Washington. "He must either have it in mind to cross the Upper Potomac, or to throw his army between mine and Washington," he wrote. Reminding

Lincoln of the army's orders of the "importance of covering Washington and Harper's Ferry, either directly or by so operating as to be able to punish any force of the enemy sent against them," he asked if he could "pitch into his [Lee's] rear, although in so doing the head of his column may reach Warrenton before I can return."[10]

Hooker did not have long to wait for a reply, for at 4:00 p.m., Lincoln wrote that he did not have the requisite military experience, and had directed the question to his general in chief, Henry Halleck. Lincoln did warn Hooker about attempting to cross the Rappahannock River to fall on the enemy's rearguard, for it would detain the troops, while Lee marched rapidly north. "In one word, I would not take any risk of being entangled upon the river, like an ox jumped half over a fence and liable to be torn by dogs front and rear, without a fair chance to gore one way or kick the other. If Lee would come to my side of the river, I would keep on the same side, and fight him or act on the defense."[11]

General Halleck weighed in about 40 minutes later, reiterating his orders of January 31, 1863, which "left you entirely free to act as circumstances...might require, with the simple injunction to keep in view the safety of Washington and Harper's Ferry." Halleck did suggest that Hooker strike any detached enemy force moving northward and destroy it.[12]

Hooker informed the secretary of war at 6:45 p.m. that Jeb Stuart's Confederate cavalry was at Culpeper Court House. He finally decided to send the VI Corps on a reconnaissance mission across the Rappahannock River to ascertain what was going on.[13]

I Corps

The men were again told to be ready to march in the morning. Canteens were filled and the men loaded three-days' rations into their haversacks. However, the orders to move out never arrived.[14]

VI Corps

General John Sedgwick was ordered to hold his corps in readiness to support the engineers who were throwing a pontoon bridge over the Rappahannock River opposite Deep Run, just south of Fredericksburg.[15]

June 6

CONFEDERATE

Ascertaining that the Federal incursion across the Rappahannock River by part of the VI Corps was not a threat, Lee put his four divisions in motion again toward Culpeper Court House. Hood's division had already reached its destination, and the others were not far away. Lee also thought it was safe enough for him to leave Fredericksburg and ride toward the rendezvous point.[1]

First Corps

The day began quietly for Hood's men. They were told to clean their guns and prepare for an inspection, but these orders were soon countermanded. Instead they were ordered to prepare three-days' rations. A frustrated Thomas Ware (Henry Benning's brigade) wrote, "so we have 3 days rations of flour to cook & no cooking utensils." The march began at noon, as the men again took the road to Brandy Station. A shower brought immediate relief as it squelched the dust and cooled the men. They marched to Stevensburg, then took the roads leading to the Rappahannock River, where a two-hour halt was permitted at 11:00 p.m. After that, they were told they would cross the river to attack the enemy.[2]

McLaws's men forded the Rapidan at Raccoon Ford and continued to march toward Culpeper Court House. When within

16

two miles of it, the column veered to the right and marched to Stevensburg, where the men camped for the night.[3]

Second Corps

Rodes's men were on the road by 5:00 a.m., but halted after marching just four miles. Reveille sounded at 3:00 a.m. in Early's and Johnson's camps, and the men were in line an hour later. They too halted for the same reason as Rodes's: a Federal thrust across the Rappahannock River had caused Ewell to halt all movements toward Culpeper Court House. Instead, the men remained in camp and were ordered to prepare two-days' rations. They could hear cannon fire from the direction of Fredericksburg and knew a fight was imminent. While Rodes's men remained in camp for the remainder of the day, Early's and Johnson's divisions continued their march at about 3:00 p.m., halting a few hours later where the Plank and Spotsylvania Roads intersected.[4]

Third Corps

The men arrived at Fredericksburg in the morning, and a picket line was thrown toward the Rappahannock River, which drove the Federal skirmishers back across the river. That night, the Federals' bands played and their soldiers shouted from across the river. General Joseph Davis's brigade arrived from the south and was assigned to Henry Heth's division.[5]

UNION

With additional sightings of rebel troops massing at Culpeper Court House, Hooker wired Halleck that he intended to send all of his cavalry and three thousand infantry in that direction to attack them. Because of the dispersed nature of this expeditionary force, the attack would not be launched until the morning of June 9.[6]

At the same time, Hooker ordered General Sedgwick's VI Corps across the Rappahannock River at Deep Run. His orders were to make a "reconnaissance in front of the bridges, and ascertain the position and strength of the enemy. Throw your corps over the river, if necessary." General Meade's V Corps was also ordered to "feel the enemy, and cause him to develop his strength....let your pickets chat enough not to tell him anything, but to find out his regiments."[7]

While Colonel Alfred Duffié, with 2,500 troopers, was sent across the river at Sulphur Springs to ascertain the enemy's position, the II and XI Corps were again told to prepare for a march with three-days' rations. Duffié ultimately came within four and one-half miles of Culpeper before turning back.[8]

A somewhat exasperated Secretary of War Edwin Stanton wrote to Hooker: "I have been trying hard to keep the women out of your camp, [but I] have given up the job. I think no officer or soldier should have his wife in camp or with the army. In other military districts, the order of the Department excludes them."[9]

Meanwhile, farther south, five thousand men under General Erasmus Keyes moved north to Walkerton, about 23 miles from Richmond. However, the proximity of General George Pickett's Confederate division retarded these movements.[10]

I Corps

James Wadsworth's division was ordered to Franklin's Crossing where it formed line of battle in support of the VI Corps, which had crossed the Rappahannock River.[11]

V Corps

Hooker's orders to the V Corps meant probing attacks against the enemy. Passing this request on to division commander George Sykes, the latter fired back, "I am opposed to any movement across the river with the forces I have....it is hardly to be expected that anything reliable would be gained, even supposing it could be obtained from such sources." Not to be put off, Hooker had the following order sent to Meade: "you are not to disregard the order to feel the enemy a little."[12]

VI Corps

General John Sedgwick received orders to make a reconnaissance near the river to ascertain the strength and disposition of the enemy. He could cross the river with one division, if necessary, and seize any civilians who might have information about the enemy's whereabouts.[13]

The sudden orders to break camp at White Oak Church caused a sense of mystery to permeate the corps. They grumbled that it was just like Hooker to keep them in the dark. Additional orders arrived for the men to prepare three days' rations, then four. The men were on the road at 2:00 p.m. It was a hot, dry, and dusty day as the column marched toward the Rappahannock River. According to Wilbur Fiske of the 2nd Vermont (Thomas Neill's brigade), there seemed to be a "dead dullness and silent gloom" hanging over the column. The men were in a rotten mood because none of them relished the idea of attacking the heights again as they had at the battle of Chancellorsville, where the corps was almost annihilated. To make matters worse, they didn't even have whiskey.[14]

As the corps approached the Rappahannock River, the men could see a pontoon bridge and knew that they would again be ordered across the river. The column halted as several batteries took position and opened a devastating fire on the Confederate rifle pits across the river. So severe was the sustained fire that Wilbur Fiske was sure the sounds could be heard in Vermont. The rebels could soon be seen scampering to safety. Now it was time to capture the rifle pits, and the 5th New Jersey and 26th New Jersey were ordered into pontoon boats for this task. The rebels still in the pits hazarded the continued artillery barrage and fired into the approaching Yanks. In the end, the Federals prevailed, capturing the pits and about 150 enemy soldiers.[15]

Other units of Albion Howe's division, and Alfred Torbert's brigade (Horatio Wright's division) crossed the river to stabilize the beachhead. The remainder of the corps remained in support on the north bank of the river. With no enemy in sight, and with nothing to do, the men dropped off to sleep with their heads on their knapsacks. During this time, General Sedgwick examined the intelligence reports and wrote to Hooker, "I cannot move 200 yards without bringing on a general fight. Before bringing over the rest of my corps, I await orders. I am satisfied that it is not safe to mass the troops on this side." In response, Sedgwick was told to keep only one division on the south side of the river. Little did Sedgwick know that he faced but one Confederate corps under A. P. Hill.[16]

June 7

CONFEDERATE

The movement of most of Lee's army continued. By nightfall, five of Lee's nine infantry divisions were concentrated at Culpeper Court House. Now under Lee's command, Imboden's cavalry brigade was ordered to attract the enemy's attention in Hampshire County and Romney (now West Virginia), and attack the Federal troops guarding the Baltimore and Ohio Railroad. In the Shenandoah Valley, General Jenkins's cavalry brigade was to ride to Front Royal, and reconnoiter northward toward Martinsburg.[1]

Lee also wanted other troops. He requested that Pickett's division join him from Hanover Junction, and that Micah Jenkins's veteran infantry brigade be mobilized from Suffolk. He believed that only 1,500 enemy occupied Suffolk, and that Robert Ransom's brigade could handle them. As an incentive, Lee hypothesized, "I think if I can create an apprehension for the safety of their right flank and the Potomac, more troops will be brought from their lines of operations in the south."[2]

First Corps

Hood's men were pleased to learn at 2:00 a.m. that they would not be called upon to cross the Rappahannock River and attack the enemy. This did not prevent Thomas Ware (15th Georgia) from writing in his diary, "thus our long & wearied march was in vane. All quite wet & no fires allowed...we suffered & some got but little sleep." The men were up at sunrise and commenced the return march to Culpeper, reaching there about noon. As they arrived, they noted that McLaws's division, which had marched from Stevensburg that morning, had joined them, and Early's division (Second Corps) was nearby.[3]

Pickett's division finally reached its camp around Hanover Court House about noon, after its march toward Tappahannock, Virginia on June 3.[4]

Second Corps

Ewell's Corps's march continued at about 4:30 a.m. Heavy rains the night before had dissipated the dust and it was cold, making the marching almost pleasant. Rodes's men finally reached Culpeper Court House at 3:00 p.m. and continued four miles to the east side of the town, where the men went into camp. Early's and Johnson's divisions waded across the Rapidan River at Somerville Ford and rested for about two hours on the Orange and Alexandria Railroad before continuing. The march finally ended when the head of the column was about three miles from Culpeper Court House. Randolph McKim of the 1st Maryland (George Steuart's brigade) noted a lack of rations and recorded that one wag said, "they put a fellow in the guard-house now for taking a drink of water; and as to eating—that's out of the question." The troops marched about 19 miles.[5]

Third Corps

Still in their rifle pits near Fredericksburg, Hill's men warily watched the Federal troops who had crossed the river.

UNION

The VI Corps remained straddled across the Rappahannock River. Despite General Sedgwick's assurances that Lee's entire army was on the south side of the Rappahannock River, Hooker was not so sure. The enemy cavalry's concentration near Culpeper, south of the Rappahannock River, perhaps concerned him most.

Hooker sent General Pleasonton orders to "cross the Rappahannock at Beverly and Kelly's Fords, and march directly on Culpeper...to disperse and destroy the rebel force assembled in the vicinity of Culpeper, and to destroy his trains and supplies of all description...." Adelbert Ames's and David Russell's brigades of the III Corps were also dispatched to assist the cavalry. Prior to leaving, Russell received 600 troops from each the I and VI Corps, and another 300 from the II Corps. While ordering the cavalry to split up during the attack, Hooker advised that the infantry remain together "as in that condition it will afford you a *moving point d'appui* to rally on at all times, which no cavalry force can be able to shake." If successful, Pleasonton was to vigorously pursue the enemy.[6]

Other troops were also put into motion, like General Julius Stahel's cavalry, which had been guarding the Orange and Alexandria Railroad, and was now sent to the Shenandoah Valley to reconnoiter. He would not leave for two days, and with only two small regiments totaling 600 men.[7]

Realizing that the Middle Military Department was too large, the Washington high command subdivided it to form the Department of the Monongahela under the command of General William T. Brooks, with headquarters in Pittsburgh. Brooks was encouraged to build fortifications using volunteer civilians. To assist in this effort, General Halleck dispatched Captain Cyrus Comstock of the Corps of Engineers there to "assist the municipal authorities and the people in preparing for their own defense." He went on to state that Comstock was to "assist and animate them in the performance of this patriotic duty, should the occasion arise."[8]

V Corps

Meade's orders to cross the Rappahannock River were clarified by General Daniel Butterfield of Hooker's staff: "the idea was to find out, if possible, what troops the enemy have at Banks' Ford, without bringing on a fight." A little later, Butterfield felt another clarification was in order: "the general [Hooker] does not desire any demonstration, and only a feeler at Banks' Ford, to ascertain, if possible, what is opposite you there."[9]

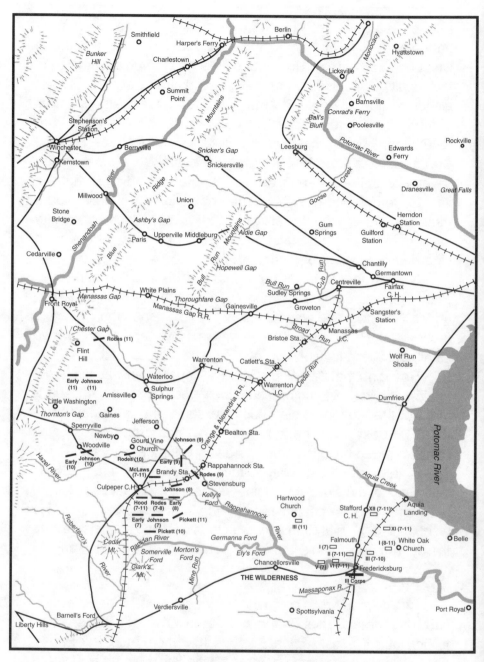

Operations June 7–June 11, 1863
(Dates in June in parentheses)

At about 11:30 p.m., Meade was able to report that there were fewer enemy pickets across the river. The Confederate pickets indicated that they were ordered to open fire on officers when the opportunity presented itself. This was against the unwritten code of ethics, and not a good sign.[10]

VI Corps

Astride the Rappahannock River, Sedgwick's VI Corps waited. Sharp picket fire erupted, but neither side chose to advance. As many as 40 men from the 6th Vermont (Grant's brigade) were killed or wounded on the picket line. Wright's division marched across the river to relieve Howe's division. The Union high command began to realize that the mission was a failure, as it was not gathering the information needed about Lee's army.[11]

June 8

CONFEDERATE

With the arrival of Johnson's and Early's divisions, Lee had two-thirds of his army at Culpeper Court House. Stuart decided to hold another grand review of his cavalry now that Lee had also arrived. Lee teased Stuart, whose horse had a wreath around its neck, "Take care, General Stuart, that is the way General Pope's horse was adorned when he went to the Battle of [Second] Manassas." After reviewing the troops, General Lee wrote to Josiah Gorgas about the condition of the men's saddles and carbines: "the former ruined the horses' backs, and the latter were so defective as to be demoralizing to the men."[1]

Lee continued to worry about his uncertainty of Hooker's position. He did know that the enemy had constructed rifle pits from the mouth of Deep Run to Mansfield. In a dispatch to General Hill, Lee wrote, "I think from what you state and other indications, that the mass of General Hooker's army cannot be very near Fredericksburg. Its exact position or intention I have not yet discovered."[2]

Lee came in mild conflict with Generals William Whiting and Daniel Hill in North Carolina. A Federal incursion on Wilmington caused them to balk at sending troops to Lee, so he wrote to the secretary of war, James A. Seddon, "I cannot suppose that so large a force [of enemy troops] as is estimated by Generals Whiting and Hill could have been thus cooped up by so small a body of men." Citing his needs, Lee continued, "I think our southern coast might be held during the sickly season by local troops, aided by a small organized force, and the predatory excursions of the enemy be repressed. This would give us an active force in the field with which we might hope to make some impression on the enemy, both on our northern and western frontiers. Unless this can be done, I see little hope of accomplishing anything of importance."[3]

First Corps

McLaws's and Hood's men remained in camp watching Ewell's Corps march past them. Hood's men were again invited to Stuart's cavalry review, but only if they behaved themselves by not taunting the horsemen.[4]

Although they had just returned to their camps at Hanover Court House the day before, Pickett's men were ordered to permanently break camp and begin their march toward Culpeper Court House. The division covered about 20 miles, camping about two miles northwest of New Market.[5]

Second Corps

While Rodes's division remained in camp, reveille sounded in Early's and Johnson's divisions' camps at 4:00 a.m., and the men were on the road within two hours. The soldiers were issued strict orders against straggling. "No man to leave ranks even for water and not at any time with his gun," noted Lt. William Kincheloe of the 49th Virginia (William Smith's brigade). Early's division passed through Culpeper Court House at about 9:00 a.m.; Johnson's entered about 90 minutes later. The column halted a short distance outside of town, where the men were permitted to rest. The two divisions finally bivouacked for the night about three miles from town. Here they finally reunited with Rodes's men.[6]

Third Corps

Heth's division increased in size by about 2,600 men when Pettigrew's brigade arrived from North Carolina.[7]

UNION

Using the cover of darkness, Pleasonton moved his troopers into position for an attack on Stuart's cavalry near Brandy Station. Buford's cavalry division and Ames's infantry brigade took position near Beverly Ford, while Duffié's and David Gregg's cavalry divisions, and Russell's infantry brigade, massed near Kelly's Ford. The rest of the army remained in their camps.[8]

Further north, all of the high-ranking officers were abuzz with speculation that Stuart's cavalry was about to launch a heavy raid into Federal territory. General Robert Milroy in Winchester suggested that the militia be called out in Maryland, Pennsylvania, and Ohio.[9]

I Corps

Wadsworth's division, which had been supporting Sedgwick's VI Corps at Franklin's Crossing, returned to its former camps near White Oak Church.[10]

June 9

CONFEDERATE

Federal cavalry, infantry, and artillery, massing near Beverly and Kelly Fords on the Rappahannock River, profoundly disturbed Lee. He informed Stuart that General Longstreet had an infantry division near Stevensburg, and General Ewell's Corps was near Brandy Station. His orders to Stuart were to "not to expose your men too much, but to do the enemy damage when possible." These orders were never carried out because Stuart was attacked by Pleasonton's Federal cavalry even before he had the chance to read them. Stuart did not expect an attack, so his units were dispersed, and few pickets were in place. The Federal attack was initially successful, but Stuart was able to regain his position toward the end of the pitched battle of Brandy Station. One Richmond newspaper reported that the battle "narrowly missed being a great disaster to our arms. Our men were completely surprised, and were only saved by their own indomitable gallantry and courage." Stuart's actions at Brandy Station, and those later in the campaign, tarnished his heretofore stellar reputation.[1]

First Corps

The attack on Stuart's cavalry brought an immediate halt to what McLaws's and Hood's men were doing. The men were ordered into line and swiftly marched toward the hostilities, where they formed into line of battle at noon. Many rigged their blankets to provide shelter from the sweltering sun. The men remained here until darkness fell, when they were ordered back to camp.[2]

Pickett's division continued its trek toward Culpeper Court House between 6:30 a.m. and 4:30 p.m.[3]

Second Corps

Rodes put his command in motion from Culpeper Court House in anticipation of orders to march toward Brandy Station in support of General Stuart's cavalry. Ewell's orders to do just that reached him a short time later. Rodes was joined by Generals Lee and Ewell at the Barbour House where they watched the swirling cavalry fight. For a moment, it looked as though the Federal cavalry would sweep through and capture the three generals. Ewell suggested that they barricade themselves in the house, but this was not necessary as Stuart's troopers finally gained the upper hand.[4]

The morning for Early's and Johnson's divisions was a quiet one. Just as several brigades were about to be inspected, orders arrived to immediately break camp and march toward Brandy Station where a cavalry fight was in progress. The column halted and formed line of battle when within one mile of Brandy Station. Nothing transpiring, the men rested on their arms for the night. James Hall of the 31st Virginia (Smith's brigade, Early's division) noted in his diary, "I expect tomorrow will tell a bad tale."[5]

UNION

Pleasonton had his troopers in position as early morning fog enveloped the area near Brandy Station. Ordered to charge, the Federal horsemen swept all before them. Confederate resistance stiffened as Stuart's veterans realized what was occurring. What followed was a pitched battle, perhaps the greatest cavalry action on U.S. soil, which ended with Pleasonton's pulling back across the Rappahannock River. One Richmond newspaper grudgingly wrote that the "Yankees withdrew slowly, disputing every foot of ground." The paper also accurately noted that the Confederate

The cavalry fight at Brandy Station

Battles and Leaders of the Civil War

troopers, who formerly had had their way with the enemy, "were astonished at their persistence, bravery, and audacity."[6]

General Hooker sent two important dispatches on June 9. The first went to General John Dix on the peninsula below Richmond, with information that Pickett's Confederate division was marching north to the Rapidan River, leaving the road to Richmond open. The second dispatch was addressed to General Halleck, informing him of the cavalry fight at Brandy Station. Hooker erroneously wrote that General Pleasonton was "not able to make head against it [Stuart's cavalry]."[7]

Hooker again asked whether he should drive south toward Richmond. Lincoln's response was swift, "I would not go south of [the] Rappahannock upon Lee's moving north of it." Lincoln wisely told Hooker, "I think Lee's army, and not Richmond, is your sure objective point." Continuing, he wrote, "follow his flank...shortening your lines while he lengthens his. Fight him too, when opportunity offers. If he stays where he is, fret him and fret him." Hooker was vindicated by historian Wilbur Nye, who strongly believed that Lee would have aborted the invasion and moved south to defend Richmond had Hooker crossed the Rappahannock River at this time.[8]

VI Corps

Still astride the Rappahannock River, the VI Corps drew the attention of the Confederate sharpshooters. The sniping became so intense at one point that two hundred Berdan's Sharpshooters were sent to quiet the enemy. With uncanny accuracy, the sharpshooters soon forced the rebels to take cover.[9]

June 10

CONFEDERATE

Lee waited 18 hours following the battle of Brandy Station to see what Generals Hooker and Pleasonton would do next. When the Federal troops did nothing, Lee ordered Ewell to continue the offensive.[1]

First Corps

McLaws's and Hood's men remained quietly in camp near Culpeper Court House. Attempting to close the distance with his two sister divisions, Pickett drove his men across the Rapidan River at Somerville Ford, and halted for the night about eight miles south of Culpeper Court House.[2]

Second Corps

Ewell's Corps returned to its former position near Culpeper Court House at about 11:00 a.m. The invasion continued when the column marched 20 miles northeast, beginning between 3:00 and 4:00 p.m. Early's and Johnson's divisions took the Old Richmond Turnpike, which ran from the capital to Winchester, while Rodes's division marched on a parallel road toward Gaines' Crossroads. The former divisions camped at Woodville; the latter at Gourd Vine Church.[3]

UNION

Hooker wrote to Lincoln that the fight at Brandy Station "crippled him [Stuart] so much that he will have to abandon his contemplated raid into Maryland, which was to have started this morning." However, in the very next paragraph, Hooker admitted that it might merely delay the invasion. With this in mind, he again requested permission to strike south against Richmond, which he believed would end the rebellion.[4]

Pleasonton's cavalry was ordered to Warrenton Junction, where it remained through June 15, guarding the nearby fords. General Halleck differed with Hooker in believing that Stuart's raid was aimed for Pittsburgh. As a result, Halleck issued orders for that city's defense. New concerns surfaced with the news that Longstreet's infantry corps was now at Culpeper Court House.[5]

General Schenck, commanding the VIII Corps in the Middle District, reported that he had 12,479 troops at Harper's Ferry and another 7,579 at Winchester, for a total of 20,058. Despite these healthy numbers, General Halleck's concern about the safety of Milroy's troops at Winchester and Berryville continued to grow. After sending a variety of vague messages about pulling back, Halleck's aide sent an order that could not be misunderstood: "you will immediately take steps to remove your command from Winchester, Va., to Harper's Ferry."[6]

A new military department was created, the Department of the Susquehanna, which included all of Pennsylvania east of Johnstown. General Darius Couch, a distinguished officer who had commanded the II Corps, commanded the new department. Never a fan of Hooker, the fiasco at Chancellorsville was the final straw. He resigned from the army and was given the new military department.[7]

II Corps

With the transfer of General Couch to the Department of the Susquehanna, General Winfield Hancock assumed command of the II Corps.

III Corps

In the absence of General Dan Sickles, who was on leave, General David Birney commanded the III Corps.

VI Corps

As is the case in most campaigns, the enlisted men near the Rappahannock River were not privy to the bigger picture. Many could not understand why the Confederates, obviously in strong numbers nearby, did not attack and crush the Federal beachhead. The stalemate was unsettling for all of them. That evening, the men were treated to a Confederate "concert," complete with bands playing and soldiers singing.[8]

June 11

In response to his constant requests for additional troops, and suggestions about the movement of others, the secretary of war wrote to Lee about the "dangers to which our destitution of a covering force to this city [Richmond] and the railroad may expose us. I have not hesitated, in co-operating with your plans, to leave this city almost defenseless." Lee's heart probably sank when he read that Jenkins's brigade (Pickett's division) would remain in North Carolina, nor would other troops be forthcoming.[1]

First Corps

McLaws's and Hood's men remained at Culpeper Court House, where drilling became commonplace. Pickett's division finally halted three miles south of town, where the men went into camp.[2]

Second Corps

Ewell's march continued at about 4:30 a.m. His destination was Winchester and Berryville, where the enemy occupied the lower valley. General Rodes called the road toward Newby's Crossroads "the worst road I have ever seen troops and trains pass over." Finding a section of the road completely impassable, and his men and horses nearing exhaustion, Rodes ordered a detour to the Richmond Turnpike. The original route was selected because it promised to be hidden from the enemy, but there were none around. Ewell's other two divisions were delayed, so Rodes did not wait for them to pass. Instead, he continued the march and finally halted his command for the night about two miles north of Flint Hill, after traveling 15 miles.[3]

Johnson's division, followed by Early's, passed Sperryville at about 11:00 a.m., and continued northward to Little Washington. Johnson's division reached it at 1:30 p.m. and went into camp; Early's division arrived about 90 minutes later. Lt. William Kincheloe of the 49th Virginia (Smith's brigade) found the town "full of pretty ladies; they employed themselves in watering the soldiers, cheering them, etc." The column marched just a few more miles before halting for the night at about 4:00 p.m. between Little Washington and Flint Hill. The temperatures soared throughout the day and thick dust choked the men. Samuel Pickens wrote in his diary, "the dust is almost intolerable & that together with the heat make the marching very severe." General Early arrested at least one officer who permitted his men to steal a visit to their nearby homes. In all, the men marched about 16 miles. That night, the three division commanders conferred with Ewell about the next day's route.[4]

Third Corps

General Hill and his division commanders were confident that the Federals did not pose a threat, so they permitted the men to pitch tents behind their entrenchments. Except for an occasional artillery shell flying overhead, the world was peaceful.[5]

UNION

Hooker's intelligence-gathering forces had done a fair job of keeping him informed of the Confederates' positions. He knew that Longstreet's Corps was at Culpeper, Ewell's Corps was north of Fredericksburg, and Hill's Corps remained opposite Franklin's Crossing. In response to General Pleasonton's request that an infantry corps move between the two armies' cavalry forces,

Hooker dispatched the III Corps from its camp at Boscobel to Hartwell Church. Here it would patrol the area between Kelly's and Beverly Fords on the Rappahannock River to the right of the V Corps. The XI Corps was sent from Brooke's Station to replace the III Corps. The other corps commanders were notified to be ready to march at short notice. Excess baggage and materials were to be deposited with the quartermasters, and all non-military personnel were to remain behind.[6]

After continual prodding by General Halleck, Schenck finally ordered Milroy to prepare to withdraw his troops to Harper's Ferry. The telegram read: "In accordance with orders from Halleck received today, you will immediately take steps to remove your command from Winchester to Harper's Ferry. You will without delay, call in Colonel McReynolds and such other outposts not necessary for observation at the front." This was not the first time that Milroy had been ordered to vacate Winchester. He also received telegrams to this effect on January 5, March 16, April 30, May 2, 8, and 29, and June 8.[7]

Milroy immediately protested, stating that he could "hold it [Winchester] against any force the rebels could afford to bring against it." He did send 114 wagons filled with supplies to safety. Milroy believed that at worst, he was facing a Confederate cavalry raid, not an attack by a seasoned infantry corps. About an hour later (1:00 p.m.), Schenck softened his original order, stating, "make all required preparations for withdrawing, but hold your position...await further orders."[8]

To the south, General Dix reported that the movement toward Richmond had halted because of the enemy's movements and "other inevitable causes."[9]

III Corps

The men received orders to break camp and prepare to march as they were finishing their noontime meal. They were on the road within an hour. The destination was Hartwood Church, about eight miles away. At first, the men were weighed down with their personal belongings, but as the march continued, more and more were shed. The men appreciated their new surroundings. "Opposite Fredericksburg, where scarcely a tree was left standing, whilest here we were in the midst of cultivated forests and sheltering groves," noted one soldier.[10]

VI Corps

Sedgwick's Corps remained astride the Rappahannock River. Enemy sniping had all but stopped because of the effectiveness of Berdan's Sharpshooters. Seldom did a rebel's head rise above his breastworks.[11]

June 12

CONFEDERATE

While the Third Corps remained in its defenses around Fredericksburg, and the First Corps remained in camp near Culpeper Court House, Ewell's Second Corps continued its march toward Winchester. Ongoing Federal activity caused Lee to order Montgomery Corse's brigade (Pickett's division) back to Hanover Junction, and to dispatch a cavalry regiment from his army to help handle the growing threat to the South.[1]

First Corps

Orders arrived at 6:00 p.m. for the men to strike their tents and prepare to march. These orders were soon countermanded, and McLaws's and Hood's men repitched their tents. Pickett's division also remained in camp.[2]

Second Corps

Reveille sounded at 3:00 a.m., and Ewell's men were on the road between 4:00 and 4:30 a.m. Rodes's division led the column, followed by Johnson's, and Early's. The column crossed into the Shenandoah Valley through Chester Gap, and continued north. The non-Virginia soldiers were dazzled by the rich countryside. Samuel Pickens of Alabama commented on the "most luxuriant clover...the splendid fields of wheat." The head of the column finally marched through Front Royal at about 11:00 a.m. The citizens were thrilled to see the troops, as Milroy's men had made frequent raids on their town. The column reached the Shenandoah River, where the men saw a disassembled pontoon bridge lying nearby. The river turned out to be shallow—only up to their knees. Many were in such good spirits, even after the 23-mile march, that they cheered as they crossed the river. The corps camped for the night just beyond the river near Cedarville. Many could be seen bathing and washing their clothes in the river that evening.[3]

While the men were resting, Ewell reviewed information about enemy troop dispositions with his three division commanders. General Robert Milroy occupied Winchester with between 6,000 and 8,000 men, and Colonel Andrew McReynolds occupied Berryville with another 1,800. Johnson's and Early's divisions would take on the larger force at Winchester, while Rodes's division, with General Albert Jenkins's cavalry brigade, would swing to the east and attempt to gobble up McReynolds. Rodes would then immediately move on Martinsburg and liquidate its garrison. These feats accomplished, the corps would cross the Potomac River and begin collecting supplies in Maryland. The day was not over for Rodes's men. Anxious to get a head start, Rodes ordered the men from their reprieve, and marched them north toward Berryville, camping for the night at Stone Bridge. Jenkins's cavalry brigade patrolled the infantry's right flank during this march.[4]

Third Corps

The men did not mind going on picket, as the unwritten truce meant a peaceful coexistence. Several men fashioned little boats they could sail across the river to trade tobacco for coffee.[5]

UNION

Hooker put several of his army corps on the march in an effort to prevent Lee from crossing the Rappahannock River east of the Blue Ridge Mountains. The I and III Corps marched to Bealton, and the XI Corps received orders to move to Catlett's Station, which they did via Hartwood Church. The XII Corps was left behind to take the XI Corps's former position. Because there was so much uncertainty about the enemy's movements, I Corps's commander, General John Reynolds, was put in command of the army's right wing (I, III, V, XI, and Cavalry Corps) until Hooker moved up and assumed command.[6]

Hooker also issued General Orders No. 62. Stern in tone, it first noted how lax the army had become, and reminded the officers of prior General Orders. Among the issues addressed were: treatment of stragglers and non-military personnel in the camps, prohibition of the use of horses and mules for non-military pursuits, and restrictions on the use of enlisted men as waiters or servants. Hooker also reminded the officers of the importance of drill at all levels of the army. This order was to be read to the men of each company and battery.[7]

Any accurate information on the enemy's movements and locations could not be attributed to Pleasonton's cavalry. Hooker was growing increasingly concerned that Pleasonton's reports were inaccurate. He finally made it very clear to his cavalry commander that his major responsibility was not to engage the Confederate cavalry, but to get "every possible information with regard to the enemy's movements....Be watchful, vigilant, and let nothing escape you." Pleasonton relied on hearsay all too often, and his patrols did not ride beyond the Waterloo Bridge. Later that day, Hooker asked Pleasonton, "how far beyond Sulphur Springs and in what part of the Valley have your scouts penetrated?...this is very important." To assist in keeping tabs on the Confederates, General Julius Stahel's cavalry was dispatched to patrol the area beyond Bull Run Mountains, toward New Baltimore, Salem, Middleburg, Dranesville, and Leesburg, and from there to the Blue Ridge Mountains, including Front Royal, and Winchester.[8]

Now that the orders to withdraw from Winchester were reversed by Schenck, Milroy was able to concentrate on the enemy's movements. Patrols were thrown out to gather information. One patrol rode south from Winchester. Seeing some Confederate horsemen approaching, the Federal troops decided to lay a trap by feigning confusion. It worked, for as the unsuspecting

Confederates galloped over a hill, they were hit by a galling crossfire. The enemy sustained 40–50 casualties. The numbers would have been higher, but the Federal troops opened fire too soon. Another patrol rode toward Front Royal. As they approached Cedarville, they saw the long lines of Johnson's Confederate infantry division. Rushing back to Milroy with the news, Colonel Joseph Moss's report was discounted by Milroy, apparently because other officers gave conflicting information.[9]

In an effort to staff the new Department of the Susquehanna, Pennsylvania Governor Andrew Curtin told Secretary of War Stanton that he would send all new recruits to General Couch, rather than form new three-year regiments. Furious, Stanton shot back a message to Couch, "I hope you have had nothing to do with such agreement. The recruiting for three years or during the war should not be postponed an hour."[10]

Governor Curtin proceeded with recruiting men in the two new departments by sending a proclamation to the citizens of Pennsylvania, with assurances that "the duties of which will be mainly the defense of our own homes, firesides, and property from devastation."[11]

I Corps

The I Corps's march north to Gettysburg began at 6:00 a.m. when it left its encampment at Fitzhugh's Plantation and White Oak Church. The corps took a detour from Pollock's Mill to avoid being seen by the Confederates around Fredericksburg. Moving west from Stoneman's Switch, about two miles from Falmouth, the column finally gained the Warrenton Turnpike. Another four-mile march brought the men to Deep Run, where they bivouacked for the night. In all, they had marched 20 miles. The weather was warm and the roads dusty. Because the men had been in camp so long, the march was especially tiring. "Tip" Wright of the 149th Pennsylvania (Stone's brigade) recalled that "I was so sore and tired that I could scarcely get one foot before the other." Many fell from the ranks, and most threw away belongings in an effort to keep up. The column apparently took the wrong road at one point, adding some unnecessary miles to the trek. Charles Davis of the 13th Massachusetts (Gabriel Paul's brigade, John Robinson's division) wrote, "this kind of foolishness does not sweeten the temper of a man who is working for $13 per month." The men of the Iron Brigade were later drawn up to watch the execution of a private in the 19th Indiana who was shot for desertion, and possibly aiding the enemy. The body lay next to its coffin as the rest of the I Corps passed. It was a silent, but pointed, reminder of the men's obligations to the government.[12]

III Corps

The men left Hartwood Church, which they had reached the night before, and were on the road to Bealton Station on the Orange and Alexandria Railroad by about 8:00 a.m. The day became exceedingly hot, and the dust hung heavily in the stagnant air. Private McCarthy recalled that "the dust combined with the heat caused great suffering. The nostrils of the men, filled with dust, became dry and feverish, and even the throat did not escape. The grit was felt between the teeth, and the eyes were rendered almost useless. There was dust in eyes, mouth, ears, and hair. The shoes were full of sand, and the dust penetrating the

Execution of a private in the 19th Indiana

Curtis, *History of the Twenty-Fourth Michigan of the Iron Brigade* clothes and getting in at the neck, wrists, and ankles, mixed with perspiration produced an irritant almost as active as cantharides." When halts were permitted, they were usually in shadeless fields. "There was sometimes a solitary oak or pine that stood upon the plain like a rock in the desert; and the limits of the shadow upon the ground enclosed a small squad that crowded together to enjoy the protection of the enlivening foliage," according to Henry Blake. Men fell out of ranks by the score. The 25-mile march ended at about 7:00 p.m. for most of the units. The exception was Joseph Carr's brigade (Andrew Humphreys's division), which was sent to Beverly Ford, reaching there before midnight. It was quite an ordeal for the men. According to Fifer Charles Bardeen, "four men in our own brigade died of exhaustion."[13]

VI Corps

Hooker finally ordered Sedgwick to remove his men from the south side of the Rappahannock River after dark. The corps was then to support the engineers as they dismantled the bridge. This retrograde movement upset not a man.[14]

XI Corps

After being held in readiness to march for the past two days, the men were told that they would begin their journey from Brooke's Station at noon. They ate lunch, then were on the road by 1:00 p.m. The destination was Hartwood Church, about 13 miles away, which they reached by sundown. John McMahon (Smith's brigade) noted that "I never sweat so in all my life."[15]

June 13

CONFEDERATE

Responding to the secretary of war's communications, General Lee wrote, "you can realize the difficulty of operating in any offensive movement with this army if it has to be divided to cover Richmond. It seems to me useless to attempt it with the force against it." He continued to ask that units from other theaters be sent to Richmond and North Carolina.[1]

While most of Lee's army was fairly inactive, Ewell's Second Corps maneuvered into position for its attacks on Winchester and Berryville. Initial contact was made at both towns.

First Corps

Because a few Federal troops crossed the Rappahannock River, McLaws's division received orders to prepare to move in that direction. The orders never materialized. Hood's men received orders to wash, clean up, and prepare to change camps at 3:00 p.m. However, the men were quickly assembled at 11:00 a.m., and with their belongings hastily assembled, marched three miles southwest to a new camp near Cedar Run. McLaws's men also marched to a new location, but later in the evening, and at a more leisurely pace. Pickett's men remained in their camps.[2]

Second Corps

With enemy troops up ahead, General Rodes decided to use the services of a local citizen as a guide. While his infantry division marched toward Millwood using a back road, Jenkins's cavalry brigade was ordered to distract the enemy by taking a more conspicuous route. The ploy didn't work as Federal cavalry observed Rodes's column. A frustrated Rodes wrote in his official report that this would have been avoided if "General Jenkins occupied Millwood during the night before, as he was ordered to do." Realizing that he had lost the element of surprise, Rodes pushed his troops through Millwood and then on to Berryville. Arriving at the latter town toward evening, Rodes learned from Jenkins that the Federal troops were in the process of evacuating.[3]

Not to be denied, Rodes immediately tried to capture the enemy. Seeing Jenkins's cavalry making feeble frontal attacks against the Federal defenses, Rodes curtly told the cavalry commander to swing his men around the left of the town to cut off McReynolds's men. At the same time, Rodes sent two of his brigades around the east side of the town, and two others around the west to cut off the Federal retreat. Louis Leon of the 53rd North Carolina (Junius Daniel's brigade) noted in his diary that "we then formed in line of battle with sharpshooters in front. We gave the Rebel yell and charged. But when we got to their breastworks the birds had flown." Realizing that he had missed his opportunity, Rodes sent his last brigade, O'Neal's, into the town. Here they helped themselves to food and supplies that McReynolds's men had left behind in their haste to reach safety. A frustrated Rodes reassembled his command and continued his march northward toward Martinsburg. Jenkins's men were already in hot pursuit. The 36th Virginia Cavalry Battalion caught up with the retreating Federal rearguard and charged. After a seesaw battle, the Confederate troopers were forced to retire. The division finally camped near Summit Point in the pouring rain, after marching about 20 miles.[4]

While Rodes was marching north toward Berryville, Ewell decided to further divide his corps by sending Early's division up the Valley Turnpike to get on Milroy's right flank. Johnson's division continued on the Front Royal and Winchester Road, where he was to confront Milroy from the south. The plan was for Johnson to distract Milroy, while Early attacked from the west. Earlier, Ewell

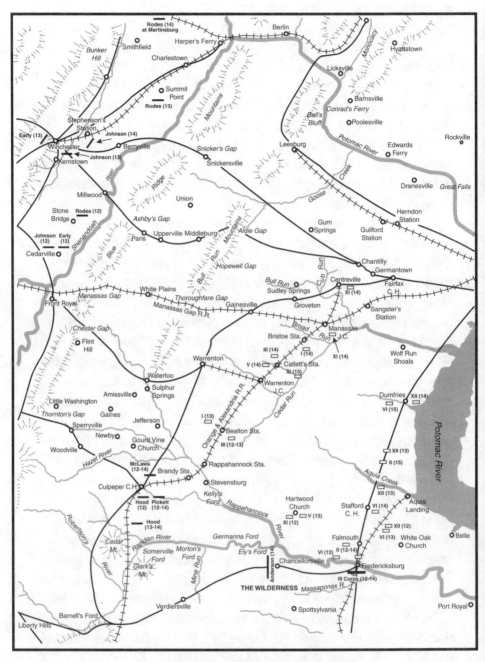

Operations June 12–June 14, 1863
(Dates in June in parentheses)

had told Johnson, "You are the operator now—I am only a looker on."[5]

On the road by 3:00 a.m., Early's division marched through Ninevel and Newtown (Stephen's City). The men were pleased to see that women had placed barrels of cool water by the side of the road for them. Reaching the outskirts of Kernstown shortly after 3:30 p.m., the men came under artillery fire from a battery on Pritchard's Hill. After forming his men on either side of the road, Early sent Harry Hays's brigade forward. As the Louisianians approached, the Federal battery wisely withdrew. Hays, however, spied the 12th West Virginia to his left, and Early immediately sent John Gordon's brigade to deal with it. Deploying his brigade, Gordon ordered his men against the enemy infantry behind a stone wall, as Hays's men also advanced. The attack drove the Federal troops from their defenses, but not before 75 of Gordon's men were killed or wounded. Only 23 West Virginians were casualties. The 12th Pennsylvania Cavalry now foolheartedly counterattacked. One of Gordon's men noted the scene: "the rattle of their steel scabbards, the clanking of their spurs, and the noise of the iron shoes of their horses as they struck the hard surface was inspiring....they came in range of Hays' Louisianans." The charge should have proved disastrous for the Pennsylvanians, but Hays's men fired too soon, giving the cavalry time to rein in and beat a hasty retreat. Early's men rested on their arms that night in a drenching rain, just south of Abram's Creek.[6]

Johnson's division also encountered the enemy on June 13. Reveille had sounded at 4:00 a.m., and as the division advanced northward along the Front Royal and Winchester Road, enemy pickets were encountered about four miles south of Winchester at about noon. The 2nd Virginia of James Walker's "Stonewall" brigade was detached as skirmishers, who quickly dispersed their counterparts. The enemy finally took position behind a stone wall, which they tenaciously held until driven back by a determined attack by the Virginians, supported by artillery. In the meantime, Johnson deployed the remainder of his division. Except for an artillery duel, this ended the hostilities for the day.[7]

Third Corps

Federal movements on the opposite side of the Rappahannock River convinced Hill that the enemy was finally withdrawing to protect Washington from Lee's invading army.

UNION

Now knowing that two powerful Confederate corps were either in, or close to, the Shenandoah Valley, Hooker realized that he could not continue to defend Washington and Harper's Ferry, and at the same time remain near Fredericksburg with part of his army. Therefore, he decided to get between the rebel army and Washington by changing his base of operations from the Aquia Creek line to Centreville on the Orange and Alexandria Railroad. Orders were subsequently sent to the right wing—I Corps (at Deep Run), III (at Bealton), V Corps (near Banks' Ford), and XI Corps (at Hartwood Church)—to rendezvous at Manassas Junction, where it would join the Federal cavalry. The other wing—II (near Falmouth), VI (at Franklin's Crossing), and XII (near Brooke's Station and Aquia Creek) Corps—were to first cover the withdrawal of government property from the depots, then march to Dumfries. The location of the enemy would dictate their subsequent movements.[8]

Since the Confederates were close to the Shenandoah Valley, Hooker ordered Pleasonton to send a cavalry brigade and a battery to Thoroughfare Gap to prevent the rebels from crossing through the mountains. Pleasonton was also ordered to send another brigade of cavalry to Warrenton to guard Waterloo Bridge. Still another brigade picketed the Rappahannock River.[9]

General Schenck announced that General Daniel Tyler would take command of the Harper's Ferry garrison. At the same time, General Benjamin Kelley headed an expedition toward Winchester to help support Milroy's men. Milroy needed all the help he could get. His men had captured several prisoners and learned that Early's and Johnson's divisions were approaching. The enemy had already driven in the troops south of town. Milroy did not seem overly concerned, for he wired Schenck, "I can hold this place five days if you can relieve me in that time. They will surround, but can't take my fortifications." Because Milroy thought the telegraph wires had been cut, he sent couriers to Baltimore with this message.[10]

To the east, Rodes's division approached Berryville. Colonel Andrew McReynolds, whose brigade defended the town, heard two cannons fire from the direction of Winchester, and knew this was the signal for him to evacuate Berryville and join Milroy. At about the same time, a patrol rushed back with news that a powerful rebel infantry column was approaching. There was no time to load all of the supplies and equipment into wagons, so only the most important were taken. As McReynolds's men were about to march north on the Charlestown Road, the Confederate cavalry arrived and made some feeble attacks against the weakly defended defenses.[11]

Making a wide detour at Summit Point, McReynolds got his men on the Martinsburg Pike at Clearbrook and finally reached Winchester just after dark. McReynolds's rearguard, composed of the 1st New York Cavalry, tangled with the 36th Virginia Cavalry Battalion, and bested it in a series of spirited fights.[12]

Pennsylvania Governor Andrew G. Curtin wrestled with a legal question that defied an answer—could he call out the militia? Becoming increasingly alarmed over the prospects of a Confederate invasion of his state, Curtin bluntly asked General Halleck whether Hooker's cavalry would enter his state after them. "My object in asking is to know whether my duty as Executive of this State ...may not require an immediate call of the militia to resist the invasion. Advise me fully." Halleck referred him to Lincoln or Stanton, as protocol prevented him from responding.[13]

I Corps

The march from Deep Run on the Warrenton Road began at about 5:30 a.m. The day soon became hotter and dustier than the one before. The men passed through several small towns with fancy names. Orson Curtis of the 24th Michigan (Iron Brigade), noted "what they lacked in size they made up with their names."

The column finally halted at Bealton Station on the Orange and Alexandria Railroad after a 12-mile march. Here it joined the III Corps. To Charles Davis of the 13th Massachusetts (Gabriel Paul's brigade), this march was worse than the longer one the day before because "the water was as scarce as whiskey, and so bad that something ought to have been provided to killed the animalcula it contained."[14]

II Corps

While the remainder of the army was on the march, the II Corps remained behind at Falmouth to watch the enemy and act as rearguard.[15]

III Corps

The men were pleased to remain in camp at Bealton Station after the 25-mile march the day before. They did have mixed emotions as a steady stream of other troops passed them to help fight the rebels.[16]

V Corps

Meade's V Corps fell under the command of General Reynolds as it began its march north. Its ultimate destination was Centreville. Heavy rains fell on James Barnes's and Sykes's divisions' camps near Banks' Ford between 6:00 and 8:00 p.m. The men were none too happy, because they were in the process of breaking camp as the first rains fell. The march began at about 8:00 p.m., and continued until midnight, when the corps reached Hartwood Church. One officer noted that "the night was very dark and cloudy, and it was with some difficulty that we found our way through the mud; and what added more to the darkness of the night, was the dense forest and narrow roads that we had to pass through."[17]

VI Corps

The withdrawal of the VI Corps from the south side of the Rappahannock River was completed on June 13. After Torbert's brigade crossed the river, it spent most of the night pulling the pontoons out of the river and loading them onto wagons.[18]

Union troops leave Falmouth

Battles and Leaders of the Civil War

Although all of the VI Corps was now safely back on the north shore of the Rappahannock River, the men did not feel safe as enemy batteries continued to fire on their camps. A very disconcerted Private Wilbur Fiske (Grant's brigade) wrote, "I dislike occupying a camp where our safety depends upon the magnanimous forbearance of our foe." Fiske was, however, confident that the powerful Federal artillery would dash the rebels' enthusiasm for causing trouble.[19]

General Sedgwick's new orders were to march toward Dumfries, and ultimately to Greenwood and Wolf Run Shoals. Howe's division began the march north just after dark. Recent rains had converted the dusty roads to a "slippery bed of mortar," according to Fiske. Periodically, a soldier fell headlong into the mud to the catcalls and merriment of his comrades. The march continued all night and ended at Brooke's Station.[20]

XI Corps

The men in camp at Hartwood Church were up by 4:00 a.m. and on the road an hour later, after cooking and eating their breakfast. The march to Catlett's Station on the Orange and Alexandria Railroad was a long one—24 miles. This was, according to John McMahon (Smith's brigade), the longest march he and his unit had ever made. The march ended at Weaverville, near Catlett's Station. Calvin Heller of the 153rd Pennsylvania (Leopold von Gilsa's brigade, Francis Barlow's division) was impressed by the countryside, which he called "beautiful...it is well-fenced and good grain of all kinds."[21]

XII Corps

The XII Corps finally broke camp on Aquia Creek near Stafford Court House at 6:00 a.m., and marched to within a mile of Brooke's Station where it was to cover the railroad from Aquia to Fredericksburg. Here the men went about preparing a more permanent camp. When it was completed, they were fatigued, but pleased with their work. After supper the men looked forward to a quiet future. The long roll suddenly sounded at about 6:00 p.m., and the incredulous men packed up their belongings and assembled on the road. First countermarching toward Stafford Court House, they struck out toward Dumfries. This was a very difficult march, as "each man was brought up short, by running against his file leader." The large number of wagons and artillery in front of them caused the continual stops. The men spent as much time standing in the road as they did marching on it. This made the men even wearier. Many men fell out of the ranks because of the extreme conditions. Division commander Alpheus Williams wrote home, "I lost a good many men, I fear, by sunstroke. It was a terrible day and my poor fellows suffered greatly."[22]

June 14

CONFEDERATE

This was a momentous day for Lee's army. A. P. Hill's Corps began its march toward Culpeper Court House, and farther to the north, Ewell's Corps engaged Milroy's troops at Winchester and Berryville. Jenkins's cavalry brigade, attached to Ewell's Corps, splashed across the Potomac River at Williamsport to attempt to capture a Federal wagon train.[1]

First Corps

Longstreet's Corps remained in its camps. According to R. T. Cole (Evander Law's brigade), the men received orders at 11:30 p.m. to be ready to march the next morning. Many of the units received three-days' rations, but were not ordered to break camp.[2]

Second Corps

General Rodes was frustrated to learn that McReynolds's brigade had again eluded him and safely reached Winchester. Ewell had not as yet responded to Rodes's requests for additional orders, so he did not know whether to forge on to Martinsburg, according to his orders, or turn to Winchester to help take on Milroy. After some reflection, Rodes decided to follow his original orders. The men began their march at 7:00 a.m., passing through Smithfield, Bunker Hill, and finally Martinsburg at about 9:00 p.m. Many men had swollen, blistered feet, after the tiring

20-mile march, which made every step miserable. Their discomfort was eased somewhat by the citizens who lined the road distributing food.[3]

Upon reaching Martinsburg, General Rodes learned that some Federal troops occupied the town. Jenkins's cavalry brigade had invested it, but had not launched any attacks. While his artillery opened fire, Rodes quickly deployed his men and sent them forward, causing the two Federal regiments to flee in the darkness. Racing after them, Stephen Ramseur's brigade captured five abandoned cannon, but the North Carolinians were unable to engage the enemy. Their cavalry and artillery had fled to Williamsport, while the infantry marched toward Shepherdstown. Rodes lamented in his report that darkness halted his operations: "Could the division have reached the town an hour or two earlier...I would have captured the whole force." Sending Jenkins's cavalry in pursuit of the enemy, Rodes took stock of the situation in Martinsburg. While most of the enemy's stores were destroyed, he was able to secure 6,000 bushels of grain, 400 rounds of rifled artillery ammunition, and a "small-quantity" of musket ammunition.[4]

According to Ewell's plan, this was the day that Johnson's and Early's divisions would destroy Milroy's command at Winchester. While Johnson drove forward from the south and east, Early's division was to circle around to the left and deliver the brunt of the attack from the west.[5]

General Early ordered one regiment from Gordon's brigade, and a second from Hays's, to advance and take Bower's Hill, just southwest of Winchester. This was accomplished in short order. Climbing to the top of the hill, Generals Ewell and Early closely studied the Federal positions around Winchester. They realized that the key to Winchester was the heavily fortified West Fort Hill northwest of town. Leaving Gordon's brigade and two batteries in position to "amuse the enemy and hold him in check in front," Early moved his other three brigades through fields around the flank of the Federals at Winchester. The plan was for Johnson's division, east of Winchester, to distract Milroy's men. Early's column moved out to the sounds of a furious artillery duel. By noon, all was quiet, and more than one Federal soldier nervously pondered what the rebels were up to. Early's three brigades were in position by 4:00 p.m., having marched eight to ten miles "without meeting with water to drink, and were very much fatigued," Early noted in his report. He now reconnoitered while the men were given a well-deserved rest. They began worrying about the coming events, and one wrote, "we all began to feel as if we had caught the elephant, and could not tell what to do with it."[6]

General Hays received word from General Early at about 5:00 p.m. that his brigade would make the assault on the Federal troops on West Fort Hill. The plan was for 20 cannon to open fire on the enemy. When the Federal troops seemed "sufficiently demoralized," Hays was to launch a bayonet attack. Early was surprised to learn that while the enemy had made preparations to receive an attack from his direction, no lookouts were posted. Early now ordered his cannon to open fire, and soon the air was ablaze with shells. Within ten minutes, one of Milroy's caissons had exploded and 50 horses were down. After about 45 minutes (between 6:00 and 6:30 p.m.), Hays ordered his men up the hill, with three regiments in front and two behind them. Smith's brigade marched 300 yards behind them, and Hoke's brigade was another 300 yards behind Smith. Hays halted his men as they reached the edge of a protective forest. Realizing that something was afoot, the 500 Yanks peering over their breastworks spied Hays's men not more than 150 yards away. They opened fire, causing a number of Louisianians to fall. Requesting permission to attack, Hays was informed that Early wanted his cannon to soften up the Federal works a bit more.[7]

Hays never received these orders, for realizing that he could not hesitate any longer, he ordered a charge. The Confederate artillery ceased fire just as Hays's men came into view. "So rapidly did this brigade push forward that the enemy had time to give us but a few volleys of musketry and only four or five rounds of canister from their field pieces," noted one of the men. There was no stopping Hays's fierce Lousianians, and soon they had captured the hill and eight cannon posted there. The latter were not easily taken, for unlike the Federal infantry, the cannoneers stood their ground and engaged in hand-to-hand combat until overwhelmed. The hill was now in Hays's hands. Seeing the enemy massing to retake the hill, two of the captured cannon were turned around and opened fire, reducing the enemy's ardor. In the meantime, Early rushed his artillery and Smith's brigade up the hill to reinforce Hays's men. Hays estimated that he lost about 80 men in this action. As might be expected, the Federal losses were lighter—about 50. One Confederate artilleryman noted that "for intrepidity, steadiness...we never saw this charge excelled, even in Lee's army." Lt. R. Stark Jackson of the 8th Louisiana wrote home, "it was the best managed affair Hayes [*sic*] ever had any thing to do with." He also noted that few Yanks were captured because they were "rather too nimble for us."[8]

While intently watching the assault, a minie ball slammed into Ewell's chest. Fortunately, it was spent, and only bruised him. So annoyed was Ewell's doctor that he took away his crutches (Ewell had lost a leg), forcing his patient to sit down and remain in relative safety.[9]

Lt. Randolph McKim of the 1st Maryland (Steuart's brigade) also watched the attack on the Federal works. "We could see the flash of his guns, sixteen discharges per minute while the Stars and Stripes waved defiantly amid the bursting shells in the rolling smoke, the sun sinking red and angry behind the western clouds, the advance and retreat of the skirmishers with the sharp crack of the rifle, while cavalry and artillery gallop into position and infantry file in column." McKim and his comrades were disappointed that they were not ordered into the fray.[10]

Upon reaching the top of the now-captured hill, Early closely observed the main Federal works around Winchester. He realized that Fort Milroy's capture would require more men than he had, so he contented himself with opening a brisk artillery fire on the Federal works. The Federal guns responded, and the artillery duel continued until dark. Tomorrow would bring the dreaded attack on the main redoubt.[11]

Earlier in the day, Walker's Stonewall Brigade (Johnson's division) moved to the east of Winchester, between the Millwood and Berryville Turnpikes, and Steuart's brigade was placed within supporting distance. The 5th Virginia of Walker's brigade was thrown forward and engaged the enemy's skirmishers. No other units were involved, and the regiment lost about 30 men in the heavy skirmishing.[12]

That night, Ewell realized that Milroy would probably retreat, so he ordered General Johnson to take three of his brigades and eight cannon and march to "a point on the Martinsburg turnpike, 2 1/2 miles north of Winchester, with the double purpose, I supposed, of intercepting the enemy's retreat and attacking him in his fortifications from that direction," noted Johnson. Accordingly, Steuart's and Francis Nicholls's brigades, along with portions of three batteries, were immediately put into motion. Walker's brigade, farther from the other two, would join them a short time later. Jones's brigade was left behind to prevent an enemy escape along a different route. As the column marched along Berryville Road, a guide told Johnson that a better position was at Stephenson's Depot, about five miles from Winchester. Here a railroad cut, masked by woods, would make a perfect place for his troops to take on Milroy. Rationalizing that the enemy would detect the men if he followed Ewell's order, Johnson decided to take the initiative.[13]

Third Corps

Scouts sent across the Rappahannock reported the Yankee camps abandoned, so Hill immediately pulled his men out of the defensive line at Hamilton's Crossing that they had occupied for the past ten days. Richard Anderson's division began the march to Culpeper Court House while Henry Heth's and William Pender's divisions remained behind. The division reached the Chancellorsville battlefield that evening. Although a resounding victory, the sights on the battlefield were horrific. J. B. Johnson of the 5th Florida (Perry's brigade) saw a pit filled with dead bodies covered by a thin layer of dirt "through which several streams of blue gas were gushing; plainly visible at some distance." Arms and legs protruded through the ground where rain had washed away the dirt over their graves. Most disconcerting was the knowledge that those body parts could have been from their fallen comrades.[14]

UNION

Time was almost up for Milroy and his division at Winchester. Believing that he had successfully halted the Confederate advance on June 13, Milroy thought that the worst was over. As a result, he did not even consider pulling his men out of Winchester during the night of June 13–14.[15]

Milroy closely watched the countryside around Winchester during the day atop a flagpole on Main Fort. He saw no Confederate activity, nor did a cavalry patrol. This serenity came to an abrupt end at approximately 5:00 p.m., when Early's division's artillery opened fire on West Fort. The bombardment continued for about 90 minutes. An irresistible attack was made shortly thereafter, resulting in the withdrawal of the infantry and loss of several cannon.[16]

A hastily convened council of war met at about 10:00 p.m. Realizing that they were all but surrounded, and having but one-day's rations and limited small arms ammunition, the group decided to finally abandon Winchester and move to Harper's Ferry. To the north, General Robert Tyler and two infantry regiments defending Martinsburg received a flag of truce from General Jenkins, who commanded a cavalry brigade attached to Rodes's division. Jenkins demanded the town's immediate surrender. Realizing that a full infantry division was also approaching, Tyler wisely decided to withdraw. Four cannon were left in the town square, and another overturned and fell into a ditch during the hurried retreat. The men made it safely back to Harper's Ferry and joined the garrison there.[17]

Scouts from the II Corps informed Hooker that Hill's Confederate Third Corps had left its positions along the Rappahannock River and was marching northwest. Lincoln had other ominous news for Hooker: "the enemy have Milroy surrounded at Winchester and Tyler at Martinsburg." Lincoln continued, "if they could hold out a few days, could you help them?" Then Lincoln added one of his most memorable lines: "if the head of Lee's army is at Martinsburg and the tail of it on the Plank Road between Fredericksburg and Chancellorsville, the animal must be very slim somewhere. Could you not break him?"[18]

Hooker rode north from Falmouth and camped at Dumfries that night. The Federal movements during the day were arduous, and two corps (I and VI) actually marched through the night and into the early morning hours of June 15. Most of the corps were concentrating in the Centreville/Manassas Junction area. The movements were: I Corps from Bealton to beyond Kettle Run, toward Manassas Junction; II Corps remained on the Rappahannock River at Falmouth; III Corps from Bealton to Catlett's Station; V Corps from Hartwood Church to Catlett's Station; VI Corps from Potomac Creek to Stafford Court House; XI Corps from Catlett's Station to Manassas and then on to Centreville; the XII Corps from Brooke's Station to Dumfries.[19]

To draw troops from Lee's army, General Halleck wired General Dix at Fort Monroe, "all your available force should be concentrated to threaten Richmond, by seizing and destroying their railroad bridges over the South and North Anna Rivers, and do them all the damage possible." Dix immediately replied that he had a large force at Blackwater and another about ten miles from White House. He promised that he would concentrate his forces at West Point and move on Richmond.[20]

Colonel Thomas Scott of Pennsylvania wrote to the secretary of war that the Federal government's decision not to pay the new soldiers was having an adverse effect on the recruitment of men for the two military departments in the Keystone state. He believed that he could secure some corporate support in the form of a loan until Congress acted. Hearing that the rebels had captured Martinsburg, Virginia, Scott again wired Stanton, this time with a request that the "President should authorize the governor to call out the militia today." Stanton snapped back the answer that Curtin had been waiting for: "has not the Governor the right...to call out the militia....this Department has no objection to his doing so." Stanton later wrote directly to Governor Curtin with the news that an enemy raid into Pennsylvania was now all but certain. Deciding that he could wait no longer for decisive action, Governor Curtin put Colonel Thomas Scott on a train for Washington. He arrived at midnight with a request for permission to recruit 50,000 troops.[21]

If General Couch was hurting for recruits, he had no trouble acquiring officers. The War Department offered a number of misfits to Couch, including Generals William Smith, Napoleon Dana, and Franz Sigel. Couch gladly accepted all of them. Hundreds of citizens also besieged Governor Curtin for commissions.[22]

Realizing that he should start constructing forts to protect the main crossings of the Susquehanna River, General Couch put together a civilian workforce numbering over a thousand for the task. He also petitioned Stanton for 4–5 batteries of artillery, which were to be sent shortly.[23]

I Corps

The march from Bealton on a road paralleling the Orange and Alexandria Railroad continued at 8:00 a.m., and the column reached Warrington at about 1:00 p.m. Lack of water continued to be a problem. Fetid marshes attracted crowds of men who greedily filled their canteens with the contaminated water, only to later suffer from severe diarrhea. More than a few died from the combined effects of dehydration and severe exhaustion. The thick dust caked the men, making their blue uniforms appear brown. The sun set, but still the men marched on. The march toward Manassas Junction slowed in the darkness, particularly because of the numerous streams in the region. Those men who slipped out of rank for a rest quickly learned their mistake. An officer, whose role was to return all men to the ranks, followed every regiment. If men were able to get past the officer, they were met by the brigade provost guard, which was bringing up the rear. The march continued past midnight.[24]

II Corps

While Hooker put the rest of his army in motion toward the Orange and Alexandria Railroad, he left the II Corps behind at Falmouth to create the impression that the defenses were still heavily manned. The men began packing up their belongings and were told to destroy anything that could be of value to the enemy. The tents were left up until after dark, when they were quickly struck, and the corps took the road at about 8:00 p.m. The drum corps was left behind to sound "Tattoo and Taps," and to keep the fires burning to deceive Hill's Confederate corps across the river. The rest of the II Corps marched about four miles north, before halting for the night, about two hours later. Gibbon's division was ordered to march back to its camps on the Rappahannock River and arrived there at midnight. This movement caused much consternation among the men.[25]

III Corps

Orders to prepare to resume the march arrived at about 4:00 a.m., but hours passed while the men waited. Because the sole source of water, a single spring, was a mile away, the men wished they could join the troops that were filing by. According to John Halsey of the 17th Maine (Regis de Trobriand's brigade) "it is difficult to get sufficient water for drinking, and as for ablutions, a mud puddle would be deemed an inestimable treasure." But there were no mud puddles as it had not rained for days. The men were finally on the road by 6:00 p.m. The corps marched through Licking Creek, Kettle Run, Warrenton Junction, and finally completed the 10-mile march at Catlett's Station by midnight. The men hated night marches, as they were "attended with additional discomforts and dangers, such as falling off bridges, stumbling into ditches, tearing the face and injuring the eyes against the bushes and projecting limbs of trees often sprung back from a soldier ahead," noted a soldier in Joseph Carr's brigade.[26]

V Corps

The corps commander, George Meade, permitted the men to rest after their uncomfortable, wet night. They slept in until after first light, then prepared breakfast, and were on the road by 10:00 a.m. The rains were replaced by soaring temperatures, which caused dense clouds of dust to hang over the column. Many men succumbed to the heat and choking dust during the 20-mile march. "Some of them fell out of the ranks, just as though they had been shot," noted one soldier from Stephen Weed's brigade. The ordeal finally ended at about 7:00 p.m., when the column reached Catlett's Station on the Orange and Alexandria Railroad.[27]

VI Corps

Stafford Court House, about seven miles north of Fredericksburg, was the assembling point of the widely dispersed VI Corps. Joseph Bartlett's brigade arrived at 2:00 a.m. and Torbert's joined it a few hours later. John Newton's division did not arrive until later in the afternoon. The night march for Alfred Torbert's men was a nightmare because of the condition of the road—an old corduroy thoroughfare with loose poles, according to Alanson Haines of the 15th New Jersey (Torbert's brigade). "We went stumbling and tripping among them with some hazard to limb and life."[28]

The men, particularly those of Newton's and Wright's divisions, thought they were to go into camp at Stafford Court House. However, between 9:00 and 10:00 p.m., they were roused out of their tents and told to break camp. Joseph Newell of the 10th Massachusetts (Henry Eustis's brigade) recalled that "wagons, heavy guns, and soldiers, all contending for the road, such whipping and swearing, such pulling and hauling, such starting and halting." The stopping and starting was particularly tiring to the infantrymen. Wilbur Fiske of Howe's division admitted that the men would rather march continuously for 10 hours than stand around and wait for half of it "unless we can sit down and rest." But they were not permitted to rest. The men kept looking for bright campfires, which would signal their bivouac site. None were seen, and the men continued marching through the night. Because of the congested conditions, the men only had progressed about five miles by daybreak of June 15.[29]

XI Corps

The march from Catlett's Station to Centreville began at 9:00 a.m. The men were permitted a two-hour halt at Bristoe Station to eat lunch, then it was off again toward Bull Run, which they reached at 6:00 p.m. The men hoped that the trek would end soon, but it didn't. It was a tough march in the heat and dust. Hartwell Osborn of the 55th Ohio (Smith's brigade) noted, "this was another dusty, hot, and waterless march, which exhausted many of the men, unused to such strenuous work." John McMahon of the 136th New York, also of Smith's brigade, added, "yesterday and today the boys fell out very fast. I saw some fall down as they were walking, unable to go farther." The march finally ended late that night about three to five miles from Centreville, after a 20-mile march.[30]

XII Corps

The all-night march of the XII Corps was a nightmare. Dense pine groves on both sides of the road caused the darkness to be "as thick as that of a subterranean dungeon," according to General Williams. Constant halts were necessitated as wagons tipped over after hitting ruts and gullies in the road. Staff officers, riding to the side of the roads, often slid down the deep gullies. The corps finally reached Dumfries at about 9:00 a.m. Here the men were permitted to rest for the remainder of the day and through the night.[31]

June 15

CONFEDERATE

Although the enemy had withdrawn from the south side of the Rappahannock River, Lee was still frustrated by the lack of clear and coherent information about the enemy's intentions. These feelings are evident in a dispatch to President Davis, in which he wrote, "the uncertainty of the reports as to threatened expeditions of the enemy along the coast of North Carolina, and between the Rappahannock and James Rivers in Virginia, has caused delay in the movements of this army, and it may now be too late to accomplish all that was desired. I am still ignorant as to the extent of the expedition said to be moving up the Peninsula, and hesitate to draw the whole of A. P. Hill's corps to me."[1]

The bold side of Lee prevailed, however, and he ordered the rest of Hill's Corps from Fredericksburg to Culpeper Court House. Longstreet's First Corps was ordered to resume its march from Culpeper Court House toward Winchester, with Stuart's troopers protecting its vulnerable right flank.

The day promised to be a memorable one for the Second Corps. Acting much like his predecessor, Stonewall Jackson, Ewell anticipated that Milroy would try to escape from Winchester under cover of darkness. Marching Johnson's division to a cutoff point, the two enemy forces tangled in the pre-dawn darkness at Stephenson's Depot. To the north, General Rodes ordered Jenkins's cavalry brigade across the Potomac River and into Pennsylvania.

The cavalry finally reached Chambersburg, Pennsylvania, at about 11:00 p.m. that night.

First Corps

The drums beating at sunrise told the men that it was time to get up and prepare to break camp. Hood's men marched north, back to Culpeper Court House, where they rested for an hour. Then marching northwest, the men headed toward Gaines' Cross Roads. The weather was brutally hot and water was in short supply, causing Thomas Ware to write, "we suffered very much & I think was the hottest days [sic] march we ever taken [sic]....A great many fell out [of the] ranks overcome by heat & several sun stroke & some died, the road side was full." A two-hour halt was finally permitted, and the men "fell about like hogs." Hood's men now crossed the Hazel River and entered the hilly country beyond. The march finally ended at 9:00 p.m., but many of the men were so exhausted they couldn't sleep. John West of the 4th Texas (Jerome Robertson's brigade) wrote, "the march was conducted by that unmerciful driver, our beloved General Hood, who simply strikes a trot and is satisfied that the Texas Brigade at least will camp with him at nightfall." West noted that two hundred men were stricken by sunstroke.[2]

Pickett's division broke camp at 1:00 p.m. and marched a short distance before camping west of Culpeper Court House. Although the distance traveled was modest, a number of men fell out of the ranks because of the excessive heat. McLaws's men had an easier time of it. They only marched about a mile from Culpeper Court House before going into camp.[3]

Second Corps

As two of his brigades approached Stephenson's Depot in the early morning hours, General Johnson decided to ride ahead to reconnoiter. After proceeding but a short distance, he heard the neighing of horses up ahead. Soon gunfire split the quiet air, and Johnson knew that he had happened upon the head of Milroy's retreating column. Quickly riding back to his men, he positioned them along a railroad cut. Scarcely had the men assumed their positions that the Yanks rushed the defenses with a yell. Johnson's men immediately opened fire, causing the attacking line to melt away with heavy losses. Continuing his attack, Milroy also sent columns against both of Johnson's flanks. The one-hour fight was desperate. General Johnson described the situation as "my infantry had expended all but one round of ammunition; the ordnance wagons were 7 miles in [the] rear. The situation was exceedingly critical...."[4]

Suddenly, Walker's Stonewall Brigade swung into view. Through some miscommunication, the brigade had not begun its march until midnight and was a mile from the depot when the fight began. According to Ted Barclay, General Johnson could be seen "galloping along the line and [he] told them [the men of Steuart's and Nicholls's brigades] the Stonewall was coming to their support and they soon rallied and in turn drove the enemy." Hurrying forward, Walker threw his brigade against a strong flanking party that was about to overwhelm Johnson's right, capturing hundreds of the enemy. Meanwhile, a flanking party led by General Milroy had fallen on Johnson's' left flank, threatening to get into his rear. The 2nd Louisiana and 10th Louisiana of Nicholls's brigade rushed over and blunted this attack as well. Now Johnson's men surged forward, and thousands of Milroy's men threw up their hands to surrender. Johnson's men scooped up almost 2,500 prisoners, 25 cannon, about 175 horses, and 11 stands of colors. John Welsh of the 27th Virginia (Walker's brigade) exclaimed, "we took more prisoners than we had men in our brigade." It was a most decisive victory for the Confederates.[5]

Back at Winchester, Early's men could see that Milroy's men had abandoned the town, as the early morning mist dissipated. One Confederate foot soldier noted, "as good fortune would have it when light came the hill was discovered to be deserted and the enemy gone." Small arms fire to the north told them that Johnson's division had caught up with the enemy, so they were ordered after Milroy. As General Early arrived at Stephenson's Depot, the masses of prisoners and captured artillery told him that Johnson did not need his help. Returning to Winchester, General Early stated in his report that he sent 108 Federal officers and 3,250 enlisted men south toward Richmond. These prisoners were guarded by the 54th North Carolina (Robert Hoke's brigade) and the 58th Virginia (Smith's brigade). In addition to the 25 cannon, a large quantity of ammunition was also secured. The men were euphoric that night. According to Lieutenant William Kincheloe of the 49th Virginia (Smith's brigade), "soon we were cooking rations and our camp became gay and cheerful, the woods a scene of delight over our successes."6

A number of units paraded through Winchester, including Walker's Stonewall Brigade, whose bands played. The citizens burst into a rendition of "Bonnie Blue Flag," causing the column to stop in its tracks. When the song was over, "their shouts rent the air, caps were waved and hurrahs resounded," recalled one of the citizens.7

Farther north, General Rodes realized that his exhausted men needed a rest. He therefore permitted them to remain in camp until 10:00 a.m. Around this time, Rodes learned of the events at Winchester, and received more frustrating news—the remnant of Milroy's division had already passed him and reached the safety of Harper's Ferry. One bright spot was that Jenkins's cavalry brigade had crossed the Potomac River and would be in Pennsylvania by evening. Leaving the 6th Alabama of O'Neal's brigade to guard Martinsburg, Rodes put his division on the road toward Williamsport at about 11:00 a.m. The division reached its destination just as darkness fell. Despite the fact that the march was only 12 miles, Rodes called it "the most trying march we have yet had; most trying because of the intense heat, the character of the road, and the increased number of barefooted men in the command." Rodes immediately sent Stephen Ramseur's, Alfred Iverson's, and George Doles's infantry brigades across the Potomac River, along with three batteries. The remainder of the command, Junius Daniel's and Edward O'Neal's brigades, remained on the south side of the river.8

Third Corps

While Pender's division remained behind, Heth's division began its movement north toward Culpeper Court House at about

3:00 p.m. and marched about nine miles to within two miles of the Chancellorsville battlefield. Anderson's division, now more than a day's march ahead, was on the move by 8:00 a.m. The men were happy to leave the battlefield, but a skull lying by the side of the road was just too tempting, and some of the men kicked it like a soccer ball as they marched along. An officer impaled it with his sword and carried it aloft, until another soldier had had enough of the desecration and buried it out of sight, behind some bushes. The column crossed the Rapidan at Germanna Ford and camped within four miles of Stevensburg. Better time would have been made had there not been obstructions leading to the ford, which forced the men to halt and clear them. Over two hours were wasted in this way.[9]

UNION

With Hooker's army dispersed at the end of June 15—the I, III, V, and XI Corps, along with the cavalry, were assembling at Manassas and Centreville, the II and VI Corps at Dumfries, and the XII Corps at Fairfax Court House—Halleck reiterated his orders: "your army is entirely free to operate as you desire against Lee's army so long as you keep his main army from Washington." Halleck also expressed dissatisfaction with the limited amount of useful intelligence that Pleasonton's cavalry were obtaining.[10]

According to modern historian Edwin Coddington, Hooker was suffering from signs of becoming demoralized and apathetic. Provost Marshal Marsena Patrick noted at this time that Hooker "acts like a man without a plan and is entirely at a loss what to do, or how to match the enemy...." This did not bode well for the Union.[11]

In Washington, Colonel Thomas Scott met with the secretaries of war and state at about 1:00 a.m. He was relieved to learn that Lincoln would issue a call for 100,000 six-month militia from the following states: Pennsylvania (50,000), Ohio (30,000), Maryland (10,000), and West Virginia (10,000). Scott did not sleep that night, instead sending telegrams to Governor Curtin and others. In one dispatch, Scott suggested that Curtin prepare a strong

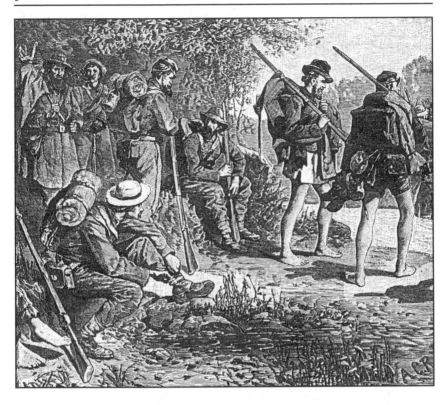

Confederates crossing a stream
Battles and Leaders of the Civil War

proclamation to the citizens of Pennsylvania, "calling upon our people to rise at once." He believed it would be most effective if issued before daylight that day. Curtin complied, noting in his proclamation that the men needed to "rush to the rescue in this hour of imminent peril." Despite its quota, Pennsylvania raised but a handful of men because of apathy. After all, the rebels were still miles away in Virginia, and most rejected the idea of serving as long as six months.[12]

Not content with 100,000 new troops, Stanton sent pleas to other governors for additional six-month militia. Each was asked how many could be sent to the cause. The responses were not positive. Iowa, Illinois, Michigan, and Connecticut expressed pessimism about raising any troops, but Stanton was delighted when New York Governor Horatio Seymour told him that he could immediately send 8,000 to 10,000 standing militia from New York City for up to three months.[13]

Stanton was making good on his commitment to Pennsylvania. General Couch requested and received five batteries, authorization to use all railroads in his district, and most importantly, militia.[14]

Milroy's retreat from Winchester began at about 1:00 a.m. Deciding that wheeled vehicles would slow the column's progress, Milroy decided to disable them and leave them behind. As the head of the column neared Stephenson's Depot at about 4:00 a.m., brilliant flashes lit up the darkness—it had encountered Johnson's Confederate division, which had swung around from the east of Winchester to cut off the Federal retreat. Forming his first brigade for an attack, Milroy sent the men forward in the darkness. The charge was repulsed, but a second, which overlapped the Confederate right, seemed to be initially more successful. However, Confederate troops rushed forward and sealed the breach.

Milroy now threw his second brigade against the Confederate left and almost engulfed it. However, the attacks were uncoordinated and ultimately failed to punch a hole through the Confederate line.[15]

Realizing that he could not drive the enemy from his front, Milroy opted to retreat in a different direction. Just then the thousand mules and horses in the rear became skittish and stampeded through the ranks. The Confederates advanced in the confusion and rounded up thousands of prisoners. Milroy escaped, but about half of his men (almost four thousand) were left behind—killed, wounded, or prisoners.[16]

Worried about the fate of the troops at Winchester and Martinsburg, Lincoln and Halleck finally learned that the latter troops, and the remnants of the former, had reached Harper's Ferry. So furious was Halleck at Milroy that he told General Schenck not to give him another command at Harper's Ferry. "We have had enough of that sort of military genius," he wrote.[17]

Lincoln was now sure that Lee meant to invade the North. The president could not have been happy with Hooker's response to this news: "if it should be determined for me to make a movement in pursuit, which I am not prepared to recommend at this time, I may possibly be able to move some corps to-morrow, and can reach the point of the enemy's crossing in advance of A. P. Hill....If they are moving toward Maryland, I can better fight them there than make a running fight."[18]

In a midnight dispatch to Lincoln, Hooker broached the subject that would ultimately be his undoing. "I request that I may be informed what troops there are at Harper's Ferry, and who is in command of them, and also who is in command of this district."[19]

One of the last dispatches that Stanton received that night must have disturbed his sleep. General Couch wrote that the enemy was detected in Pennsylvania, nine miles south of Chambersburg. He also noted another column (Early's division) on the road to Gettysburg.[20]

It was actually worse than Couch realized, for Jenkins's Confederate cavalry brigade thundered into Chambersburg at about 11:00 p.m. that night. Hundreds of African Americans fled ahead of the rebels in an effort to avoid being captured and returned to slavery. Civilians captured two officers, who were later released. Among Jenkins's first acts was a demand that all citizens relinquish their weapons.[21]

I Corps

The I Corps's long march, which had begun at 8:00 a.m. on June 14, finally ended at about 3:30 a.m., when the column reached Manassas Junction. The men had marched approximately 25 miles in almost 20 hours. According to A. P. Smith of the 76th New York (Lysander Cutler's brigade), "no man who endured that march will readily forget it." Smith found the frequent stops along the way, caused by troops or trains in front of them to be especially tiring. By the time the men finally halted, they had shed all but their most important personal belongings—guns, ammunition, rations, canteens, and rubber blankets.[22]

The men were up and on the road again at about 8:30 a.m., after only a five-hour reprieve. A short stop was permitted when the men reached Bull Run, and many used the time to bathe in the cool waters and fill their canteens. Here they could witness some of the gruesome sights of the battle of First Bull Run. A 14-mile march brought the men to Centreville at about noon, where they were permitted to rest. According to Henry Clare, the officers set a fast pace because the men knew to "get ahead as fast as you can or be taken prisoners."[23]

II Corps

Most of the II Corps continued its march from just north of Falmouth at about 2:00 a.m.; John Gibbon's division, which had returned to the Rappahannock, started out a few hours later. The head of the column reached Stafford Court House by midmorning—just in time to see the courthouse in flames. According to R. Holcombe of the 1st Minnesota (William Harrow's brigade), it was "fired by some wretches from the preceding column." The men were permitted to rest here until about 2:00 p.m., when the march continued to a point about one mile beyond Aquia Creek. The 20-mile march was made on one of the hottest days the men had ever experienced. According to a soldier from Thomas Smyth's brigade, the thermometer registered 102 degrees. Many fell from the ranks and straggled behind the column, or fell by the road side. Only 53 men of the 15th Massachusetts were present when the march ended, causing the regiment's commanding officer to write, "I never saw anything like it. The men would go as long as they could stand and then fall." Lieutenant Colonel Richard Thompson of the 12th New Jersey (Smyth's brigade) wrote home that he would rather fight a pitched battle than make a forced march. "Men fall from exhaustion, clothes wet, faces and teeth black with dust, lips parched, eyes sunken, feet blistered, and then driven on at the point of the bayonet."[24]

The men were unaccustomed to this type of forced march and their behavior reflected it. Charles Cowtan of the 10th New York noted:

> On the morning's start the regiment was noisy with conversation, and loud jokes....Later in the day words grew fewer

and laughter and song more scarce...now late in the afternoon, the soldiers have no stomach or spare wind for words,
and scarcely anything is heard but the groan of some suf-
ferer from blistered feet, or the steady click of the bayonet
swinging at the left side against its neighbor the canteen.[25]

III Corps

The men were on the road at 7:00 a.m., bound for Manassas
Junction. At least part of the march was along the Orange and
Alexandria Railroad. The temperatures soared as the day wore
on. According to John Halsey of the 17th Maine (DeTrobriand's
brigade), "the air was almost suffocating...the dust in the road
was scalding...the soil of Virginia was sucked into our throats,
sniffed into our nostrils, and flew into our eyes and ears until our
most intimate friends would not have recognized us." Charles
Bardeen (Carr's brigade) recalled, "never again did I suffer for
water as on this day." General David Birney wrote to a friend, "the
country is barren of good water, and men would gather on the
road side, lapping up like dogs anything like liquid." Those men
still in the ranks were most grateful when a halt was ordered near
Bull Run at about 10:00 p.m. The stream provided welcome relief
to the parched and weary men.[26]

V Corps

Reveille sounded at 3:00 a.m., and the V Corps was on the
march about two hours later. The entire march was along the
Orange and Alexandria Railroad. The column passed through the
First Bull Run battlefield, which still bore the effects of that bloody
fight, and reached Manassas Junction by noon. The men were
given an hour's rest here. Back on the road, the combination of
the extreme heat and rapid pace caused scores to fall by the side
of the road with heatstroke. The conditions became so severe
that Meade permitted the men to halt prior to reaching Centreville
after marching 12 miles. Sergeant Charles Bowen of the 12th
U.S. (Hannibal Day's brigade) knew of at least seven men who
died as a result of these severe conditions.[27]

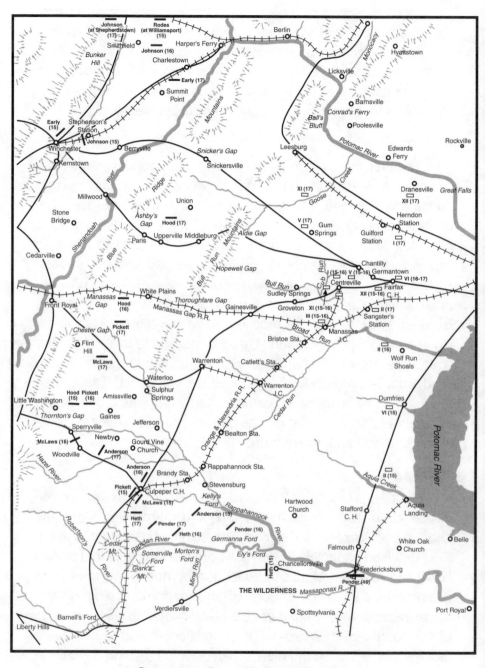

Operations June 15–June 17, 1863

(Dates in June in parentheses)

VI Corps

The column, which had marched all night from Stafford Court House, finally found a clear road, and began making better time at daybreak. A halt was finally permitted at Aquia Creek, where the men prepared breakfast. According to Wilbur Fiske of the 2nd Vermont, "those who had preferred sleep to breakfast lost the latter for a very pitiful allowance of the former." On the road again, the heat became unbearable, and coupled with the intense clouds of dust and scarcity of water, the men were miserable. They felt that the dust that caked them actually intensified the effects of the sun. Ambulances were soon filled with men who could not keep up, and the dead lined the road. Newton's division at the head of the column finally reached Dumfries between 11:00 a.m. and noon; the rearguard did not reach it until 5:00 p.m. By this time, some of the regiments could count less than a third of their men present. After resting for a while, the coffeepots appeared, and the men felt that their brews never tasted better.[28]

XI Corps

The corps was up at 3:00 a.m., but it did not begin its march until 6:00 a.m. The men reached Centreville about three hours later. After passing through the town and marching a short distance beyond it, the men were delighted when they were ordered to halt and prepare to bivouac for the night. John McMahon marveled in his diary, "we have come 63 miles in all in 2½ days, which I think is well for such hot weather."[29]

XII Corps

Up at 2:30 a.m., the men were soon on the road from Dumfries. Many grumbled about not having a chance for breakfast. Several horses that had been brought into camp now carried the men's knapsacks. One Virginia farmer stormed up to General Henry Slocum, complaining that someone had taken his horse. After asking him if he was a loyal Union-man and hearing that he was not, Slocum asked him, "Did they burn your house and barn, and kill all your cattle?" When the farmer replied that they hadn't,

Slocum told him, "Well, sir, you ought to thank God, and consider yourself fortunate."[30]

The weather was extremely hot during the 25-mile march to Fairfax Court House, and many fell by the side of the road with heatstroke. Edmund Brown of the 27th Indiana (Colgrove's brigade) related that General Henry Slocum appeared during one of the short breaks. Officers began yelling, "Clear the way, there!" Slocum kindly said, "Never mind, boys, don't get up: my horse is not as tired as you are. We can go around." The march finally ended at about 9:00 p.m. As Archibald McDougall's brigade arrived at its bivouac site, a brass band struck up military airs, which seemed to invigorate even the most tired men.[31]

June 16

CONFEDERATE

All three of Lee's corps were in motion for the first time since the campaign began. Longstreet's men continued their march east of the Blue Ridge Mountains where they screened the Second Corps, which was marching toward the Potomac River. Far to the south, Hill's corps approached Culpeper Court House.

Imboden's Confederate cavalry brigade entered Cumberland, Maryland. After rounding up horses and visiting stores, the Confederate raiders burned the telegraph office. Amazingly, they did not touch the railroad shop. The relieved citizens watched the Confederate column ride out of town at about 10:30 a.m.[1]

Jenkins's Confederate cavalry brigade left Chambersburg and rode north about four miles, stopping at Shirk's Hill. Here they formed into line of battle. Meanwhile, Jenkins returned to Chambersburg and demanded $900 for the horses and equipment taken from the two captured officers that had not been returned. The town complied, paying in Confederate script. While Jenkins was in town, foraging parties combed the region for horses, cattle, and useful supplies.[2]

First Corps

Hood's men were on the march at first light. After traveling three miles, they were permitted to rest for an hour. The march continued, occasionally across fields. As the men approached

Jenkins's cavalry brigade in Chambersburg

Battles and Leaders of the Civil War

the mountains, they could see the devastation caused by Federal troops all around them. The temperature began to soar, and the dust was thick. Before long, men began falling from the ranks. Fatalities apparently occurred as the situation was exacerbated by the scarcity of water. Thomas Ware estimated that one hundred men from his 15th Georgia fell by the wayside. Most rejoined the regiment later that night. The march finally concluded at 9:00 p.m. at Marcum Station on the Manassas Gap Railroad.[3]

McLaws's men were on the road by 4:00 a.m., and unlike Hood's men's march up ahead, theirs was almost pleasant. Robert Moore of the 17th Mississippi (William Barksdale's brigade) reported, "have traveled more than 20 miles yet the boys complain but little of being fatigued." Gentle breezes cooled the men ali day—breezes that were less evident in the hilly country now being traversed by Hood's men. The column bivouacked for the night near Sperryville.[4]

Pickett's men did not begin their march until 7:00 a.m. They crossed the Hazel River and eventually camped near Gaines' Crossroads after the 20-mile march. Surgeon Charles Lippitt noted that while the ground here was not as fertile as that around Culpeper Court House, "the mountain scenery by far [is] more grand & beautiful."[5]

The march was a hot one. Randolph Shotwell of the 8th Virginia (Richard Garnett's brigade) vividly described what it was like to march in such hot weather:

> The dust is almost suffocating...it forms a fine impalpable powder, sufficiently light to fill the air like smoke; and penetrate the eyes, ears, nostrils, hair, and skin, until its power of annoyance is unbearable. Then, when one's clothing is utterly saturated with perspiration mixing with the dust in a grimy paste; and above all weighs the heavy musket...and the chafing canteen straps, is it strange that one sees hundreds of men gasping for breath, and lolling out their tongues like mad men?[6]

Second Corps

Johnson's men were up by 6:00 a.m. and ordered to cook two days' rations. The march toward Shepherdstown began around 3:00 p.m. and ended just south of Smithfield. Here Jones's brigade was detached to destroy canal boats, grain, and generally put the Chesapeake and Ohio Canal out of commission.[7]

While Johnson's division marched toward the Potomac River, Early's men remained in camp near Winchester. Many wandered into town, hoping to secure some supplies. Much to their displeasure, the captured supplies were guarded by quartermasters, who liberally helped themselves to the goods. Lieutenant William Kincheloe fumed, "this was the reward brave soldiers received for taking the place."[8]

General Rodes permitted his division to rest near the Potomac River. The halt at Williamsport was necessary because his men's feet were "bruised, bleeding, and swollen," yet none complained, and all tried to keep up. The quartermaster was busy scrounging about for supplies, sending two tons of leather, 35 kegs of black powder, 1,500 horses, and 2,000 head of cattle south to Virginia.[9]

Third Corps

Pender's division finally began its march at 4:00 a.m., making it the last of Lee's divisions to embark on the invasion. The division marched about 15 miles and crossed the Rapidan River at Ely's Ford. Heth's division began its march at about 3:30 a.m., and marched approximately 18 miles, halting within 12 miles of Culpeper Court House. This was a difficult march for the men. According to J. Caldwell (Abner Perrin's brigade), "the weather was intensely hot and close, and it was with difficulty that the men, fresh from camp, and burdened with unnecessary baggage could be kept up."[10]

Anderson's division finally reached Culpeper Court House and marched about two miles beyond it. Because of the excessive heat, a number of men fell by the side of the road with heatstroke. The route of the march was lined with discarded blankets and clothing, as the men made a valiant effort to keep up.[11]

UNION

Only the two corps well south of Washington were on the march today. The VI Corps marched from Dumfries to Fairfax Station, and farther south, the II Corps marched from Aquia Creek via Dumfries to Wolf Run Shoals. The rest of the army was given a well-deserved rest. The I and XI Corps were in camp near Centreville, the III camped near the old Bull Run battlefield, the V Corps camped near Warrenton Station, and the XII Corps was concentrated near Fairfax.

In a candid note to Lincoln, Hooker apologized for some of his recent remarks, stating, "they were suggestions merely, for I have not the data necessary to form an enlightened opinion in this case." He also indicated a growing problem: "I have not enjoyed the confidence of the major-general [Halleck] commanding the army....as long as this continues we may look in vain for success." Seeking to correct the errors in his previous dispatches, Hooker wrote, "it may be possible now to move to prevent a junction of A. P. Hill's corps with those of Ewell and Longstreet. If so, please let instructions to that effect be given to me." This was a very strange message, given Halleck's expansive orders about the use of the army. Lincoln could not have felt good about Hooker's growing timidity.[12]

Hooker later wired Lincoln that he would put the army in motion at 3:00 a.m. the following day to relieve the Harper's Ferry garrison. Lincoln fired back, "to remove all misunderstanding, I now place you in the strict military relation to General Halleck....I shall direct him to give you orders and you to obey them." Halleck followed with a dispatch about 15 minutes later: "I have given no directions for your army to move to Harper's Ferry. I have advised the movement of a force, sufficiently strong to meet Longstreet, on Leesburg, to ascertain where the enemy is, and then move to the relief of Harper's Ferry, or elsewhere, as circumstances might require." He further attempted to clarify Hooker's role by stating, "you are in command of the Army of the Potomac, and will make the particular dispositions as you deem proper. I shall only indicate the objects to be aimed at." Halleck explained that there were no reports of enemy troops approaching Harper's Ferry, so there was no reason for Hooker to move his army there.[13]

In a subsequent telegram, Hooker asked Secretary of War Stanton to tell the media that his army was moving south to the James River, as a way of throwing a scare in Lee. Stanton quickly rebuffed him, writing "the very demon of lying seems to be about these times, and generals will have to be broken for ignorance before they will take the trouble to find out the truth of the reports."[14]

A frustrated Governor Curtin noted that Philadelphia had not responded to his proclamation, yet the enemy was beyond Chambersburg and advancing rapidly toward Harrisburg. "Our capital is threatened, and we may be disgraced by its fall, while the men who should be driving these outlaws from our soil are quarreling about the possible term of service for six months."[15]

All-out panic began to grip Harrisburg. Records, portraits, and other valuables were removed from the State House and sent to safety. Shops were boarded up and merchandise sent to Philadelphia for safekeeping. Bankers did the same with their currency. Thousands thronged to the railroad station, hoping to catch a train. It didn't matter where, as long as it was miles from the approaching rebels. One observer wrote that the movement "[is] no longer a flight—it is a flood." The roads south of Harrisburg were deluged with people walking or riding in wagons. The latter were loaded high with valuables. In the hysteria, several citizens thought to be Southern sympathizers were arrested.[16]

The panic also spread to other cities. Baltimore impressed all African Americans into service to build entrenchments and forts without payment, while Philadelphia raised over $51,000 for labor and materials to build theirs.[17]

General Dix's plans crystallized. One column of 7,000 men under General George Getty would march to Hanover Junction and destroy bridges over the North and South Anna Rivers, while a second column of 5,000 under General Erasmus Keyes would move from White House to secure Bottom's Bridge on the Chickahominy. This would leave a clear path for Getty's men to advance on Richmond.[18]

I Corps

The exhausted men were permitted to rest throughout the day at Centreville. It became a "wash" day for both the men's bodies and their clothes. The lack of news of Lee's movements and intentions led to wild rumors. Some made the men exceptionally nervous, like the story that had Lee crossing into Pennsylvania. Some units were ordered to participate in a dress parade.[19]

II Corps

Up at 3:00 a.m., the men were on the road from Aquia Creek an hour later. The column reached Dumfries at 8:00 a.m. Here the men were permitted to rest for two hours before moving on to Wolf Run Shoals, which they reached at dusk. This too was a hard march, and the roads were lined with stricken men. Captain

George Bowen (12th New Jersey) noted in his diary, "one would scarce have recognized his best friend through the sweat and dust, our faces would be wet with perspiration, the dust would settle on it, then a drop would start running down and wash a path through, this would soon fill, and again it would be washed off."[20]

III Corps

The men were given another day of rest. Many toured the old Bull Run battlefield, still littered with debris and skeletal remains.[21]

V Corps

The men were grateful to have a day of rest near Centreville, where they were joined by hundreds of stragglers. The soldiers roamed the countryside, which contained many old Confederate forts built during the first year of the war.[22]

VI Corps

The march began again after midnight on June 16. As with the day before, the men marched through the night, and were

Union troops reach Manassas Junction

Battles and Leaders of the Civil War

given a breakfast break in the morning. Many of them were too tired, even for coffee, and slept instead. Then it was on to Wolf Run Shoals on the Occoquan River for a longer halt. The men found a large measure of relief in the cool waters, using it to bathe their blistered feet, cool their hot, throbbing heads, and satisfy their thirst. They were back on the road at 3:30 p.m., after their three-hour rest, and reached Fairfax Station in the evening, when they went into camp.[23]

XII Corps

The men were given a day of rest near Fairfax Court House, and told that they would be breaking camp at 3:00 a.m. the following morning.[24]

June 17

CONFEDERATE

Lee continued to be frustrated by his lack of knowledge about Hooker's movements. He had every reason to be concerned because his army stretched over one hundred miles. Ewell's Second Corps straddled the Potomac River, Hill's Third Corps was en route to the Shenandoah Valley from Culpeper Court House, and Longstreet's First Corps was between the two in the Shenandoah Valley. Lee complained to General Longstreet in a dispatch that "I have heard nothing of the movements of General Hooker either from General Stuart or yourself, and, therefore, can form no opinion of the best move against him." He was particularly concerned about Ewell's Second Corps, which was preparing to invade Maryland. To Ewell he wrote, "repress marauding. Take what is necessary for the army, and give citizens of Maryland Confederate money or certificates. Do not expose yourself. Keep your own scouts."[1]

Lee had not heard from General Stuart because he had his hands full with Yanks. Assigned to guard Longstreet's flank, Stuart had deployed his brigades so they blocked the vital Aldie and Thoroughfare Gaps through the Blue Ridge Mountains. A pitched battle was fought with Federal cavalry and infantry at Aldie, who pushed Stuart's troopers out of the pass. Pickett's and Hood's divisions (First Corps) rushed over to support the cavalry.[2]

First Corps

Hood's exhausted men were re-energized when they learned of Ewell's decisive victory at Winchester. Still marching parallel to, and east of, the Blue Ridge Mountains from Marcum Station, the men followed the railroad east for a few miles, then struck north again on a rocky and hilly road. While difficult, the march was made easier by the abundance of the cool mountain water. Upon reaching Piedmont Station (now Delaplane), the local citizens treated the men to delicacies, but it was not much more than a gesture. Thomas Ware reported that one local woman presented two gallons of milk and a bucket of ham and biscuits to his regiment, which numbered over three hundred men. Once again, the temperatures soared and scores of men fell by the side of the road. Ware estimated that over half of the men in his company fell out of the ranks: "I never saw men so much fatigued & it was [the] hottest march we ever done." The men were finally permitted to rest briefly at Upperville, then continuing on for two miles before halting for the night.[3]

McLaws's men now experienced what Hood's had on June 16—hilly roads with little water. Robert Moore recorded in his diary, "have a very fatiguing march to-day. A great many have broken down & a good number have been sun stroke." The march, which began again at 4:00 a.m., passed Little Washington and Gaines' Crossroads.[4]

The 22-mile march of Pickett's division began at 5:00 a.m. and ultimately ended at Brice's Crossroads. Randolph Shotwell noted the difficult conditions, writing, "flesh and blood cannot sustain such heat and fatigue....it is terrible....I have seen men dropping, gasping, dying, or already dead." The hot, dry weather caused quite a commotion when the column reached a source of water. According to Shotwell, men "crowding you at each elbow, stepping on you from behind, and getting in your way in front; like a flock of sheep, frightened and confused..."[5]

Second Corps

Reveille sounded in Johnson's division's camps at 3:30 a.m., and the men were on the road an hour later. The column halted for the day at noon, three miles south of Shepherdstown, after the 12-mile march.[6]

Early's division remained in camp near Winchester. Some of the men again tried their luck at getting needed supplies, and this time, at least some were successful. Lieutenant Kincheloe was pleased with his new pair of pants and boots. Gordon's, Hays's and Smith's brigades left Winchester around noon and marched toward Charlestown, camping about four miles south of the town.[7]

General Rodes ordered Daniel's brigade across the Potomac River in the early afternoon to join the three that had crossed on June 15. O'Neal's brigade was left behind on the Virginia side. Quartermasters scoured the countryside, looking for provisions, which Rodes said were "obtained, in a proper manner." Among the goods secured were 35 kegs of powder and 2,000 head of cattle. He could not vouch for the behavior of Jenkins's cavalry, however. Rodes noted that the horses they took "were rarely accounted for." He also reported that Jenkins's men engaged in some violence at Greencastle.[8]

Third Corps

Leaving Culpeper Court House, Anderson's division crossed the Hazel River and camped on the opposite side. Several heat-induced deaths were reported.[9]

Both Heth's and Pender's divisions began their marches between 4:00 and 4:30 a.m. The weather was exceptionally hot again, causing several deaths. Heth's division finally reached Culpeper Court House around 10:00 a.m. and camped about two miles beyond it. Pender's division marched about 12 miles that day but was still south of Culpeper.[10]

UNION

Hooker's frustration with conflicting reports about Lee's movements, and even those of other Federal troops in the area, continued to escalate. He knew from General Couch that approximately 1,500 enemy cavalry were in Chambersburg and had heard of enemy activity near Hagerstown, Maryland. That night, Hooker shot off a note to Halleck, saying, "all my cavalry are out, and I have deemed it prudent to suspend any further advance of the infantry until I have information that the enemy are in force in the Shenandoah Valley." That day, the I Corps marched from Centreville to Herndon Station, the II Corps continued its march to Sangster's Station, the III Corps moved a short distance from the Bull Run battlefield to Centreville, the V Corps broke camp at Warrenton Junction and marched to Gum Springs on Goose Creek, the VI Corps was permitted to rest at Fairfax Station, the XI Corps marched from its camp near Centreville to Goose Creek near Leesburg, and the XII Corps broke camp at Fairfax and marched to Dranesville. During the next week, these troops would essentially remain inactive waiting until, according to Hooker, "the enemy develops his intention or force."[11]

In utter frustration, Hooker's chief of staff, Daniel Butterfield, sent a wire to General Rufus Ingalls in Washington: "Try to hunt up somebody from Pennsylvania who knows something, and has a cool enough head....[rebel] cavalry enough is reported to have appeared to fill up the whole of Pennsylvania and leave no room for the inhabitants."[12]

Hooker ordered Pleasonton to send General David Gregg's cavalry division to Aldie, and then on toward Winchester to learn more about the enemy's movements and strength. Pleasonton immediately complied. One regiment ran into Fitz Lee's brigade, and after a heated battle, drove the Confederates backward. It was later set upon by another Confederate cavalry brigade and almost annihilated. Judson Kilpatrick's brigade ran into Thomas Rosser's brigade at Aldie, and after a lively fight, defeated it. Losses were high, particularly among Kilpatrick's Federal cavalry brigade, which lost about 20 percent of its men. Late that night, Hooker ordered Pleasonton to continue pushing against the enemy cavalry to see what was behind it.[13]

Jenkins's Confederate cavalry brigade remained in Chambersburg for a third day. Officers ordered the stores to be opened at 8:00 a.m., so the men could "shop." Suddenly a courier rushed in with news that the Yankees were coming. Jenkins quickly collected his men and rode south toward Greencastle. It turned out that the "Federal troops" were only curious citizens from a nearby town who were paying a visit to Chambersburg to see the invaders.[14]

The Union high command's hope of a foray against Richmond from the Peninsula unraveled. In what appears to be a series of excuses, the commander of the expedition, General Erasmus Keyes, told General Dix that he was concerned about maintaining the flow of supplies as he moved north. "If we advance further we must establish depots, and guard them," he wrote. Then he outrageously second-guessed his superiors by stating that if Lee was crossing into Pennsylvania, his troops should abandon their mission and march north to help halt the enemy invasion.[15]

A new source of troops began to materialize. At 1:10 a.m., Governor Curtin sent a wire to Stanton asking whether the 172nd Pennsylvania, whose term of enlistment had expired, and was about to leave Yorktown for home, could re-enlist as a six-month regiment. At about 10:20 p.m., Stanton received another telegram asking whether he could use the services of the 800-strong 27th New Jersey, whose term of enlistment had also expired. Both invitations were gladly accepted.[16]

With enemy raiders in Pennsylvania, thousands of citizens from the Keystone state finally answered the call for militia. Approximately 8,000 men eventually reached Camp Curtin, outside of Harrisburg, and participated in the campaign. Here they were equipped and mustered into Federal service. In all, about 37,000 Pennsylvanians were mustered in during this period.[17]

Stanton continued to receive queries from governors about Lincoln's call for six-month volunteers. An example was a telegram from Rhode Island's Governor James Smith, who asked if these men would be credited to his state under the Conscription Act, and if returning nine-month regiments could receive a bounty for enlisting in six-month regiments.[18]

Other governors, like Joel Parker of New Jersey, were ready to act. He issued a proclamation that began, "Jerseymen! The

State of Pennsylvania is invaded! A hostile army is now occupying and despoiling the towns of our sister State. She appeals to
New Jersey...to aid in driving back the invading army."[19]

I Corps

The men were back on the road between 5:30 and 6:00 a.m.
after a short reprieve. Their destination was Herndon Station on
the Alexandria and Loundoun (Leesburg) Railroad, which they
reached at about 4:00 p.m. after a 14-mile march. A. P. Smith
(Lysander Cutler's brigade) noted that "the roads were filled with
wagons, batteries, cavalry, infantry, artillery, all rushing, halting,
sweating." Air circulation was restricted as the men marched
through dense groves of pines. The results were predictable. According to Smith, "the dust arose in suffocating clouds, was in-
haled at every breath, and settling upon faces from which the
perspiration flowed at every pore, soon rendered the face of the
most intimate friend indistinguishable in the surging crowd." The
conditions were almost unbearable, and the roads were lined with
prostate men. Those still in the column were overjoyed to see the
cool clear springs near Herndon Station. Within moments, thousands were splashing cool water on their steaming faces and
necks.[20]

II Corps

The men were permitted to sleep in, so the march did not
begin until 9:00 a.m. The road took the men through the Bull Run
battlefield, where they could see the remnants of that great battle.
The column finally reached their campground at Sangster's Station on the Orange and Alexandria Railroad, near Fairfax Court
House, at 4:00 p.m. It was another difficult march. One sergeant
from the 14th Connecticut (Smyth's brigade), recalled, "it was a
terrible day, the weather being hot and sultry. The roads were
ground to powder by the thousands of men who had preceded
us, which made our process very slow, and strong men wilted
down as though blasted by something in the air....the ambulances
were soon filled with used up men, while hundreds of others had

to be urged along, as we were not allowed to leave one living man behind." The rearguard collected discarded items that could be used by the enemy, arranged them in piles, and burned them.[21]

III Corps

No one was upset when the morning passed without orders to resume the march. The men were on the road by 3:00 p.m. and marched only three miles to Centreville, arriving there at about 5:00 p.m. "The heat is truly infernal, and only the shortness of the march saved many of us from sunstroke," wrote John Halsey (de Trobriand's brigade). The men could not complain, however, as they were now camped in the shade with ample fresh water nearby. Rampant rumors had General George McClellan assuming command of the army again.[22]

V Corps

Reveille sounded at 3:30 a.m., and the men were on the road by 6:00 a.m. The road surface was a good one for marching, and although the pace of this march was more moderate, Ira Pettit of the 11th U.S. (Sidney Burbank's brigade) noted in his diary, "tremenduous [sic] falling out of the men...awful dusty." John Parker of the 22nd Massachusetts (William Tilton's brigade) wrote, "there was nothing but slimy mudholes to drink out of, and the suffering was intense." Sergeant Charles Bowen of the 12th U.S. was one of the men who fell from the ranks, noting that "my sight began to fail & my head swim [sic] & I had to drop under a shade tree. I lay here some two hours...." After passing through Centreville, the 10-mile march continued to Gum Springs near Goose Creek, where the men went into camp at about 4:00 p.m. According to Francis Parker, the 32nd Massachusetts (Jacob Sweitzer's brigade) started the march with 230 men and ended it with 107. "Even this poor showing was far ahead of most regiments composing the division," he wrote.[23]

The two-division corps was to be joined by another: Crawford's Pennsylvania Reserves, which had been on guard duty around Washington since February. A participant in many bloody battles of the war, it was sent to guard the capital and restock its depleted ranks, as it was a "mere skeleton." Beginning on June 15, the men could see long lines of wagons and infantry pass their lines. Not able to accept their inactivity any longer, the officers of William McCandless's brigade sent a plea to their commanding officer: "We, the undersigned...having learned that our mother State has been invaded by a Confederate force, respectfully ask, that you will, if it be in your power, have us ordered within the borders of our State for her defense....we now wish to meet him [the enemy] again where he threatens our homes, our families and our firesides." The men did not know it, but orders were already being cut for their return to the Army of the Potomac.[24]

VI Corps

The VI Corps was permitted to rest at Fairfax Station after its rigorous marches during the past few days. Here the men counted and nursed their blisters, scrapes, and sores. They also worried about the location of the Confederate army, not sure "where our crafty foes are in the front or rear."[25]

XI Corps

The men were up between 2:00 and 3:00 a.m. and told to prepare to march. They were on the road to Leesburg by 4:00 a.m., marching at a "lively gait." The day was exceptionally hot and dusty, and men fell by the score. Wagons following the corps picked up these unfortunates until they become full. According to William Shimmers (von Gilsa's brigade), "every shady nook and corner was occupied by squads who, overpowered by the heat, were unable to keep up with the marching column." The column halted at 11:30 a.m., and the men ate lunch. The corps finally halted at Goose Creek, near Leesburg, after the 23-mile march. Many men refreshed themselves in the creek as soon as the march ended. Some of the more fortunate were treated to a sheep supper, when some of these animals roamed into the camps. John McMahon noted, "the boys went out and killed them without leave or license."[26]

XII Corps

True to their word, the XII Corps officers ordered the bugles sounded at 3:00 a.m., and the men were on the road from Fairfax Court House within an hour. It was an easy 10-mile march. The men went into camp at 11:00 a.m., about 2–3 miles southeast of Dranesville. It was just as well, for the heat was unbearable, even in the shade. The men were occasionally rousted when the grass and woods caught fire.[27]

June 18

CONFEDERATE

Lee finally ascertained that Hooker's entire army had at last pulled back from the Rappahannock River and was concentrating near Centreville. This gave him additional confidence that Richmond was not Hooker's target.[1]

The cavalry battles over the Blue Ridge Mountain gaps continued as the enemy advanced as far as Upperville, where a battle was waged. Lee ordered Hood's division to march from Upperville to relieve Early at Winchester, so the latter could rejoin Ewell's Corps in its march through Maryland. However, enemy activity on the road to Snickersville forced Lee to send Hood's division instead to protect Snicker's Gap through the Blue Ridge Mountains. While Ewell was in the northern part of Virginia, Longstreet was to protect the mountain passes, so that the enemy could not get between the rest of the army, and A. P. Hill's Corps was now marching toward the Shenandoah Valley.[2]

First Corps

Hood's march began early, and before long the men had reached Paris, where they were permitted to rest for two hours. The column traversed Ashby's Gap and entered the Shenandoah Valley. They waded the two hundred-yard wide, waist-deep Shenandoah River. An additional mile brought Henry Benning's and Robertson's brigades to their campsites. Laws's and

Anderson's brigades were detached at the river and sent down to guard Snicker's Ford. The men appreciated that they only marched eight miles that day.[3]

Pickett's men were on the road again by 5:00 a.m. and soon passed Piedmont and reached Paris at about 11:00 a.m. Surgeon Charles Lippitt was most impressed by the scenery: "I was never more struck with the grandeur of mountain scenery than on this march. No other scenery can equal it." Randolph Shotwell marveled at how the weather had changed from blistering hot to cool. "This evening we are positively shivering around our campfires, with hail and sleet falling...," he noted.[4]

Possibly because of the hard march the day before, McLaws's men did not begin their trek until 5:00 a.m. Men began dropping from the ranks even before they had marched 10 miles. The still air intensified the heat and clouds of choking dust. The column finally ground to a halt for the night near Piedmont Station on the Manassas Gap Railroad. Heavy evening rains helped cool things down a bit.[5]

Second Corps

Johnson's division's leisurely march northward did not continue until 2:00 p.m., and two hours later, the column crossed the Potomac River at Boteler's Ford. One soldier from the 1st Maryland noted in his diary, "when we caught sight of the river, a shout arose." John Stone of the regiment found the current to be very strong. "On this side we gave three rousing cheers," he noted. Their brigade commander, General George Steuart, also a Marylander, jumped off his horse and kissed the earth. The march continued for about three miles to the edge of the Sharpsburg battlefield, where the division went into bivouac. Many men left their camps to visit the old battlefield. The 1st and 3rd North Carolina of Steuart's brigade marched to the site of their comrades' graves. A chaplain conducted a burial service, and a military salute was fired. In all, the division marched about six miles that day.[6]

While Robert Hoke's brigade, accompanied by General Early, finally left Winchester, the rest of the division approached the

Potomac River. The weather was miserable. Lieutenant Kincheloe described the men as becoming "jaded and the whole of us much oppressed by heat." As the men passed through Leestown, they were somewhat energized by the local women, who turned out to provide encouragement. The main body camped about two miles from Kearneysville on the road leading to Shepherdstown.[7]

While Rodes's men were again resting and collecting supplies, Ewell visited their commander with momentous orders. The division would break camp on June 19 and head for Hagerstown. The men would then march south, as though they were about to attack Harper's Ferry. Their actual destination was Chambersburg, Pennsylvania.[8]

Third Corps

The corps was again on the march. While Anderson's division reached the vicinity of Flint Hill, Heth's division passed through Sperryville and camped between it and Gaines' Crossroads. Pender's division passed through Culpeper Court House and camped about four miles beyond it.[9]

UNION

After hearing that Confederate cavalry was at Point of Rocks, Maryland, Hooker dispatched the XII Corps to Leesburg to secure the fords in the area. Colonel Elijah White, 35th Virginia Cavalry Battalion, had already destroyed a "first class" engine and 22 cars, and had captured a cavalry company under Captain S. C. Means. According to General Daniel Tyler, the train was "sacrificed by carelessness and bad management."[10]

In preparation for crossing into Maryland, Hooker ordered pontoon bridges thrown across the Potomac River. He also sent a circular to his commanders outlining materials that could not be brought along on the march, including excess baggage, wooden benches, and cooking stoves. Only two days' supplies of food for the men, and three days' forage for the animals were to be carried in the limited number of wagons. In a backhanded slap against

Hooker, Halleck wrote that "officers and citizens are on a big stampede. They are asking me why does not General Hooker tell where Lee's army is; he is nearest to it."[11]

In the growing confusion over the use of the Harper's Ferry garrison, Halleck wrote to Hooker, "General Schenck has been notified that you have control of any of his forces that are within the sphere of your operations. If you want anything of General Schenck [commanding the Middle District, which included Harper's Ferry] or General Heintzelman [overall commander of the Washington defenses], telegraph them direct."[12]

This was primarily a day of rest for the Army of the Potomac. All of the corps remained in camp, except for the VI Corps, which made a short march, and the XII Corps, which made a longer one to Leesburg. Hooker's aides reported that by the end of the day, the I Corps was near Guilford Station, the II Corps was at Sangster's Station, the III Corps was near Centreville, the V Corps was at Gum Springs, the VI Corps was at Germantown, the XI Corps was on Goose Creek, and the XII Corps was at Leesburg.[13]

After tangling with his Confederate counterparts the day before at Aldie, General Pleasonton sent two strong reconnaissance columns out in search of the enemy. One went toward Ashby's Gap by way of Middleburg, and the second rode toward Snicker's Gap by way of Philomont. The two sides fought a series of skirmishes on the east side of the Blue Ridge Mountains.[14]

Colonel John Mosby's Confederate irregulars continued to be a problem. General Butterfield, Hooker's chief of staff, wrote to General Meade, "Catch and kill any guerrillas, then try them, [it] will be a good method of treating them."[15]

Hooker was also frustrated by the amount of accurate information about his army's movements that was finding its way into Northern newspapers. He finally asked the Associated Press to distribute a telegram to all editors, asking them not to print the locations of his units, nor official reports. "After any fight the reports can open their fire as loudly as they please, but avoid...giving the designations of forces engaged," he wrote.[16]

Patriotic fever was especially common among the African Americans living in Pennsylvania, and many wished to enlist. When asked if he would accept black recruits, General Couch merely replied that he had no authority to do so. In a note to Stanton, he expressed his concern that such an act would be bitterly opposed in many communities. Stanton, who was also receiving heat on this issue, snapped back that Couch should accept any recruit "without regard to color." Possibly rethinking the matter, he softened his position to a recruiting officer stating, "if there is likely to be any dispute about the matter, it will be better to send no more." Stanton understood the sensitivity of the issue and knew that these troops could be used elsewhere.[17]

I Corps

Excited about the prospect of another day's rest, the men were disappointed when they were ordered to break camp and form into column. It turned out that they were only changing their camp to Guilford Station on Broad Run, about four miles to the west.[18]

V Corps

The V Corps remained in camp near Gum Springs. A severe thunderstorm drenched the men at about 4:00 p.m. It was the first rainfall in about six weeks.[19]

VI Corps

The VI Corps broke camp in the morning and marched five miles to a half mile beyond Fairfax Court House, where the men halted and prepared breakfast. They waited through the day for orders to continue to march, but they never arrived. It started to pour at 5:00 p.m., thoroughly soaking the unprotected men. The easy conditions over the past several days had done wonders for the men. They felt rejuvenated and their ranks were back to normal, as the stragglers had slowly returned. Some of the men reflected on the waste of government property. Marching with the rearguard, Reverend Alanson Haines (Torbert's brigade) noted, "the corps which had preceded us in the march had been most prodigal. Hundreds of thousands of dollars' worth of property had been destroyed by the flames, or thrown away, to be gathered by the enemy, should they follow."[20]

XI Corps

The men were assigned the task of providing support for the Federal cavalry. Up at first light and ready to march. They were later told to break ranks, as they were not going to travel that day. Heavy rains pelted the men as they threw their tents up in the afternoon. "Rain at length—refreshing rain—is delighting this parched country. It is the first rain since our recrossing the Rappahannock on the 6th of May," wrote Frederick Winkler of the 26th Wisconsin (Wladimir Krzyzanowski's brigade).[21]

XII Corps

The corps was ordered to make a 20-mile march to Leesburg, where it watched the fords over the Potomac River. The march began at about 7:00 a.m. under oppressively high heat and humidity. The men passed through Dranesville and continued on the road to Leesburg. A welcome shower soaked the soldiers at about 1:00 p.m., which had the effect of relieving their bodies that were soaked with sweat and caked with dust. Williams's division in the van was pelted by hail as it forded waist-deep Goose Creek. It finally reached Leesburg at about 4:00 p.m., where the corps remained for about a week. Slocum first put his men to work rebuilding old breastworks. The countryside yielded a bounty of vegetables, fowl, pork, and grains that energized the men. The old Ball's Bluff battleground was nearby, and most of them toured it during their stay here.[22]

June 19

Lee's army was becoming much less dispersed each day. Ewell's Corps was in southern Maryland and northern Virginia, and Hill's had entered the Shenandoah Valley. Longstreet's Corps was in between, guarding the gaps through the Blue Ridge Mountains.

Lee received disappointing news from President Davis that Jenkins's infantry brigade (Pickett's division) would not join the invasion. According to the president, the brigade was "relied upon by General D. H. Hill, not only to protect Petersburg, but to support the positions occupied by him farther south, and he insists that without it his line cannot be defended."[1]

General Albert Jenkins sent Colonel M. J. Ferguson on a raid to McConnellsburg. The horsemen reached Mercersburg as darkness fell on the town and continued through the night to McConnellsburg.[2]

First Corps

Hood's men were ordered to cook their rations in the morning. Officers suddenly yelled for their men to "fall in," as the division was ordered to seize Snicker's Gap, about ten miles away. Because the food was not ready, details were left behind to complete the task. They caught up with the rest of the division that night. Hood's men were being sent to support Stuart's cavalry, who were trying to fend off their Federal counterparts. The division forded the Shenandoah River at about 1:00 p.m. and finally marched into Snickersville, where the soldiers found the citizens in a frightened way. Federal troops were in the area, and many of the townspeople had abandoned their homes, lest they get in the middle of the fight. Law's and Jerome Robertson's brigades took up defensive positions at Snicker's Gap, while Hood's other two brigades remained at Snickersville for the night. A heavy fog and mist descended upon the brigades up on the gap, and then heavy rains began falling.[3]

McLaws's men did not begin their march until 7:00 a.m. The rains made the roads muddy and the march difficult. The column passed Paris and finally reached Ashby's Gap at about 3:00 p.m., after the 12-mile march. The heavy rains and strong winds that night collapsed several tents.[4]

On the road at 11:00 a.m., Pickett's men thought they would cross Ashby's Gap into the Shenandoah Valley. Instead, they kept marching on the east-side of the Blue Ridge Mountains toward Snicker's Gap. They occupied the area between Hood's and McLaws's divisions.[5]

Second Corps

This was a quiet day for most of Ewell's Corps. Johnson's division rested in southern Maryland. Early's men waited in camp near Shepherdstown while their commanding officer, with Hoke's brigade, marched to join them. The men savored the rest and the cover from the pouring rain, which had begun the prior night and continued unabated through the day.[6]

Prior to continuing its march north, Rodes's division waited until its final brigade, O'Neal's, crossed the Potomac. The Alabamians first removed their pants and underwear before wading into the river. Samuel Pickens of the 5th Alabama noted that the water reached above the men's knees and was "swift & beautifully clear." Finally intact, the division struck north for Hagerstown at about 8:00 a.m. The bands struck up "Bonnie Blue Flag" as the men proudly marched through the streets after the seven-mile

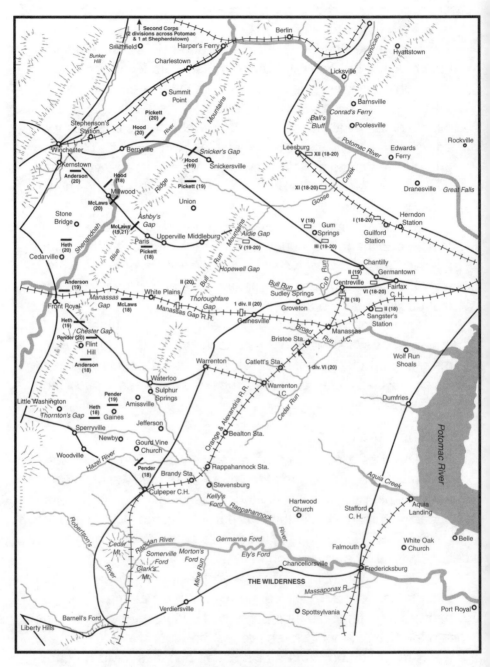

Operations June 18–June 20, 1863
(Dates in June in parentheses)

march. The soldiers found that the men of the town treated them "very shabby, but the ladies quite the reverse," recalled Louis Leon of the 53rd North Carolina (Daniel's brigade). The division marched another two miles to near Funkstown on the road to Boonsborough, where it went into camp at about 2:00 p.m. on the banks of Antietam Creek.[7]

Earlier in the day, a tollgate keeper lowered his bar across the road as Rodes's infantry approached. "Who is going to pay for the horses and wagons I see coming?" he asked an officer. The officer quickly responded, "I am....I'll give you an order on President Davis. Take it to Richmond and get the money." Realizing that he was no match for a eight thousand-man Confederate division, the gate keeper reluctantly raised the bar.[8]

Third Corps

Anderson's division crossed the Blue Ridge Mountains at Chester Gap and marched on Front Royal, where the men went into camp. The reprieve was a short one, as orders arrived at 4:00 p.m. to resume the march. That night, the division crossed both branches of the Shenandoah River. A second set of orders to halt for the night were most welcome, until many of the men realized that mud was everywhere. As a result, most spent the night sitting or standing.[9]

While Heth's division reached Chester Gap in the Blue Ridge Mountains, Pender's division marched all day, crossing the Hazel River, and finally camped at Gaines' Crossroads. The rains caused James McElvany of the 35th Georgia (Edward Thomas's brigade) to record in his diary, "had a very bad time of it." The night was not much better. Surgeon Spencer Welch wrote home: "we were in an open grass field and so we had to stand up and take it....I sat up the entire night on a rock and kept dry with an oilcloth." He noted that he was one of the lucky ones who at least had a rock to sit on.[10]

UNION

Seeking to clarify Halleck's claim that he could use Schenck's and Heintzelman's troops, Hooker asked his commander, "are orders for these commands to be given by me where I deem it necessary? The nature of the control to be exercised by me I would like to have distinctly and clearly fixed and understood by Generals Heintzelman and Schenck, that I may not seem to avoid proper channels or to act discourteously toward them." It actually turned out that Hooker was given control over the latter, as Halleck only deemed the defense of the capital to be too important to be turned over to a field commander.[11]

Hooker reported that his cavalry had clashed with the enemy's again, this time near Middleburg and Upperville. The Confederate horsemen had again been shoved backward. Four of the infantry corps remained in camp: I Corps at Guilford Station, VI Corps at Fairfax Court House, XI Corps at Goose Creek, about four miles from Leesburg (toward Aldie), XII Corps at Leesburg. The V Corps was sent from Gum Springs to Aldie to support the Federal cavalry there. The III Corps marched from Centreville to take its place. The latter's position at Centreville was taken by the II Corps, which marched from Sangster's Station. Pleasonton's reports still led Hooker to doubt that Lee was going to cross the Potomac River.[12]

After exchanging telegrams with General Slocum of the XII Corps about where the pontoon bridges over the Potomac should be built, General Daniel Butterfield decided on Edward's Ferry. He had initially considered Noland's Ford, but given the uncertainty of Lee's position and his respect for Slocum, Butterfield chose Edward's Ferry.[13]

In a later telegram, Hooker expressed his dissatisfaction that the New York Herald was accurately reporting his army's movements. "Is there no way of stopping it?" The Northern press had become a veritable gold mine of accurate information, and Confederate commanders actively sought out the papers during the invasion. Halleck replied that there was no way, except by expelling the reporters from the camps, which Grant had done in Mississippi.[14]

Now that Confederate troops had visited Chambersburg, and would possibly do so again, General Curtin assigned General Joseph Knipe to command a newly arrived brigade of New

York troops. He placed the eight hundred-man unit on a train from Harrisburg bound for Shippensburg.[15]

I Corps

The I Corps remained in camp near Guilford Station. The men enjoyed watching, and then eating, the plentiful fat sheep in the area.[16]

II Corps

The II Corps's all-day rest on June 18 continued until late afternoon, when the men broke camp at Sangster's Station and took the road to Centreville. The head of the corps reached the town at 5:00 p.m.; the rearguard, several hours later. R. I. Holcombe of the 1st Minnesota (Harrow's brigade) referred to the town as "well known and not pleasantly remembered." Thomas Galway of the 8th Ohio (Samuel Carroll's brigade) recalled that by the time his unit reached its destination at 9:00 p.m., the night was black and rainy, and since the men did not know how long they were to stay here, they merely thrust their bayonet-fixed rifles into the ground and spread their blankets over them.[17]

III Corps

The men's lice and flea infestations had reached epic proportions, making life miserable. At about 2:00 p.m., the men were on the road to Gum Springs (Arcola), about ten miles away. Rains fell on the parched fields at sunset. While the men welcomed the rain, they did not care for the resulting ankle-deep mud. It became so dark during the night march that "bats ran into each other." Edwin Houghton of the 17th Maine (deTrobriand's brigade) recalled that "only by continually shouting could we keep our places in the ranks." The head of the column finally reached its destination at about 9:00 p.m. and went into camp. The soaked men lay down on their wet blankets and tried to sleep. However, a commotion during the night brought the men to their feet. Grabbing their muskets, they fixed bayonets and prepared to repel the enemy charge. Suddenly, a spooked herd of cattle that had been hidden in a small forested area swung into view. The relieved men broke ranks and permitted the cattle to enter their lines. All sacrificed their lives for the Union cause.[18]

V Corps

The V Corps remained in camp near Gum Springs until about 3:30 p.m., when the men were told to pack up their belongings. The march began at about 6:00 p.m. and continued for about six miles along the Winchester Turnpike toward the Blue Ridge Mountains. The corps went into camp at Aldie, just as the first rains began falling. The mountain air and clear, crisp waters helped to invigorate the men.[19]

VI Corps

The men received orders to break camp at Fairfax Court House in the afternoon and await word to begin the march. These orders never arrived, so the soldiers put up their tents again.[20]

XI Corps

The men remained in camp near Goose Creek. The weather was cool and intermittent rains hit the area. The storm was so severe that night that some men were flooded out of their tents.[21]

XII Corps

The XII Corps remained in camp near Leesburg, where they were ordered into formation to watch the execution of three soldiers for desertion. Two were from the 46th Pennsylvania, and the third was from the 13th New Jersey. The number of desertions was becoming alarmingly high, so the Union high command decided that a few executions might act as a deterrent. It seemed to work, for as the men marched past the bodies, they realized the "enormity of their crime might be more emphatically and indelibly stamped upon our minds and consciences," noted Lawrence Wilson of the 7th Ohio (Charles Candy's brigade).[22]

June 20

While Ewell's Corps remained in its camps in northern Virginia and southern Maryland, Hill's Corps continued its march northward in the Shenandoah Valley. Just ahead, Longstreet was ordered to pull his men from the passes and march for the Potomac River.

Lee received welcome news that Imboden's cavalry brigade had destroyed a number of Baltimore and Ohio Railroad bridges between Cumberland and Martinsburg, and gathered large quantities of horses and cattle. Lee was most excited about the latter and wrote to Imboden that "they [cattle] are not only important but essential, and I request that you will do all in your power to obtain all you can." Lee also told Imboden that if the opportunity arose, he should cross the Potomac into Maryland. Knowing that General Imboden's troops were undisciplined, Lee told him to "repress all marauding, take only the supplies necessary for your army...give receipts to the owners, stating the kind, quantity, and estimated value of the articles received, the valuation to be made according to the market price in the country where the property is taken."[1]

Reaching McConnellsburg, Pennsylvania, at 4:00 a.m., Ferguson's detachment of Jenkins's cavalry brigade awoke an astonished citizenry with orders to open their stores so that "purchases" could be made. The Confederate currency was almost as good as play money, but the terrified merchants gladly accepted it so their stores would be spared. The troops also rounded up about $12,000 worth of cattle, 120 horses, and several African Americans. The raiders then retreated through Mercersburg, Pennsylvania.[2]

First Corps

General Longstreet received orders to be ready to march in the direction of the Potomac River. To prepare for this movement, Longstreet ordered his men to recross the Shenandoah River. Earlier in the day, at 9:00 a.m., Benning's and Anderson's brigades (Hood's division) took the road and reunited with Hood's remaining two brigades at Snicker's Gap. The troops began constructing breastworks composed of three-foot-high piles of rocks with brush in front of it. The men remained here through the evening, when they were ordered to abandon their positions and recross the Shenandoah River. Thomas Ware complained, "so this makes the 3d time we have crossed the river in 36 hours." Many of Benning's men were cooking their rations when ordered to leave, so they had to navigate the river holding half-cooked rations of beef in their hands. As rains swelled the river, turning it into a torrent, cavalry detachments were sent down river to catch any unfortunate infantryman who was swept along with the current. The soldiers were ordered to ford the river without disrobing. Some of the men obeyed the order (e.g., Laws's brigade), others did not (e.g., Benning's brigade). Either way, the men were wet and miserable when they reached the opposite side. When the division bivouacked within a mile of the ford, they began looking around for wood to make fires. None could be found, so they began eyeing the fences. The officers initially rejected this idea. They soon relented, but not before each company compensated the fence's owner for the wood used. Soon warm fires could be seen throughout the camps. Most of the men were finally dry by midnight. The cooking continued and most men got little sleep that night.[3]

Pickett's men thought they were to march at first light. Indeed, one brigade had formed into line and the others were preparing to do so, when orders to fall out arrived. The column finally re-formed again at about 1:00 p.m., and the march continued. The initial segment of the march took them through Snicker's Gap. After several miles, the men were permitted to halt and build fires to warm their drenched bodies. The division crossed the Shenandoah River at Snicker's Ferry, which Surgeon Charles Lippitt believed to be the deepest ford on the river; the heavy rains had made the river swift, cold, and armpit deep. A number of men were swept downstream, and many more rifles were lost and ammunition ruined. The men halted just beyond the ford. Randolph Shotwell noted, "we were half frozen and dripping with water when we presented ourselves to the fair feminines [*sic*] of Berryville."[4]

Possibly because of the heavy rains, McLaws's men were not on the road until 5:00 p.m. As the column descended the mountain, the weather moderated, until it was actually sunny at its base. The men next waded the waist-deep Shenandoah River at Berry's Ford and went into camp on the other side. More than a few men were swept up by the strong current and needed to be rescued. Major R. C. Maffett of the 3rd South Carolina (Joseph Kershaw's brigade) reported that his regiment lost 2,370 rounds of ammunition during the crossing.[5]

Second Corps

Johnson's men were told to pack up and prepare to march at 8:00 a.m., but the orders were countermanded two hours later. Some of the men did change the location of their camps, though. Early's and Rodes's divisions also remained in camp—the former still in Virginia, the latter in Maryland. Many men were out foraging, despite the pouring rain. Whiskey apparently flowed freely, causing many of Rodes's men to become drunk.[6]

Third Corps

Because of darkness and rain, not all of Anderson's division's wagons crossed the Shenandoah River on June 19.

Therefore, the men did not continue their march until close to noon on June 20. Once begun, the men marched about two miles beyond White Post, where they bivouacked for the night.[7]

Heth's division, now in the Shenandoah Valley, passed through Front Royal, crossed the Shenandoah River, and camped near White Oak. Pender's division, bringing up the rear, continued its march through Flint Hill, and then camped near Chester Gap in the Blue Ridge Mountains. The steep and muddy roads made the ascent very difficult.[8]

UNION

Hooker's army's positions were unchanged, except for the II Corps and VI Corps. Two divisions of the former marched to Thoroughfare Gap (with a division at Gainesville) to support the cavalry, while Howe's division of the VI Corps marched to Bristoe.[9]

Many Federal troops were now in Colonel John Mosby's territory. Because these rebels knew the area like the backs of their hands, they were able to launch lightning hit and run attacks on the Federal troops. General John Reynolds was nearly captured during one of these raids, so he became especially emphatic about hunting down these irregular troops.[10]

The 2,300-man remnant of Milroy's division assembled in Bedford and Bloody Run, Pennsylvania. Most were without weapons, and Milroy was not initially with them. When Milroy arrived, he consolidated his troops and reported his position to General Couch. The VIII Corps commander, General Schenck, wired Milroy with orders to "inform me where you are, with what force..." Milroy asked Couch for clarification about his situation. Pleased to have a fairly large body of veteran troops in his district, Couch wired back that "you will not obey the orders of any general but myself, no matter what may be his rank." General Halleck seemed to settle the matter when he wrote to Schenck, "Major-General Milroy will be placed in arrest...." Schenck wavered somewhat later in the day and told Milroy, "take your orders for the present and get your supplies from General Couch. Stanton received the welcome news

Pennsylvanians digging entrenchments near Harrisburg

Battles and Leaders of the Civil War

that Couch had concentrated over four thousand militia at Altoona, and General John Foster volunteered to send 10 of his regiments from New Berne, North Carolina, to Baltimore or Fort Monroe.[11]

With the defenses around Harrisburg completed, General Couch manned them with New York militia regiments. The undisciplined soldiers soon wore out their welcome by looting nearby houses and stores.[12]

I Corps

The I Corps remained in camp. Some of the units were told at 2:00 p.m. to await orders for a march to support the cavalry at Aldie. Some, like Henry Baxter's brigade (John Robinson's division) did begin the march, but they were not needed, and were ordered back to camp. Periodic thunderstorms rumbled through the area.[13]

II Corps

The II Corps was on the road from Centreville at noon. Earlier, some of the men had raided the 9th Massachusetts Battery's sutler. General Alexander Hays ordered two pieces of the battery deployed and called out a regiment to disperse the crowd. "It was a great time and afforded much fun," noted Andrew Ford of the

15th Massachusetts. The men passed the two Bull Run battlefields during their march, where they saw numerous unburied and partially buried bodies. Joseph Ward of the 106th Pennsylvania (Philadelphia brigade) wrote in disgust that "it seemed hard enough to give one's life for their country and harder yet, so long after the battle, not to be decently buried, or at least have enough dirt to cover one's bones." The march took the men through Gainesville as the sun went down. William French's division remained here, while Gibbon's and Caldwell's divisions continued on to Haymarket. The Philadelphia brigade, which arrived at about 8:00 p.m., thought it was going into camp here, but was dismayed to be ordered to continue to Thoroughfare Gap after a short rest.[14]

III Corps

The men remained in camp near Gum Springs. Reports of bushwhackers caused the men to stay close to their camps.[15]

V Corps

The V Corps remained in camp near Aldie. Samuel Keene described the day as "a mainly misty day—rather uncomfortable upon the whole—and blue lonesome day."[16]

VI Corps

The VI Corps remained in camp near Fairfax Court House. Rumors about the two contending armies were much more prevalent than official orders. The day was not a quiet one for Howe's division, which marched 18 miles to Bristoe Station. The men were not impressed with their surroundings, which consisted of "a two-story house, which probably answered for a dwelling-house and a depot, and a woodshed."[17]

XI Corps

The rains of the night before were so heavy that Smith's brigade, which had camped on the opposite side of Goose Creek, was ordered to rejoin the rest of the corps before the bridge washed away. Cannonading could be heard to the north, but it was otherwise a quiet day for the men.[18]

June 21

CONFEDERATE

The aggressiveness of the Federal cavalry and their infantry supports caused Lee to countermand Longstreet's orders to continue its march toward the Potomac River. Instead, Hood's and Pickett's men remained in camp, ready to support the cavalry, while McLaws's division was rushed to Ashby's Gap. Hill's Corps began reaching Berryville, while Ewell's remained in camp.[1]

General Lee issued General Orders No. 72 to prevent pillaging as his army entered Northern territory. Among the most important sections were that only officers had the authority to order the taking of supplies and market value was to be paid. If the person refused, the goods could be confiscated. The entire text is in the endnote.[2]

Most of the men were unhappy with this order. John Casler of the Stonewall Brigade (Johnson's division) wrote, "when we crossed the Potomac we thought we would have a fine time plundering in the enemy's country, and live fine; but General Lee had orders read out that we were not to molest any of the citizens, or take any private property, and any soldier caught plundering would be shot." Casler recalled that "the infantry did not have much chance to plunder, as we were kept close in ranks and marched slowly. We would camp every night near some town; but there would be a guard in the town, and we could not get in without a pass, and after we got in were not allowed to disturb anything. Of

115

course we could go to the houses and get all we wanted to eat without money, for they did not want our money, and were glad to give us plenty through fear." Casler noted that the "cherries were ripe while we were in Pennsylvania, and there were a great many trees along the road. We stripped them both of cherries and limbs, leaving nothing but the trunks. General Lee was more strict on us than while in Virginia."[3]

General Micah Jenkins agitated to be permitted to return his infantry brigade to Pickett's division. He correctly observed Federal troops withdrawing from Suffolk. What he didn't know was that these 20,000 troops had massed near Yorktown and appeared poised for an attack on Richmond. Equally troubling to the Richmond authorities was the fact that General D. H. Hill had but three cavalry regiments to patrol a three hundred-mile front in North Carolina.[4]

First Corps

This was a confused day for Hood's division. The men had orders to break camp and be ready to march by sunrise. The drums beat at the appointed time, and the men formed into line. They waited past noon, and many slept with all of their accouterments. General Hood rode through the camps ordering inspections. He told General Henry Benning to find a more appropriate camp and expressed concern over the men's wet ammunition. Before long the men were washing and preparing for a dress parade. These activities completed, the troops were told to be ready to leave. They waited until after dark, but when no further orders arrived, the men unrolled their blankets and went to sleep for the night.[5]

Pickett's men remained in camp. A supply of new clothes arrived, which were distributed to some of the men.[6]

Recrossing the Shenandoah River at about 4:00 p.m., McLaws's men halted, formed line of battle at Ashby's Gap, about two miles east of Paris, and prepared to repel a Federal cavalry attack. They were almost immediately set to work constructing breastworks. Before long they could see the disordered ranks of Confederate cavalry that had been roughed up by their Federal counterparts. The Federal attack never materialized, however, and the men spent a miserable night here. Fires were prohibited because of the proximity of the enemy, and the men had left their blankets back at camp.[7]

Second Corps

Many of Ewell's men participated in religious services. Ewell was excited because he had the go-ahead to march into Pennsylvania, now that Hill's and Longstreet's Corps were near at hand. That evening, Early's and Johnson's men were also told to be ready to move out in the morning.[8] Rodes was told to continue his march toward Chambersburg on June 22.

Third Corps

On the road by 6:00 a.m., Anderson's division reached Berryville at about noon. While the rains brought cooler weather, mud replaced the heat as an impediment to the march. Here the men finally learned that their destination was Pennsylvania. Frank Foote of the 48th Mississippi (Carnot Posey's brigade) explained after the war that "...we were braced by a consciousness of superior valor and a contempt for our foe, which in the end proved our ruin. The idea of making the North feel some for the rigors and hardships was uppermost in our minds...."[9]

Heth's division also continued its arduous journey north, reaching Berryville that evening. Now in the Shenandoah Valley, the morale of Pender's division improved. The intense heat subsided and the men were rewarded with breathtaking views. One soldier in John Lane's brigade called it "the prettiest country I ever saw." The division marched through Front Royal and waded the Shenandoah River. Thomas Littlejohn of the 1st South Carolina (Perrin's brigade) recalled that the river was "one-half thigh deep." The men were pleased to see two officers' canoe overturn in the middle of the river, dumping both unceremoniously into the water. The division spent the night near White Post.[10]

UNION

The Army of the Potomac was again fairly inactive, as all but one division remained in their camps. The exception was Barnes's division of the V Corps, which supported Pleasonton's cavalry. Believing that only Stuart's cavalry was on the east side of the mountains, Pleasonton had requested permission to throw his entire cavalry at it and "cripple it up." The Federal forces attacked Stuart's cavalry at 7:00 a.m., driving Stuart's troopers through Upperville into Ashby's Gap, with the loss of at least one cannon.[11]

A 1,340-foot pontoon bridge was thrown over the Potomac River at Edward's Ferry in preparation of the army's crossing into Maryland. Meanwhile, Federal signal corps officers reported that the rebels had captured herds of cattle in Maryland, and were driving them across the Potomac.[12]

The situation with Milroy became muddied again as General Schenck wired General Couch, "you are to place him [Milroy] at once in arrest."[13]

I Corps

The I Corps remained in camp near Guilford Station as thunderstorms continued to batter the area. The men could hear the sounds of battle coming from Upperville, where the cavalry tangled.[14]

II Corps

The II Corps remained near Thoroughfare Gap. Their responsibility was to ensure that no enemy troops crossed through the mountains at that strategic point.[15]

III Corps

The men remained in camp near Gum Springs where some of the units engaged in drills. They could clearly hear the sounds of the cavalry battle in the distance.[16]

V Corps

While Sykes's division remained in camp near Aldie, Barnes's division was on the road at 3:00 a.m. The men did not know it, but

Union cavalry at Upperville

Battles and Leaders of the Civil War

they were marching to support General Alfred Pleasonton's Federal cavalry, which was tangling with the enemy over the vital Blue Ridge Mountain gaps. Marching to Middleburg, the infantry covered about nine miles. At this point they began passing thousands of Federal cavalry. Colonel Strong Vincent's brigade was detached and sent to accompany General David Gregg's cavalry division. Forming line of battle to the left of the cavalry, Vincent's men could see dismounted rebels behind a stone wall. While advancing three regiments against the wall, Vincent sent the 16th Michigan against the enemy's flank, causing the Confederates to flee. The Confederates stubbornly defended one stone wall after another in a series of skirmishes. During one of these attacks, the Federal troops were able to capture a Blakely cannon. After a series of withdrawals, the Confederates remounted and rode toward Upperville.[17]

The fight between the two cavalry forces was inspiring to Colonel Vincent, who had never witnessed such an event before. "The triumphant strains of the bands, as squadron after squadron hurled the enemy in his flight up the hills...gave us a feeling of regret that we, too, were not mounted and could not join in the chase."[18]

While this was transpiring, Tilton's brigade was ordered to Ashby's Gap to support the cavalry stationed there. It was a time of great anxiety for the men, as they did not know what they would encounter. Colonel Tilton was told that his men would go into action as soon as they arrived at the gap. The enemy did not cooperate, however, pulling out before Tilton's men arrived.[19]

Hearing that the rebel ranger, John Mosby, was to visit a local farm to receive information about the Federal movements, General Meade sent a contingent of 100 men from the 14th U.S. Infantry and 30 troopers from the 17th Pennsylvania Cavalry to ambush and capture the pesky partisan. Taking position, the men did not have long to wait before their prey, with about 25 men, approached. To the infantry's horror, the cavalry opened fire before the trap was sprung. After recoiling, Mosby and his men attacked, driving the Pennsylvanians back in disarray. The Federal infantry now opened fire, but many of their cartridges were wet because of the rainy conditions. Seeing that he was outnumbered, Mosby beat a hasty retreat, causing General Meade to write, "thus the prettiest chance in the world to dispose of Mr. Mosby was lost."[20]

VI Corps

This Sabbath was a quiet time for the men at Fairfax Court House. Many attended church services, and a few of the units changed the location of their camps. Howe's division at Bristoe Station could hear the sound of firing from the Blue Ridge Mountain gaps where the two armies' cavalries were battling.[21]

June 22

Lee expressed his concerns about Hooker and his army to Jeb Stuart: "Do you know where he is and what he is doing? I fear he will steal a march on us, and get across the Potomac before we are aware. If you find that he is moving northward, and that two brigades can guard the Blue Ridge and take care of your rear, you can move with the other three into Maryland, and take position on General Ewell's right, place yourself in communication with him, guard his flank, keep him informed of the enemy's movements, and collect all the supplies you can for the use of the army."[1]

In a note to General Ewell, who was near Hagerstown, Lee gave orders to continue sweeping north toward Pennsylvania. "If you are ready to move, you can do so. I think your best course will be toward the Susquehanna, taking the routes by Emmitsburg, Chambersburg, and McConnellsburg....if Harrisburg comes within your means, capture it." Ewell's Corps would therefore march on three parallel roads.[2]

Emboldened by Hooker's passivity and the disappearance of the enemy's cavalry from the mountain passes, but worried that Ewell's Corps could be cut off and destroyed, Lee ordered the rest of his army across the Potomac and into Northern territory.[3]

About half of Lee's army was on the move. The First Corps continued its march toward Winchester, and farther north, the

Third Corps concentrated near Charlestown. Ewell's Second Corps marched through Maryland. Rodes's division finally crossed the Pennsylvania state line and reached Greencastle at 1:30 p.m. Pickett's (First Corps), Johnson's (Second Corps), and Heth's divisions (Third Corps) remained in camp.

During a meeting with Lee, General Stuart outlined a bold plan in which he would take all but one or two of his cavalry brigades, pass through a gap in the Blue Ridge Mountains, ride between Washington and the Army of the Potomac, and ultimately rejoin the army in Northern territory.

First Corps

Hood's men were somewhat skeptical when told they would break camp at 6:00 a.m., since those had been their orders the day before. The march began at the appointed time for all but Anderson's brigade, which was left behind to guard Snicker's Gap. The three brigades reached Snicker's Ford on the Shenandoah River by noon and rested for two hours. Marching southwest, the division finally reached Millwood at about 5:00 p.m., where it went into camp about a mile beyond. Winchester was up ahead.[4]

With the Federal cavalry threat gone, McLaws ordered his division back across the Shenandoah River in the late afternoon. Although Pickett's men were told to be ready to march at 3:00 a.m., they remained in camp all day.[5]

Second Corps

Early's division was on the road again at sunrise. Heavy rains had apparently swelled the Potomac River, causing a delay in Early's crossing. The division's goal was to link up with Johnson's division, still in camp near Sharpsburg. Lieutenant Kincheloe (Smith's brigade) recalled that "the road is enlivened by many secession ladies and demonstrations." Entering Shepherdstown, the men were pleased to see women waving Confederate flags. The soldiers then splashed across the hip-deep Potomac River at Boteler's Ford before 8:00 a.m., and marched through Sharpsburg and Boonsborough, camping about three miles from the latter town. Here, the 17th Virginia Cavalry of Jenkins's brigade joined the division. During the march through Maryland, Lieutenant Kincheloe was less than taken with the appearance of the women. "They looked as if they had been smoked for half a century and then dried. They were chunky and nearly as long one way as the other."[6]

Rodes's division was also on the road, breaking camp at 8:00 a.m. Iverson's brigade was the first brigade to cross the line into Pennsylvania at Middletown at 11:00 a.m. Jenkins's cavalry brigade rode ahead of Rodes's division. It encountered Federal cavalry, and dashing back, deployed for action, while Rodes's division did the same. The Federal cavalry wisely did not follow, and Rodes put his men back on the road to Greencastle, entering it at about 1:30 p.m. "The people seemed downhearted, and showed their hatred to us by their glum looks and silence," recalled Louis Leon of the 53rd North Carolina (Daniel's brigade). The division camped at 1:00 p.m., about two miles beyond the town after the 13-mile march. The men helped themselves to the abundant cherries.[7]

Third Corps

Anderson's men were pleased to remain in camp through the morning. The reprieve gave them time to write home. These letters usually complained about the hot and dusty roads, and the great fatigue and exhaustion that attended the march. The men were probably disappointed when they were ordered back on the road at 2:00 p.m. The division approached Charlestown that night.[8]

Heth's division was given a rest, spending the day near Berryville. Pender's division, bringing up the rear, had no such reprieve, and was again on the move at 4:30 a.m., marching through White Post toward Berryville.[9]

UNION

This was an exceptionally quiet day for the Army of the Potomac. All of the units remained in camp, except for Barnes's division, which returned to the V Corps at Aldie.

Confederates enter Pennsylvania
Battles and Leaders of the Civil War

After driving the Confederate cavalry back from the Blue Ridge Mountain passes, Pleasonton finally reported that most of the enemy infantry was scattered north of Winchester. This was not true—General Couch wired Stanton, "Rodes' division of infantry are reported as entering Greencastle at 12:30 p.m. this day. Their cavalry advancing upon Chambersburg."[10]

As a result, General Couch nervously contemplated the size of his military district and the scarcity of troops to defend it. He wrote to Stanton that "you will readily understand what kind of a force I have, when a few regiments, with a sprinkling of nine-months' men in them, are the veterans." Two New York regiments were stationed at Carlisle, and a Pennsylvania unit was at Gettysburg. While these troops looked good, they were completely green and did not have much confidence in themselves.[11]

Because he needed Milroy's services, Couch chose to put off General Schenck's request that the shamed division commander be arrested. Couch wrote to Schenck, "he [Milroy] cannot be relieved at this moment."[12]

Couch was not the only officer worried about his ability to carry out his mission. Pleasonton was increasingly concerned about the worsening condition of his horses. He estimated that it would take 1,500 horses to simply replace those lost in the last 15 days through battles and hard exertion.[13]

General Knipe's New York brigade arrived in Chambersburg. The citizens were overjoyed to see friendly troops after the town had been occupied by Jenkins's Confederate cavalry brigade. Knipe immediately put his men to work building barricades and digging rifle pits.[14]

To the south of Chambersburg, Captain William Boyd's company of the 1st New York Cavalry ran into a company of Jenkins's 14th Virginia Cavalry and gave chase. The rest of Jenkins's brigade lay in the grass, waiting to ambush the Federal troops. Captain Boyd had a funny feeling about the situation and halted his men before the trap was sprung. However, one of his troopers, Corporal William Rihl, fell—the first Federal soldier killed in the campaign. Boyd quickly returned to Chambersburg with word that a heavy column of Confederate infantry was approaching. This caused a general panic among Knipe's irregular troops, who were later marched back to the railroad, where they entrained.[15]

President Lincoln was becoming deeply concerned about Hooker's inability to stem Lee's movements. He could not have felt worse when he began hearing the sounds of battle to the northwest.[16]

III Corps

The men continued to idle near Gum Springs. Eradication of lice and fleas took up most of the men's time, and the rest was devoted to drilling, card playing, and eating.[17]

V Corps

Barnes's division returned to Aldie and reunited with Sykes's division at about 4:00 p.m.[18]

VI Corps

Reveille sounded at 5:00 a.m. It was the first time it had sounded in quite awhile. The men prepared breakfast and waited for orders to break camp. These orders never came, and the men remained where they were. Water was scarce, causing some of the men to try digging their own wells. The men knew it was just a matter of time before they met Lee's army on the battlefield. J. F. Hartwell (Joseph Bartlett's brigade) anticipated a battle with "cool dread (not fear)." He had seen the ranks of his regiment reduced by three-quarters and wrote to his wife that "if you were to see our regt. today marching past your house with its ranks so greatly thinned by death & exposure as they are you could not well suppress a pitying tear or a feeling of reverence...."[19]

XI Corps

Although the men did not receive marching orders, they were told to be ready to leave their camps at Goose Creek at a moment's notice.[20]

June 23

Lee was able to report to President Jefferson Davis that General Ewell's Corps was moving toward the Susquehanna River, A. P. Hill's Corps was marching toward the Potomac River, and Longstreet's Corps was west of the Shenandoah River with orders to follow A. P. Hill. He also reported that Fauquier and Loudoun Counties in the Shenandoah Valley provided his army with rich supplies. Lee was, however, concerned about the scarce forage for his horses, forcing them to subsist on local grass. This took valuable time and was not nearly as nourishing as grains.[1]

After contemplating Stuart's plan presented the day before, Lee ordered his cavalry commander to leave two of his brigades at the Blue Ridge Mountain passes and ride north with the rest of his command. Stuart was permitted to cross the Potomac River at Shepherdstown and move to Frederick. "You will, however, be able to judge whether you can pass around their [Hooker's] army without hindrance, doing them all the damage you can, and cross the river east of the mountains. In either case, after crossing the river, you must move on and feel the right of Ewell's troops, collecting information, provisions, &c.," he wrote. Imboden's cavalry brigade was to remain on the infantry's left.[2]

In another attempt to secure additional troops for the invasion, Lee sent President Davis a letter. He noted that it was getting late in the season for new Federal operations in the South, and he could see no benefit "derived from maintaining a large force on the southern coast during the unhealthy months of the summer and autumn." Instead, he suggested that General Pierre G. T. Beauregard's army be transferred to Culpeper Court House, where it could threaten Washington from another direction. He also noted that Hooker had thrown a pontoon bridge over the Potomac River.[3]

First Corps

Hood's men were up early, expecting to continue their march. Nine o'clock arrived, and found the men still lying about. Orders arrived at 10:00 a.m. to clean up and rest for the day, which brought considerable rejoicing. Several men went out to forage, but came back with little. The men also learned that wood was scarce, as was water. That night they were told that the march would continue early the next morning. According to Thomas Ware, the orders also included the following information: "No stragling [*sic*], no pressing private property, evry [*sic*] man [should] keep his place as we are going in M'd [Maryland]." Although Ware did not say it, the men were probably ambivalent about an invasion. While they were excited to take the war to the North, they recalled the bloody battle of Antietam that resulted from their last incursion.[4]

While General McLaws permitted his men to remain in camp, he ordered them to wash and prepare for a dress parade in the evening. Brigade Commander Joseph Kershaw was pleased when wagons bearing 503 rifles captured at Winchester arrived and were distributed to his men. The men knew that they would be marching come morning. Pickett's division also remained in camp.[5]

Second Corps

After a four-day rest, Johnson's division was on the road again at 4:00 a.m. The column reached Hagerstown at about 11:00 a.m. John Stone of the 1st Maryland (Steuart's brigade) wrote home that "at each place the inhabitants seemed most astonished at seeing so many soldiers. Some expressed the belief that nearly

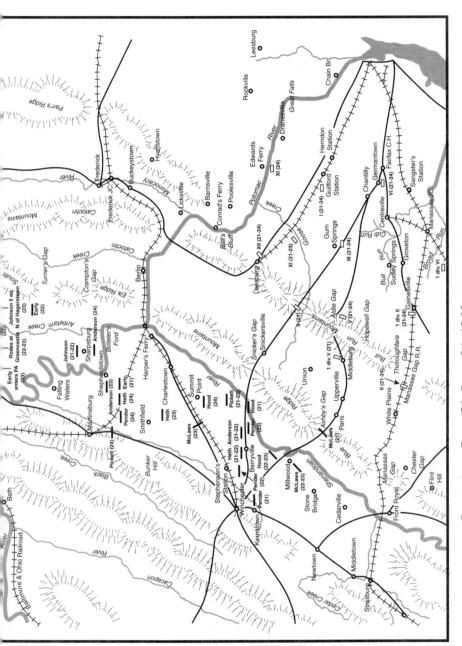

Operations June 21–June 24, 1863 *(Dates in June in parentheses)*

the entire world had turned out to pay them a visit." Cherries were everywhere, but George Buswell of the 33rd Virginia (Stonewall Brigade) proudly wrote home that "we did not steal them. We asked the owner, an old man, for them. He told us to help ourselves." Continuing northward for about five miles, the division went into camp at 3:00 p.m., after the 17-mile march. The Pennsylvania border was within a few miles.[6]

Early's column marched through Cavetown, Smithburg, Ringgold (Ridgeville), and finally entered Pennsylvania at Waynesborough. Lieutenant Kincheloe noted that the nearer they came to the border, the grimmer the citizens became. He noted that they were "bad enough looking by nature, [but now] fear had tortured them into the ugliest of creatures." The march finally ended about 3:00 p.m., when the men were ordered to halt for the night and cook three days' rations.[7]

General Rodes's division remained in camp near Greencastle, where he demanded large quantities of food and other useful items. The town's leaders found the demands so excessive that they did not even attempt to satisfy them. This caused Rodes's men to search the town, where they found a variety of items. Those soldiers reading the *Philadelphia Press* probably sneered when they learned that Pennsylvania Governor Andrew Curtin had called out the militia.[8]

Third Corps

Anderson's men were on the road by daybreak. During the march through Charlestown, the flags were unsheathed, the bands played, and the men marched smartly with their guns at "right shoulder shift." So excited were the women that General Carnot Posey was forced to dismount so they could kiss him. The march halted shortly after noon, when the division reached Shepherdstown, within a couple of miles of the Potomac River. During this leg of the march, the countryside's beauty awed the men. Nearby was Harper's Ferry, where the men could see the white Yankee tents dotting the hillsides.[9]

Heth's division was also on the road, reaching Charlestown that night. Pender's division, still lagging behind, finally entered

Berryville, and continued marching north before stopping for the night.[10]

UNION

The Army of the Potomac again remained in camp while Hooker pondered Lee's intentions. General Stahel, whose cavalry division had reconnoitered the Rappahannock River fords without finding any rebels, was ordered back to Fairfax Court House.[11]

The Federal signal corps reported that the enemy camps around Sharpsburg, Maryland were gone, and that a long line of enemy infantry was approaching Charlestown from the south. In preparation for the army's move into Maryland, General Henry Benham, who headed the Engineers, was ordered to prepare to throw a pontoon bridge across the mouth of the Monocacy Creek in Maryland.[12]

Jenkins's Confederate cavalry brigade rode again into Chambersburg. Unlike the first time, the troopers arrived in broad daylight and rode slowly and confidently into town. General Jenkins demanded provisions, which were brought to the courthouse. To the south, Ewell's commissary officers were demanding goods from Greencastle.[13]

Not satisfied with General Couch's response about Milroy, General Schenck's aide sent a wire to the latter with direct orders to return to Baltimore with the remnants of his division. To the south, Dix's movement toward Richmond continued.[14]

III Corps

The III Corps continued to lie in camp near Gum Springs. The scarcity of rations began to make the men grumble. Some had nothing but hard bread and a half-ration of salt pork.[15]

V Corps

The V Corps remained in camp near Aldie. Those men who went off to forage without permission were often caught and sent out on guard duty as punishment.[16]

General Samuel Crawford, commander of the Pennsylvania Reserve division stationed around Washington, was excited when he was ordered to hold his men in readiness for a reunion with the Army of the Potomac.[17]

XI Corps

The XI Corps remained in camp along Goose Creek. The inactivity was affecting many of the men. According to Frederick Winkler (Krzyzanowski's brigade), "I get a little homesick, when we are here so idle and uncomfortable, in every way disagreeably situated, deprived of everything. I rather wish that we march continually; this idleness is unendurable, but I must not complain."[18]

June 24

CONFEDERATE

While Ewell's Corps flooded into Pennsylvania, Hill's Corps began crossing the Potomac River into Maryland, and Longstreet's Corps was not far behind. General Stuart finalized his plans for the grand movement around Hooker's army. As he moved north with most of his command, he ordered William Jones's and Beverly Robertson's cavalry brigades to remain behind to guard Ashby's and Snicker's Gaps. General Robertson was ordered to oversee both brigades' operations, and Stuart ordered him to "watch the enemy; deceive him as to our designs, and harass his rear if you find he is retiring. Be always on the alert; let nothing escape your observation, and miss no opportunity which offers to damage the enemy." After the enemy had crossed the Potomac River, Robertson was to leave pickets at the mountain passes, cross the River, and follow the Confederate infantry.[1]

First Corps

General Longstreet's orders were to put his men on the road toward Maryland in the early morning hours. Pickett's division led the column, followed by the Reserve Artillery battalion, then Hood's division, and McLaws's division brought up the rear.[2]

Although reveille sounded at 3:00 a.m. in Pickett's camps, the column did not move out until 5:00 a.m. The division marched through Berryville and halted for the night at about 4:30 p.m. near Darkesville.[3]

The drums beat in Hood's camps at 2:00 a.m., and the men were on the road at daybreak. A march of about six miles brought them close to Berryville, where the men were permitted to rest and eat breakfast. They were joined here by Anderson's brigade, which had marched from Snicker's Gap. With music playing, the division marched through Berryville. The men could see the devastation wrought by the Yanks, particularly among the outhouses and fences, which were all burnt. The column now struck out toward Shepherdstown, marching eight miles in that direction before halting for the night at Summit Point. The men noted that much of the lush country was uncultivated owing to the fact that the owners had fled their farms or joined the army. McLaws's men began their march from Berry's Ford early, passing through Berryville, and finally camping near Summit Point on the Harper's Ferry and Winchester Railroad.[4]

Second Corps

Reveille sounded at 4:00 a.m. in Johnson's division's camps, and the men were on the road an hour later. They crossed the Pennsylvania State line, headed for Greencastle, which one Maryland soldier called a "pretty hard looking place." From here they struck out toward Chambersburg, halting for the night when within three miles of the town. Many soldiers commented on the difference between Virginians and Pennsylvanians. According to Rev. James Sheeran of the 14th Louisiana (Nicholls's brigade), "here you find none of that grace of manners, high-toned sentiment, or intellectual culture that you find in old Virginia. Indeed, with all their wealth they appear little advanced in civilization."[5]

Food was so scarce during this march that many men took to scrounging from local citizens. One soldier from the 2nd Louisiana wrote home that over 30,000 men were infected with "sore mouth," which he said resulted from fresh meat and vegetable deficiencies. The men were also on the lookout for hats to protect them from the blazing sun. Spying one on a young, one-armed civilian, a Confederate soldier approached, only to be told, "you took my arm at Fredericksburg, but I'll be damned if you'll take my hat." Steuart's brigade was detached and sent to McConnellsburg via Mercersburg, on the opposite side of Cove Mountain, to collect supplies, particularly livestock. Arriving at Mercersburg, the Confederates assembled the town officials and informed them that all goods must be surrendered on demand. The men then dispersed among the shops, using Confederate currency to compensate the storeowners. The brigade left for McConnellsburg that night. They encountered Federal militia, who quickly ran for safety.[6]

On the road at about 7:00 a.m., Early's column marched from Waynesboro to Quincy, Altodale (Mont Alto), and then on to Greenwood (Black Gap). Strict orders were issued against straggling, and no one was to leave the ranks, except at halts, and only then to secure water. Private property was also to be respected. The officers were not impressed with the quality of the local citizens. Colonel Clement Evans of Gordon's brigade noted that the citizens were "generally living in pretty good style, but [are] coarse, uneducated, and apparently having little knowledge of the outside world."[7]

Rodes's division broke camp at 5:00 a.m. and finally reached Chambersburg at noon. General Jenkins again frustrated General Rodes because he was unable to hold the town before the infantry arrived. As a result, most of the usable supplies were removed prior to the infantry's arrival. The march continued for about three miles, when the division camped on the Conococheague River after the 14-mile march. General Ewell met with the town's leaders at the National Bank and demanded 5,000 suits of clothing, 100 saddles and bridles, 10,000 pounds of leather, 5,000 bushels of grain, 50,000 pounds of bread, 500 barrels of flour, and a host of other items. When the citizens told him they could not possibly secure the items in the amount of time allocated, Ewell told his officers to take what they needed by force. "The people gave everything to the soldiers as they said our money would do them no good," recalled Samuel Pickens of the 5th Alabama (O'Neal's brigade).[8]

With the infantry now in Chambersburg, Ewell sent Jenkins's cavalry brigade toward Carlisle by way of Shippensburg. Fired upon by a detachment of the 1st New York Cavalry, Jenkins panicked and sent for immediate assistance. Daniel's brigade of Rodes's division was ordered to assist Jenkins at midnight.[9]

Third Corps

Anderson's division finally crossed the Potomac River in the morning. The men could not contain their excitement, and many sang "Maryland, My Maryland," as they forded the waist-deep river. The march took the men through the old Sharpsburg battlefield. Although nine months had passed since the battle, they could easily see that a major battle had been fought here. Low mounds covering the bodies, scarred trees, furrowed ground, and new fence-rails were much in evidence.[10]

Pender's division continued its northward march, camping within two to three miles of the Potomac River, near Shepherdstown. Here it rejoined Heth's division.[11]

UNION

Hooker now knew only too well where Lee's army was located, and with the completion of a pontoon bridge over the Potomac River, he was ready to move his army into Maryland. The XI Corps broke camp at Goose Creek and marched to Edward's Ferry where it would cross the Potomac. Otherwise, it was a quiet day for the Army of the Potomac, as the other units remained in camp. The same could not be said for the engineers, as they were ordered to throw a second bridge over the river.

In a remarkable dispatch, Hooker concluded to Halleck that General Ewell had crossed the Potomac River for "purposes of plunder. The yeomanry of that district should be able to check any extended advance of that column, and protect themselves from their aggression." Hooker never explained how they were to

Harper's Ferry

Battles and Leaders of the Civil War

accomplish this task. He planned to send a corps toward Harper's Ferry to sever Ewell from the balance of the rebel army. He also informed Halleck that if Lee did not throw any further infantry across the Potomac River, and Washington could be secured, then he would "with all the force I can muster, strike for his line of retreat in the direction of Richmond." Little did he know that Ewell was not the only Confederate corps across the river at this time.[12]

Despite the fact that enemy troops were deep in Federal territory, Halleck formulated plans to arm the clerks and send them to guard storehouses, relieving the troops there for duty in Washington's defenses. General Stahel's cavalry was dispatched into Maryland to keep an eye on the enemy there. Later in the day, General Couch confirmed Lincoln's worst nightmare—at least 10,000 rebels were in Pennsylvania.[13]

As a Confederate infantry brigade under General George Steuart approached the Cove Mountains on its way to McConnellsburg in search of supplies, a small Federal force assembled to block its passage. Colonel Jacob Szink placed a battalion of "emergency" troops at each mountain pass, supported by the 12th Pennsylvania Cavalry. Szink apparently did not think to construct barricades or breastworks to aid in his defense. Seeing the cavalry suddenly withdraw as the enemy approached, the infantry followed. Barely a shot was fired at the Confederates, who entered McConnellsburg and remained unmolested for two days.[14]

Two Confederate divisions were now in Chambersburg, Pennsylvania, where a list of demands for provisions was presented to the town's leaders. In exasperation over what they considered to be excessive demands, one official exclaimed, "it is utterly out of our power to furnish these things, and now, if you are going to burn us out you will only have to do it." The Confederates assured him that they had no intention of torching the town. Instead, the soldiers moved from house to house in search of the needed supplies.[15]

A number of command changes were made. General William French, formerly a division commander in the II Corps, was assigned command of the Harper's Ferry garrison. The Middle Department was further divided to form the Department of West Virginia under the command of General B. F. Kelley.[16]

I Corps

The men were told to prepare for a march, so they dutifully struck their tents and packed their belongings. The hours passed. Some regimental commanders decided to conduct drills while waiting. When orders did not arrive, the men re-erected their tents.[17]

II Corps

The II Corps remained near Thoroughfare Gap. The Third Division commander, General William French, left the army to take command of the Harper's Ferry garrison and was temporarily replaced by Colonel Samuel Smyth.[18]

V Corps

The V Corps remained in camp near Aldie. Some of the troops were camped near President James Monroe's mansion, but guards prevented potential visitors from entering the house. Two U.S. regulars had their heads shaved and were drummed out of camp for cowardice.[19]

Secretary of War Edwin Stanton finally ordered the Pennsylvania Reserve division, near Washington, to join the V Corps. In anticipation of this order, the men had already packed up their belongings and were ready to strike their tents.[20]

VI Corps

Still at Bristoe Station, General Howe ordered a three-hour division drill. Not happy with the results, he conducted another one the following day. Eustis's brigade was detached and sent to Centreville, where it relieved Hays's brigade (soon to become George Willard's). The rest of the corps remained at Fairfax Court House.[21]

XI Corps

The men were on the road to Edward's Ferry in the morning and arrived there by 1:00 p.m. The exceptionally slow march covered but six miles. In a mental muddle, Hooker continually changed Oliver Howard's orders during the day. First, Howard was to cross the river and proceed to Harper's Ferry, then Hooker changed his mind and ordered the XI Corps to remain at Edward's Ferry, where it was to support the VI Corps. Next he decided to allow the corps to cross the river and remain near it, guarding the bridge and stores. Finally, he permitted Howard to cross the Potomac and march toward Sandy Hook. This would not occur until June 25, however.[22]

XII Corps

The XII Corps remained in camp near Leesburg. Twice the telegraph wires had been cut in Leesburg, causing General Slocum to warn citizens that he would shell and burn the town if it happened again.[23]

June 25

CONFEDERATE

Threatening reports reached the secretary of war of about 17 gunboats and transports steaming up the York River toward White House, about 25 miles from the capital. Here they disembarked approximately six thousand Federal infantry. Another force was supposedly marching up the peninsula toward Richmond as well.[1]

The First Corps continued its march toward the Potomac River, passing by Martinsburg. Pickett's division crossed the river, while the other two camped nearby. Already in Pennsylvania, Rodes's and Johnson's divisions (Second Corps) remained in camp near Chambersburg, while Early's division was near Greenwood. Just to the south, Anderson's division (Third Corps) approached the Pennsylvania border, while Pender's and Heth's divisions camped within eight miles of Hagerstown.

Stuart's cavalry moved out at about 1:00 a.m. on its ride around the Army of the Potomac. The men rode light, necessitating frequent halts to permit the horses to graze. As the troopers approached Haymarket, Virginia, they encountered the Federal II Corps on the march. A battery deployed, but it quickly limbered up when the Federals reciprocated and also sent infantry against it. Sometime during the day, Stuart sent a courier to Lee with the news that the entire Federal army was on the march. Lee never received this vital message as the courier was either killed or captured.[2]

Having crossed the Potomac River, General Imboden's cavalry brigade raided into Maryland. Its mission was to block the traffic on the Chesapeake and Ohio Canal, the Baltimore and Ohio Railroad, and to disrupt Federal communications. The men did a very good job completing this task.[3]

First Corps

Hood's and McLaws's divisions were on the march early. Continuing north, they marched through Smithfield, Clarkesville, and passed by (not through) Martinsburg at about noon. The two divisions finally camped at 5:00 p.m., not far from the Potomac River in a drizzling rain. They had marched over 20 miles and were ready to cook their one-day's beef rations. Tally Simpson of the 3rd South Carolina (Kershaw's brigade) complained that the rations were getting short again—one-quarter pound of beef per man. "I ate my day's rations at one mouthful—not one meal," he wrote.[4]

Pickett's division was on the road at 4:00 a.m. and soon marched through Martinsburg. John Dooley of the 1st Virginia (James Kemper's brigade) noted that he "perceive[d] at once that we are not treading friendly streets." Not everyone shared this assessment, as some saw citizens waving handkerchiefs. The division halted briefly at Falling Waters before crossing the Potomac River about four miles below Williamsport at about 2:30 p.m. Although the river was only thigh-deep, the men were disappointed that they could not wait to use the pontoon bridge being constructed nearby. A heavy shower soaked the men, as they continued for about a mile before halting for the night after completing their 21-mile march. That night, Garnett's brigade was drawn up in three sides of a square to watch the execution of a deserter. Private John Riley had perfected a moneymaking scheme in which he accepted money as a substitute, then deserted, only to repeat the process again. He did this three times before being caught. A member of the 56th Virginia noted that "it was a sad scene indeed."[5]

Confederate troops destroy the Chesapeake and Ohio Canal

Battles and Leaders of the Civil War

Second Corps

While most of Rodes's and Johnson's divisions rested near Chambersburg, Steuart's brigade of the latter division remained at McConnellsburg. Samuel Pickens (O'Neal's brigade) said the men were "to impress every thing found there necessary for the use of the army." Samuel Firebaugh found the citizens of the town "scared nearly to death. Give the last thing they have if we only spare there [*sic*] lives."[6]

After marching three long days, Early's division was permitted to rest at Greenwood. General Early rode over to confer with General Ewell at Chambersburg and was told to cross the South Mountains to Gettysburg, proceed to York, and cut the Northern Central Railroad, which ran between Baltimore and Harrisburg. He was also to destroy the bridge over the Susquehanna River at Wrightsville/Columbia, then rejoin the corps at Carlisle, by way of Dillsburg. Colonel Elijah White's 35th Virginia Cavalry Battalion, called the "Comanches," joined Early on this expedition.[7]

Third Corps

Rain falling on Anderson's division did not affect the troops, as they were using an unmuddy, modern road. The march began at noon, and the men passed through Hagerstown, and finally to Middleburg on the Pennsylvania border. Some bushwhackers suddenly appeared near Hagerstown and fired on the column, narrowly missing General Ambrose Wright. This was not the reception they expected—they had been told that many Marylanders would volunteer and swell their ranks.[8]

Heth's and Pender's men were pleased by the warm reception they received as they passed through Shepherdstown. The town had been under Yankee rule for two years, so the soldiers assumed that the citizens had changed sides. As the division approached the Potomac River at Blackford's Ford, the men were permitted to remove their pants and underwear. Most gladly complied before wading into the four hundred-yard-wide river. J. Caldwell of the 1st South Carolina noted that it was "not a spectacle fit for female eyes, for most of the men stripped off their nether clothing." The crossing was completed by noon, and the Confederates continued to the Antietam battlefield. Only when they came within eight miles of Hagerstown were they permitted to camp for the night. Thomas Littlejohn of the 1st South Carolina (Perrin's brigade) was dismayed to find that many wells were locked to keep the men from refreshing themselves.[9]

UNION

Hooker now ordered the entire army into Maryland in pursuit of Lee's army. General Reynolds received orders to take command of the III and XI Corps that day, in addition to his own I Corps. He was also assigned a brigade of Stahel's cavalry, which was to cross the Potomac River and seize Crampton's Pass and Turner's Gap. Hooker's orders were to cross the Potomac River and proceed toward Middletown in two lines, where he would guard the vital mountain passes and protect the left of the army against an attack. The I Corps was to move to Barnesville, and the next day proceed through Adamstown and Jefferson; the III Corps was to march to the mouth of the Monocacy, and eventually to Point of Rocks, Petersville, and Burkittsville. Poised to cross the river, Howard's XI Corps was to march to Point of Rocks and then to Jefferson.[10]

Three of the other corps remained in camp: the V Corps was near Aldie, where it continued to support the cavalry; the VI Corps, minus Howe's division, remained near Centreville; and the XII Corps watched the army's left flank. The II Corps marched from Thoroughfare Gap to Gum Springs, where it replaced the III Corps.

Because of the poor condition of the Army of the Potomac's horses, Halleck gave Hooker orders to seize all serviceable animals from Loudoun County, Virginia, and the adjacent portions of Maryland. Another reason Halleck gave was to "save them from the enemy."[11]

The tug of war over General Milroy and his command continued. Schenck sent another wire to Milroy at 9:30 a.m. with orders to report immediately to Baltimore. Couch responded for Milroy shortly thereafter, saying it was impossible to comply as the troops were needed in the Pennsylvania mountains. Schenck retorted at 11:15 a.m., "in their present, unsupplied, disorganized, and necessarily ineffective condition, I fear Milroy's men, if you keep them where they are, will only come to grief." Schenck indicated that he only wanted to refit the remnants of the command and reunite them with his other commands being sent to Frederick. Schenck, in utter frustration, ended the wire with, "I will submit the matter to the General-in-Chief." Schenck did just that, explaining to Halleck that of the 2,346 officers and men left in Milroy's command, one-fifth were without arms and many were shoeless.[12]

Halleck was becoming even more cranky than usual. After receiving a question from General Schenck about whether he should send the newly arriving New York militia directly to Washington, Halleck snapped back, "my order to send troops to Washington means precisely what it says. I cannot make it more definite."[13]

With the rebels pouring into Pennsylvania, General Couch was told by Secretary of War Stanton, "you will furnish arms, ammunition, subsistence, transportation, and all needful supplies (excepting uniforms) to any troops placed under your command." This applied to troops not yet sworn into service with the government.[14]

In a confidential letter to General Samuel Heintzelman, commander of the Washington District, General John Barnard, chief engineer of the city, reiterated that the city could not be held by the forts alone—troops were needed between them as well. He felt that only the Army of the Potomac could save Washington from capture, and was confident that Hooker would do just that. However, he did suggest that local citizens be armed and sent to the forts. He estimated that the 12,000–15,000 men raised in this way could have an impact.[15]

I Corps

The men were awakened at 3:00 a.m., struck camp, and were on the road by 8:00 a.m. This was a tough march because the pace was slow, causing frequent starting and stopping, and continual bunching up. The column reached the pontoon bridge over the Potomac River at Edward's Ferry by about 2:00 p.m., but had to wait for the XI Corps's wagons to cross. The corps immediately crossed the river when the bridge cleared and continued on to Poolsville. Here school-aged children lined the roads, waving flags and shouting encouragement. The men's spirits were high, now that they were in friendly territory. "It seemed pleasant once more to see smiling faces and to be greeted with friendly words," noted Charles Davis of the 13th Massachusetts (Paul's brigade). Rain fell intermittently as the march continued through Barnsville at 8:00 p.m., where the men spent a wet night after the 15-mile march. Cutler's brigade spent the night in a cornfield where 3–6 inches of water had accumulated between the rows. A. P. Smith explained, "of all the songs and rhymes written [about]...the beauties of the different seasons...we do not remember of any in which the author fell into ecstasies over sleeping in a mud-puddle." Fortunately, division commander General Wadsworth had straw delivered.[16]

II Corps

Finding Stuart's cavalry division on its flank, the II Corps left its position at Thoroughfare Gap at 10:00 a.m., and headed toward Gum Springs. As Gibbon's Second Division approached Haymarket, Confederate cavalry appeared with two batteries and opened fire. A number of men were killed and wounded, and several prisoners were taken. Federal artillery galloped into position, and Webb's Philadelphia Brigade halted, formed line of battle, and advanced on the enemy. The rebel batteries were ultimately forced to withdraw. This affair did not amount to much, but did relieve the men's boredom.[17]

The march continued to Gum Springs, which the head of the column reached that night at about 9:00 p.m. The men marched about 23 miles that day. They were soaked from the drenching rain, and the mud was deep. One consolation was that the rain cooled the air, and fewer fell by the side of the road with heat prostration. The men spent a thoroughly miserable night as they lay down on the wet ground in their wet clothes, covered by their wet blankets. The scarcity of wood made fires out of the question.

General Alexander Hays's New York brigade reinforced French's division at Gum Springs. Several of these regiments had had the indignation of being captured at Harper's Ferry during the prior autumn and were itching for redemption. The men were fully stocked with clothing and assorted knickknacks, which they quickly discarded as the march continued. The II Corps veterans gleefully picked through the goods, so it became Christmas in June.[18]

III Corps

After five days of inactivity at Gum Springs, the men finally broke camp at 6:30 a.m. and marched toward Edward's Ferry. The route took them past Mount Hope and Farmwell, and across Goose Creek. Fortunately, a pontoon bridge had been thrown across it, so the men did not get wet. The head of the column reached Edward's Ferry at about 11:00 a.m., where they were given a break. Thinking this was a lunch break, many of the soldiers built fires and began preparing coffee. However, they soon received orders to cross the river, causing many to curse both their officers and their bad luck. The march was now along the Chesapeake and Ohio Canal. Rain began falling in the afternoon, soaking the men to the skin, and making the roads slippery. They had marched about 25 miles that day. The ranks were lighter, as many had fallen by the wayside. Thomas Marbaker of the 11th New Jersey called it a "terrible experience." Some lost their footing and fell into the canal, and many openly wondered why they were marching on this narrow road when a more passable one was nearby. Wyman White of the 2nd U.S. Sharpshooters (Hobart Ward's brigade) considered this part of the march to be most treacherous, feeling that it was "the same as walking on the glarest [sic] of ice. In order to keep on our feet we were obliged to take short steps." The ordeal continued until 10:00 p.m., when Birney's division reached the Monocacy Aqueduct. Humphreys's division did not arrive for another two hours. Colonel Regis DeTrobriand recalled that night: "without shelter, without supper, in a driving rain, we slept in the mud that sound sleep which is known only to soldiers worn with fatigue."[19]

V Corps

The V Corps remained in camp near Aldie. Mosby's guerrillas continued to be active, which made the men nervous and reduced their interest in foraging away from the main body. The steady rains also contributed to this feeling.[20]

The Pennsylvania Reserve division finally broke camp at Upton's Hill near Washington at 2:00 p.m. and began its march north. The division spent its first night at Ball's Crossroads on the road to Leesburg. Even the pouring rain could not dampen the men's soaring spirits.[21]

VI Corps

Howe's division was on the road from Bristoe Station at 7:00 p.m. Its destination was Centreville. The men complained that it was dry all week that they spent in camp, but now that they were on the road, it began to rain. According to Wilbur Fiske of Grant's brigade, this gave them "the luxury of another night's march in the slippery mud."[22]

XI Corps

The XI Corps was up at 3:00 a.m. and on the road about 90 minutes later. Its immediate goal was to cross the Potomac River at Edward's Ferry. Krzyzanowski's brigade unfurled its flags and broke into song as it crossed the long pontoon bridge to Maryland. One private wrote that "we have left the deserted fields of Virginia and come to a smiling, happy, thrifty land, to Maryland." The 24-mile march that day took them through Poolesville. Here "the women cheered us and waved their handkerchiefs [as] well. This is the first place for them to do so," noted John McMahon (Smith's brigade).[23]

XII Corps

The XII Corps remained in camp near Leesburg. From their camps, the men could see long lines of troops and wagons crossing the river at Edward's Ferry.[24]

June 26

CONFEDERATE

As Hill's Third Corps crossed into Pennsylvania and approached Chambersburg, Lee ordered Rodes's division, and then Johnson's, from that town to Carlisle. From here they were to advance on Harrisburg. Pickett's and Hood's divisions of the First Corps also passed into Pennsylvania, while McLaws's got as far as Maryland. Ironically, the latter was the first division to begin the invasion, but the last to cross the river.[1]

Stuart's cavalry raid continued. Finding enemy troops in his path, Stuart rode farther east than he had planned, moving to Brentwood and Wolf Run Shoals. He crossed Bull Run, then halted to graze his horses.[2]

After occupying Hancock, Maryland, General Imboden's cavalry brigade crossed into Pennsylvania where it rounded up hundreds of head of cattle near McConnellsburg. The men were not well disciplined and stole from the local citizens.[3]

First Corps

Although ordered to march at 4:00 a.m., the ongoing rain, which had fallen all night, caused Pickett's officers to delay the march until sometime between 5:00 and 6:00 a.m. The division halted after marching about three miles, and filed off the road so A. P. Hill's Corps could pass. The march continued through Hagerstown, where some of the citizens waved handkerchiefs.

Surgeon Charles Lippitt noted that the "men are smaller & the women obsequious, boring even at a distance....all seem afraid we will injure them knowing how well they deserve it." Thomas Pollock of Kemper's brigade observed that not all of the citizens had this countenance. Some "look fierce and angry and tell us confidently we will never get back." The division finally crossed into Pennsylvania, marching through Middleburg and camping about a mile from Greencastle. Here they first experienced the Pennsylvania Dutch, who often said, "take de horses, take de cattle, take everything, but don't burn de barn, de houses...." It was a dreary 20-mile march for the men as the steady, cold rains made the roads muddy and slippery, and dampened their spirits.[4]

A light rain fell as McLaws's and Hood's men prepared to break camp and leave at sunrise. Their destination was Williamsport on the Potomac River, which Pickett's men had crossed the day before. The road toward the Potomac River was becoming muddy, but at least it was only about four miles away. Reaching the ford at midday, the men were not permitted to strip before crossing the river. Thomas Ware of the 15th Georgia described the river as a "little over one knee deep & 200 yards wide." He did not mind fording it fully clothed as he was soaked from the rain anyway. It appears that the men of Robertson's brigade may have been permitted to strip, as during the crossing, the soldiers passed two young ladies in a buggy who were also fording the river. One member of the 1st Arkansas exclaimed, "it was not everyday of the week that 50,000 men passed in review without their trousers on." According to Augustus Dickert (Kershaw's brigade), the men celebrated when they reached the Maryland side of the river. "Here was shouting and yelling. Hats went into the air, flags dipped and swayed, the bands play 'Maryland, May Maryland,' while the men sang 'All Quiet Along the Potomac Tonight.'" After a brief break on the Maryland side, the men marched to Williamsport. Another two miles brought the men to a grove of trees, where they halted. Robert Moore (Barksdale's brigade) recorded in his journal, "have experienced a very disagreeable day."[5]

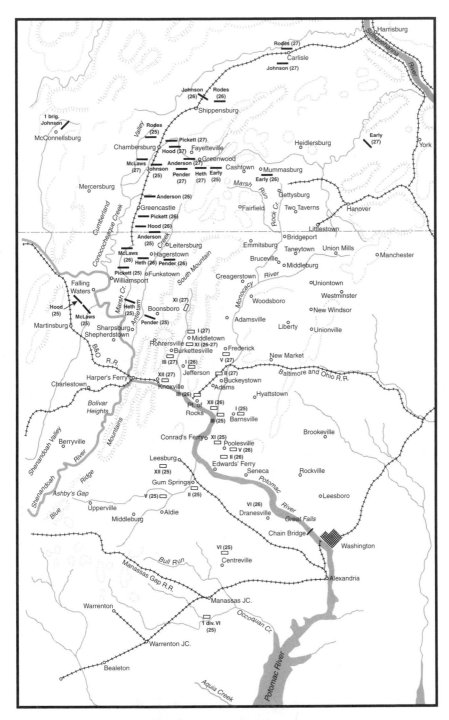

Operations June 25–June 27, 1863
(Dates in June in parentheses)

The men's spirits brightened when they were issued captured Federal whiskey. The tops of the barrels were removed, and the men dipped their cups as they passed. Many added it to the contents of their canteens to make the treat go further; others drank it straight and cajoled their comrades for theirs. As a result, many became drunk and fights broke out. John Stevens of the 5th Texas (Robertson's brigade, Hood's division) reported that

> there were more drunk men...than I think I ever saw in my life...some cried, some hooped and yelled. Some cussed and swore, others ripped and tore....It kept the sober boys busy to keep the drunk ones from killing each other. Soon some fell by the wayside helpless and were dumped into wagons and ambulances and hauled the balance of the day. Some others were not seen for 15 hours afterwards and when they caught up with their commands, they were quite sober but their eyes looked like two burnt holes in a blanket.[6]

One can easily imagine the road from Williamsport lined with prostrate Confederate soldiers that night. While most of the officers chose to look the other way, Colonel Van Manning of the 3rd Arkansas "ordered the sober ones to dunk the drunken ones in the creek to bring a reaction," recalled Miles Smith of the 4th Texas.[7]

As it continued its march, Hood's division shifted to a small muddy side road, but the going was slow. Most of the men did not mind, though, as they were feeling the whiskey's warmth. After another seven miles the column reached the Pennsylvania border. The column finally halted for the night near Greencastle, Pennsylvania. The more creative men wrote that "we had breakfasted in Virginia, dined and wined in Maryland, and taken supper in Pennsylvania," and "we were in four states that day, the fourth being in a state of intoxication."[8]

McLaws's division, marching in the rear, passed through Williamsport, Maryland, and camped just beyond it. As a result, it did not cross into Pennsylvania.[9]

Second Corps

Rodes's and Johnson's divisions' new destination was Carlisle. On the road at 6:00 a.m., the column marched, actually slogged along, in heavy rains to Shippensburg. Samuel Pickens found it to be a "common looking place & is inhabited by common looking people, principally Dutch." On reflection, he noted that "I have not seen any nice, refined people since we have been in the state." Rodes's division halted for the night at Dykeman Spring, a short distance beyond Shippensburg, after the 11-mile march. Here they reunited with Daniel's brigade, which had been dispatched to support Jenkins's cavalry. Johnson's division, marching behind Rodes's, camped approximately half a mile west, on Timber Hill. While most of the men were content to rest, some went into town in search of supplies.[10]

Steuart's brigade left McConnellsburg at 4:00 p.m. to begin the 24-mile march back to Chambersburg, and the rest of Johnson's division. The route was through Loudonton (Fort Loudon) and St. Thomas. Two soldiers left behind surrendered without a fight, but were killed in cold blood by recently discharged Federal soldiers. Near St. Thomas, Maryland cavalry under Major Harry Gilmor captured 60 head of cattle, 40 horses, and a handful of mules. The brigade halted when within about a mile of the latter town.[11]

Early's expeditionary force was to be on the road at daybreak. However, heavy rains delayed its departure from Greenwood until about 8:00 a.m. The column was traveling light, as the wagons had been sent to Chambersburg. Accompanying the troops were the ambulances, one medical wagon for each brigade, the regimental ordnance wagons, and one wagon for each regiment, carrying its cooking utensils. Fifteen empty wagons for collecting supplies also accompanied the division.[12]

General Early ordered his men to destroy the Caledonia Iron Works near Greenwood, owned by ardent abolitionist Thaddeus Stevens. This was composed of a furnace, forge, and a rolling mill. The manager implored Early not to destroy the works, as it made little money, and only operated to provide jobs and housing for the poor. Early retorted, "Yankees don't do business that way. They carry on their operations to make money." The mill laborers could only sadly watch as their source of income went up in flames. Early justified this act by saying that he was simply reciprocating for the Union army's acts of aggression against Southern citizens, which were promoted by Congressman Stevens. After reaching Cashtown, General Early learned that a Federal force occupied Gettysburg. Halting his division, Early sent Gordon's brigade and White's cavalry battalion toward Gettysburg, where they would "amuse and skirmish with the enemy." The remainder of the division marched along a parallel road through Hilltown to Mummasburg, and thence to Gettysburg, where Early would get on the enemy's "flank and rear, so as to capture his whole force," he noted in his report.[13]

Upon arriving at Mummasburg, Early dispatched Hays's brigade toward Gettysburg, while his two other brigades went into bivouac. General Early rode toward Gettysburg and learned that White's cavalry battalion and Gordon's brigade had encountered the eight hundred-man 26th Pennsylvania Militia along Chambersburg Pike. The green soldiers fled, leaving behind about 175 prisoners. The cavalry and two regiments of Hays's infantry were sent after the fleeing militia. The cavalry caught up with the militia's rearguard, and a brisk skirmish took place. The growing darkness, and a concern about the size of the militia force, caused Colonel White to break off the engagement.[14]

Assembling the prisoners in the town square, Early told them, "You boys ought to be home with your mothers and not out in the fields where it is dangerous and you might get hurt." He then paroled them with instructions that they go home and stay out of further trouble.[15]

In the meantime, Gordon's men marched into Gettysburg with bands merrily playing "Dixie." Professor Michael Jacobs, a faculty member at Gettysburg's Pennsylvania College, described the rebels' appearance as "most of the men were exceedingly dirty, some ragged, some without shoes, and some surmounted by the skeleton of what was once an entire hat."[16]

General Early now turned his attention to another goal: collecting supplies. He demanded that the town officials hand over all usable bounty, but they replied that the town held little. A search of the town confirmed this information. Early did find about two hundred rations in railroad cars, which were issued to Gordon's men. The 10–12 cars were then burned, as was a small railroad bridge nearby. This was no easy task as it was rainy, and mud was everywhere. Early now ordered Gordon to march his brigade to York at first light, while Colonel White was to ride with his cavalry battalion to Hanover Junction on the North Central Railroad, destroying railroad bridges along the way. He was then to rejoin Gordon at York, burning more railroad bridges in the vicinity.[17]

Meanwhile, the rest of Early's division bivouacked at Mummasburg. For the first time since entering Northern territory, the men were permitted to use fence rails to build fires. In but a few moments roaring fires began drying the drenched men. Lieutenant Kincheloe of the 49th Virginia (Smith's brigade) recalled that the column passed many terrified citizens during the march. "All they ask is to spare their lives, all else is at our will."[18]

Third Corps

Citizens lining the road told Anderson's water-logged men when they crossed the Pennsylvania border, and the soldiers responded with cheers. As the division entered Greencastle, the men were confronted by a mass of women, all waving the Stars and Stripes. The column camped two miles beyond the town. That night the men were given a large ration of whiskey. According to Frank Foote the whiskey was "as foul as the average Northern estimate of Jeff Davis and his cause."[19]

Many men in Heth's and Pender's divisions were getting pretty disgusted with the rain that had continued to fall for two days. The roads were becoming impossibly muddy, making the marching much more difficult. The march ended just south of Hagerstown, Maryland.[20]

UNION

Now settled on sending his entire army across the Potomac, Hooker painstakingly laid out their routes, particularly their movement across the river over the two closely situated pontoon bridges. He knew that without great care the river crossing could become a tangled mess. His marching orders were as follows: The XII Corps at Leesburg was to march at 3:00 a.m. to Edwards Ferry, cross the bridge over the Potomac and proceed to Point of Rocks, Maryland, and then to Middletown. A detachment was to be left behind at Leesburg until relieved by the V Corps. The latter corps, at Aldie, was to march at 4:00 a.m., cross Goose Creek at Carter's Mill and proceed to Leeburg, then cross the Potomac River at Edwards' Ferry and march toward Frederick. The II Corps was to leave Gum Springs at 6:00 a.m. and march via Farmwell and Franklin, cross the Potomac River, and also march on Frederick. The VI Corps was to march at 3:00 a.m. from Centreville and Fairfax via Chantilly, Frying Pan, Herndon Station, and Dranesville, cross the river at Edward's Ferry, where it was to support the engineers' removal of the bridges. Then it was to follow the II

Union troops cross the Potomac River

Battles and Leaders of the Civil War

Corps toward Frederick. Already in Maryland, the III Corps was to march to Point of Rocks. The XI Corps was to march to Middletown (with one brigade each at Crampton's Gap and Boonsborough Gap), and the I Corps was to follow it.[21]

One division of Pleasonton's cavalry covered the army's flank at Aldie, and the second division covered the three roads from Aldie to Gum Springs. General Reynolds complained that the brigade of Stahel's cavalry assigned to him "does nothing. They go into camp behind the infantry, and send out small squads from them."[22]

The militia regiments were active. The 26th Pennsylvania Militia arrived in Gettysburg at about 9:00 a.m., and after a quick breakfast prepared by the grateful citizens, marched three miles west of town to assume defensive positions. The unit soon encountered the 35th Virginia Cavalry Battalion, which lived up to its name, "The Comanches," as its men let out "barbarian yells" as they advanced. Realizing that they were no match for these veterans, the militia pulled back to safety. The Comanches then entered Gettysburg. According to Professor Michael Jacobs, the rebels were "yelling and shouting like so many savages...firing their pistols, not caring whether they killed or maimed man, woman, or child." Other units from Early's Confederate division pressed the militia, and a brief skirmish ensued. Militiaman Henry Shriver noted, "such confusion I never saw—everyone gave orders and no one obeyed—we were all green and knew nothing about regular forming." The militia again retreated, and the growing darkness cut off the pursuit. About 175 men were captured but later paroled.[23]

Knipe's two New York regiments erected barricades and dug rifle pits on the road to Carlisle. The town's militia was called out and lent a hand. However, Knipe wisely pulled his men back to safety as two powerful Confederate divisions (Rodes's and Johnson's) approached.[24]

The employees of the Quartermaster's and Commissary Departments in Washington were organized into units for the purpose of defending the capital. General Heintzelman believed that they needed to be mustered at least once or twice a week to become accustomed to their new role.[25]

With the enemy deep into his state, Governor Curtin issued another proclamation calling for 60,000 men to come forward to defend Pennsylvania. Curtin wrote that "I will not insult you by inflammatory appeals." Then in the next sentence, he did just that: "A people who want the heart to defend their soil, their families, and their firesides, are not worthy to be accounted men."[26]

I Corps

The men were up at about 4:30 a.m., and on the road from Barnesville by 6:00 a.m. The march took them over the Catoctin Mountains to Jefferson, where they spent the night after the 18-mile hike. Rains made the roads muddy and slippery, but the men remained in good spirits. This was caused, at least in part, by the countryside. One soldier wrote that "we have passed through as nice country as I ever saw....the valley is as beautiful as nature could make it." Another soldier from Stone's brigade wrote, "we suppose we are near the Rebel army and think it is very probable we will have something to do soon. May God give us success and enable us to help secure our country's rights."[27]

II Corps

The march began from Gum Springs at about 6:00 a.m. in intermittent rains. The column marched through Farmwell Station and Frankville and reached Edward's Ferry that night. Here it crossed the Potomac River on pontoon boats between 10:00 p.m. and the early morning hours of June 27. All was confusion around the bridges because of the massive numbers of wagons trying to cross. The march continued into Maryland for a mile or two before ending. The exhausted men fell to the ground, too tired and muddy to pitch their tents. Charles Fuller of the 61st New York (Edward Cross's brigade) recalled that "the men were tired, but they were marched and countermarched, and halted and started, and placed and unplaced until it was fair to conclude that someone was drunk."[28]

III Corps

So exhausted were the men from the march the day before that few erected shelter tents when they went into camp. "It was too dark, and we had no stakes or pins," explained Captain Charles Mattocks of the 17th Maine (de Trobriand's brigade). As a result, the men awoke with their blankets wet because a light rain had fallen during the night. Charles Bardeen's (Carr's brigade) woolen blanket was so heavy that he was forced to leave it behind. The column was on the road by 10:00 a.m., and within five hours, had marched six miles to the Baltimore and Ohio Railroad near Point of Rocks. Rain falling during the march made the roads slippery. Despite the fact that local citizens were selling "horrid pies," the men "snapped them up at high prices." Some of the men also found whiskey and became drunk.[29]

V Corps

Reveille sounded at 2:00 a.m. and the men were on the road by 6:00 a.m. A halt was permitted at Leesburg after the 13-mile march in the steady rain. The men prepared dinner, then left for Edwards' Ferry, about nine miles away, reaching it at 6:00 p.m. They crossed the Potomac River on the pontoon bridges, and "as we stepped upon the Maryland shore, many were the ejaculations of joy at getting off the sacred soil of old Virginia," wrote Corporal William Read of the 118th Pennsylvania (Tilton's brigade). The march continued for another four miles, when the men finally camped for the night near Poolsville. It was a long 26-mile march, made more difficult by the scarcity of letters from home. Samuel Keene recorded in his diary, "who's [sic] fault is it? The fault of the government. Poor management, imbecility, etc."[30]

The Pennsylvania Reserve division, marching to rendezvous with the rest of the V Corps, broke camp at Ball's Crossroads at 5:30 a.m. and passed the VI Corps at Dranesville. The men were exhausted by 4:00 p.m., so their officers let them bivouac for the night at Goose Creek. Although veterans of many battles, they had become accustomed to the soft life of picket duty.[31]

VI Corps

Bringing up the rear of the army, Howe's division was already on the march during the first moments of June 26. It reached Centreville at 1:00 a.m., where the men were permitted a few hours of rest. Although everything was wet, the men spread their blankets on the saturated ground and promptly fell asleep. At first light they were on the road again without having had breakfast or even coffee. The march was horrendous, as explained by Private Fiske (Grant's brigade): "blistered and raw, every nerve was magazine of pain, and every step exploded them." The column finally halted that night at Dranesville.[32]

The rest of the VI Corps broke camp near Centreville at about 3:00 a.m. Marching approximately 15 miles, they passed through Dranesville, halting just a mile beyond it. Eustis's detached brigade at Centreville was also up at 3:00 a.m. and told to pack up and prepare to march. It finally moved out four hours later and rejoined the VI Corps at Dranesville at about 5:00 p.m., after the 17-mile march.[33]

XI Corps

Von Gilsa's brigade (Francis Barlow's division) was detached in the morning and sent ahead to secure Crampton's Gap through South Mountain near Burkittsville. One of Adolph von Steinwehr's brigades was sent to Boonsborough Gap. Both brigades had a battery with them. The men were overjoyed with this duty, as according to William Simmers of the 153rd Pennsylvania, "the prospect of a speedy deliverance from the odious yoke of Billy Barlow filled every heart with joy." Passing through Jefferson in the morning, Simmers noted that "the numerous flags thrown to the breeze told us that we were once more where the hearts of the people were with us." The inhabitants of Burkittsville were so excited to have Federal infantry in their midst that they generously provided them with bakery goods.[34]

Because of the wet conditions and the men's fatigue, the rest of the corps was permitted to rest until 9:00 a.m. and did not begin its march until shortly before noon. The column reached

Jefferson at 2:00 p.m. Some of the men behaved poorly, according to Henry Henny of the 55th Ohio (Smith's brigade): "I was some[what] demoralized to see some of the soldiers destroy property and pillage everything they coveted. Surely where there is a Union sentiment we should respect private property." The column finally halted near Middletown, at about 5:00 p.m., after marching only seven miles that day. The men were impressed by the patriotic reception they received from the latter town.[35]

XII Corps

After spending seven full days in Leesburg, the XII Corps finally broke camp at 4:00 p.m. and marched toward Edward's Ferry on the Potomac River. Here the corps crossed the river on the pontoon bridges, marched to the canal, and struck its towpath in a steady drizzle. The soldiers followed the route the III Corps had taken before them through Poolesville to the Monocacy Aqueduct, where the men finally went into camp after the 15-mile march. Abundant quantities of cherries along the route made the march somewhat easier to bear.[36]

June 27

CONFEDERATE

Riding several miles in front of Rodes's division, Jenkins's cavalry brigade entered Carlisle. The town's leaders asked Jenkins to spare the community. Jenkins had no intentions of destroying the town and merely requested rations for his 1,500 men and forage for their horses. After collecting these supplies, Jenkins rode off with his men. Before the day was over, Rodes's and Johnson's divisions entered the town from different directions. The frightened citizens remained in their homes with doors locked and windows shuttered. The troops again collected supplies while here.[1]

With Carlisle in Confederate hands, and Longstreet's and Hill's Corps's arrival at Chambersburg, Lee prepared orders for Ewell's capture of Harrisburg. Imboden's cavalry brigade was ordered to McConnellsburg and Jenkins's was sent toward Harrisburg to make a reconnaissance of that city's defenses. The troopers camped about halfway to Mechanicsburg. Colonel White's "Commanches" entered McSherryville and Hanover, halting at the latter town to "shop" for supplies.[2]

General Isaac Trimble, newly returned to the army after receiving a debilitating wound during the Second Manassas Campaign, recalled a conversation with Lee. Looking down upon a map of the region, Lee purportedly rested his finger near Gettysburg and said, "Hereabouts we shall probably meet the enemy and fight a great battle. And if God gives us the victory the war will be over....."[3]

While in Chambersburg, Lee issued another general order against pillaging:

GENERAL ORDERS, No. 73.

Chambersburg, Pa., June 27, 1863.

The commanding general has observed with marked satisfaction the conduct of the troops on the march, and confidently anticipates results commensurate with the high spirit they have manifested.

No troops could have displayed greater fortitude or better performed the arduous marches of the past ten days.

Their conduct in other respects has, with few exceptions, been in keeping with their character as soldiers, and entitles them to approbation and praise.

There have, however, been instances of forgetfulness, on the part of some, that they have in keeping the yet unsullied reputation of the army, and that the duties exacted of us by civilization and Christianity are not less obligatory in the country of the enemy than in our own.

The commanding general considers that no greater disgrace could befall the army, and through it our whole people, than the perpetration of the barbarous outrages upon the unarmed and defenseless and the wanton destruction of private property, that have marked the course of the enemy in our own country.

Such proceedings not only degrade the perpetrators and all connected with them, but are subversive of the discipline and efficiency of the army, and destructive of the ends of our present movement.

It must be remembered that we make war only upon armed men, and that we cannot take vengeance for the wrongs our people have suffered without lowering ourselves in the eyes of all whose abhorrence has been excited by the atrocities of our enemies, and offending against Him to whom vengeance belongeth, without whose favor and support our efforts must all prove in vain.

The commanding general therefore earnestly exhorts the troops to abstain with most scrupulous care from unnecessary or wanton injury to private property, and he enjoins upon all officers to arrest and bring to summary punishment all who shall in any way offend against the orders on this subject.[4]

Most of the men in the ranks were unhappy with Lee's orders. Charles Bachelor of the 2nd Louisiana (Nicholls's brigade) wrote home after the battle of Gettysburg that "it makes my blood boil to hear the many depredations committed by Yankees—and just to think we invaded their country passing into Pennsylvania almost to Harrisburg...without doing them the least harm and whenever it was necessary for us to take anything they were paid for it its true value. The conduct of our government is really discouraging to us and shows a great want of nerve to become equal to the emergencies now existing."[5]

After riding to Fairfax Court House, Stuart ordered his men across the Potomac River, at Rowser's Ford. The river was deep here, forcing the cavalrymen to drag the cannons and caissons into the water and tow them to the Maryland shore.[6]

General Lee and his staff in Chambersburg

Hoke, *The Great Invasion of 1863*

Per Lee's request, General Samuel Jones sent an expeditionary force toward Beverly, West Virginia, to threaten, and possibly capture it. Jones made it clear that he could not commit too many of his troops, for he was charged with safeguarding the Virginia and Tennessee Railroad and the saltworks in the area.[7]

First Corps

Pickett's men continued their journey into Pennsylvania at about 5:00 a.m. Entering Greencastle, they found the citizens looking very serious. One farmer along the way told the men that "he could not blame our army for taking horses, etc., for he had heard the yankees boast of what they had taken from the southern people." The march took the men through Chambersburg. Charles Lippitt noted that the women looked very "common." As the column moved to the bivouac area about three miles north of the town, some of the men caught some chickens. Their officers immediately forced the men to compensate the owners with Confederate script. The division marched about 15 miles that day.[8]

Hood's men were on the road again before 8:00 a.m. As they marched through Greencastle at a quick-time pace with music playing, they could see the great contrasts with Virginia. Thomas Ware noted that the citizens looked "mad & sullen at our appearance, a great many closed doors; stores all closed…every thing is cheap." Outside of town, the dreary march continued, this time on a narrow, muddy road. The soldiers had different perceptions of their comrades' behavior during this march. Captain Henry Figures (Law's brigade) reported that "some of the army treated the citizens very badly, stole their chickens, milk, butter etc." Figures was particularly repulsed by the waste. "There were a great many sheep killed that were not used," he wrote. Thomas Ware also noted that the men occasionally marched through fields of wheat and corn, tearing down fences along the way. Tally Simpson of the 3rd South Carolina wrote home, "Wofford's Brig. of this div [*sic*] stole so much that they could not carry what rations they drew from the commissary." R. T. Cole (Law's brigade) swore that he did not see any such actions committed by the men.[9]

A 12-mile march brought Hood's men to Chambersburg. Thomas Ware called it "as fine a town as I ever saw," and compared it in size to Atlanta. The townspeople had the same reaction to the invaders as those in Greencastle. To Colonel Robert Powell of the 5th Texas it was a "city of banners...a Union flag surrounded every house...every lady held a flag in her hand, varying in size from a postage stamp to a table cloth." One particularly well-endowed woman stood on her porch with a large banner draped across her chest. A Texan in Robertson's brigade yelled out to her, "Take care, Madam, for Hood's boys are great at storming breastworks when the Yankee colors is on them." Another woman shouted to John West, "Thank God, you will never come back here alive," to which he responded, "No, we intend to go to Cincinnati by way of New York." The woman beat a hasty retreat into her house and slammed the door. The Confederate soldiers often swapped their hats for newer ones from the heads of local citizens. When asked the whereabouts of their hats, the local citizens replied, "We have had some experiences." Many of the men were frustrated to see guards stationed on every corner to prevent looting. This did not, however, prevent many of the men from slipping away to procure needed supplies. The march continued for about three miles beyond the town, where they rejoined Pickett's division camped in a large grove of trees. Although the division had marched about 17 miles, many of the men still had enough energy to slip away to forage.[10]

McLaws's division continued its march early as well, beginning several miles behind Hood's and Pickett's. The column marched through Hagerstown, Middleburg, and crossed into Pennsylvania around midday. The division continued through Greencastle, where townspeople lined the streets to watch the Confederates pass "with as much apparent curiosity as if we had been orangoutangs [sic] or baboons," noted a soldier in the 10th Georgia (Paul Semmes's brigade). "We were clad in garments very much damaged by hard usage," noted the soldier. Overhearing a smirk about their clothes, one soldier merely said, "we don't put on our best clothes when we go out to kill hogs." The division finally stopped for the night at Marion, about six miles south of Chambersburg.[11]

The men were very impressed with the thickly populated countryside and found that the land was rich enough for the people to live on small farms. Many farms were only 6 to 20 acres in size, without even one tree stump visible in the fields. Colonel James Fremantle observed that the men widened the road by opening the fences that lined it, to permit more rapid movement. He was most impressed by the self-restraint of the men—no citizen was molested, and no property destroyed.[12]

Second Corps

Rodes's division was on the move at 6:00 a.m. on the last leg of its trip to Carlisle. Because of the condition of the wet roads, Samuel Pickens (O'Neal's brigade) called the 23-mile trek "worse than 30 on a good dry road." As the division approached the town, two militia regiments fired into it, and then scurried to safety. As he entered the town, Pickens felt "completely broken down & my feet hurt me very much." When the men realized that they were within 20 miles of Harrisburg, the fatigue suddenly seemed less omnipresent. Daniel's, Iverson's and Ramseur's brigades made themselves comfortable in the U.S. Barracks, while Doles's brigade bivouacked on the campus of Dickinson College, and O'Neal's was left about one and one-half miles from town on Baltimore Pike to watch for the enemy. General Ewell immediately made a number of demands on the town. The townspeople felt the requirements were excessive and could not comply. Ewell merely told them that he would let loose his soldiers to locate and take these supplies.[13]

A group of local ministers found their way to General Ewell, now resting in the Carlisle Barracks, and asked whether they could conduct religious services on Sunday. "Certainly," replied Ewell, "I wish myself to attend Church." The ministers departed, but soon returned with another request. Would the general have objections if they said a prayer for President Lincoln at the service? "Not at all," Ewell replied, "I know of no man who is more in need of your prayers."[14]

Johnson's division, minus Steuart's brigade, broke camp and was back on the road by 7:00 a.m., where it followed Rodes's division to Carlisle. Reverend Sheeran of the 14th Louisiana (Nicholls's brigade) noted that "it was remarkable to see how orderly our men conducted themselves on this march. It is true many of them helped themselves to poultry, vegetables, milk, etc., but I saw no wanton destruction of private property." Charles Brown, a German immigrant in the 2nd Louisiana, straggled during the march, and was reportedly killed by civilians. Meanwhile, Steuart's brigade arrived in Shippensburg too late to catch up with the rest of the division. It therefore continued its march toward Carlisle, passing through Stoughstown and Springfield along the way, covering about 20 miles.[15]

General Early's division, minus Gordon's brigade, marched from Mummasburg, leaving between 6:00 and 7:00 a.m. The column trudged through Hunterstown, New Chester, Hampton, and East Berlin, and camped for the night a short distance from the latter town. White's Comanches, riding in advance of Gordon's brigade during its march toward York, rode through McSherrytown at about 10:00 a.m. and continued on to Hanover. Colonel White addressed the citizens in the town square, saying that while his men were roughly dressed, they were gentlemen fighting for a just cause. The men then dismounted and visited the stores. Moving through Hanover Junction, the cavalry burned the railroad equipment there, after first driving off the militia. Meanwhile, General Early rode the four miles to Gordon's camp to discuss the capture of York. Although there were no reports of Federal troops in this large town, Early wanted Gordon to be ready. After securing the town, Gordon was to proceed 12 miles to the Columbia bridge and secure it. This would be the passageway across the wide Susquehanna River to Harrisburg.[16]

That evening, Mr. Arthur Farquhar passed through the Confederate picket line and conferred with General John Gordon. He was permitted to return to his home in York only if he agreed to return with information about whether there would be any resistance when Gordon's men entered the town. A subsequent

conference among the town leaders resulted in a grudging real-
ization that the town must be surrendered.[17]

Third Corps

As Anderson's division marched through Chambersburg, the
Stars and Stripes fluttered from most windows. Occasionally, a
small Confederate flag was thrown from a window, only to be
pulled back in within a few seconds. As the regimental bands
played, some soldiers broke ranks and nonchalantly plucked hats
off the heads of unsuspecting citizens lining the road, replacing
them with their tattered ones. The men were not surprised by
their reception here, and Private Holt reflected that the Pennsylvanians liked them even less than the Marylanders. He also observed that few citizens spoke English and noted that the women
were "insolent and ugly" and wondered if they were the models
for the "comic pictures they put in the almanacs." Colonel Francis
Fleming of the 2nd Florida (Perry's brigade) called them "low
Dutch," and wrote to his brother, "I have scarcely seen a refined
and highly intelligent person since I have been in the state."
Anderson's men finally halted for the night at Fayetteville, proud
of the scarcity of stragglers.[18]

As Heth's, and then Pender's divisions passed through
Hagerstown, the men could see many Southern sympathizers
being closely watched by their Union neighbors. Many Confederate flags could be seen inside the doors. The long column now
entered Pennsylvania, where the men were amazed at the bounty
of the land and the barns that were larger than the houses. Samuel
Hankins of the 2nd Mississippi (Davis's brigade) noted that many
of the houses were abandoned, and in their haste to get away,
the inhabitants had left the front doors open. Pender's division
finally halted about a mile from Fayetteville, where it finally caught
up with the rest of the corps, but it paid the price. George Hall of
the 14th Georgia (Edward Thomas's brigade) noted that "my feet
was so sore I could hardly put them to the ground." General Dorsey
Pender wrote to his wife that night, "I never saw troops march as
ours do; they will go 15 or 20 miles a day without leaving a straggler

and hoop and yell on all occasions." He was also proud of his men's restraint. "They have done nothing like the Yankees do in our country. They take poultry and hogs but in most cases pay our money for it." A. J. Dula of the 22nd North Carolina (Scales's brigade) remembered the night of June 27. Several of his comrades woke him after returning from a foraging expedition, loaded down with chickens, geese, and ducks. The rest of the night was spent cooking these delicacies.[19]

UNION

The entire army was on the move. The left wing (I, III, and XI Corps) were near the South Mountain passes (particularly Turner's and Crampton's), while the rest of the army was moving toward Frederick. The I Corps marched from Jefferson to Middletown; the II Corps travelled from just inside the Maryland border, through Poolsville, Barnsville, and finally camped near Monocacy Junction on the Baltimore and Ohio Railroad. The III Corps marched from the latter railroad through Jefferson and Burkittsville. The V Corps took the road from Poolsville to Buckytown, camping at Ballinger's Creek, near Frederick. The VI Corps marched from Dranesville to Edward's Ferry, where it crossed the Potomac River—the last corps to do so. The XI Corps remained near Middletown and the vital South Mountain passes, and the XII Corps marched from the Monocacy Aqueduct to Point of Rocks, Petersville, and Knoxville.[20]

Grossly overestimating the size of Lee's army, Hooker persistently asked for additional troops on June 25. He had sent his chief of staff, General Daniel Butterfield, to Washington to see Halleck and Lincoln to request more men. Butterfield forwarded his recollections of the meeting to Hooker on June 27. Halleck was resistant, as he did not wish to strip any additional men from the capital's already meager defenses, and Lincoln supported him. Next, Butterfield traveled to Baltimore to see General Schenck, who also portrayed his department as being undermanned. Butterfield returned, frustrated and empty-handed.[21]

A morning dispatch from Hooker to Halleck again despaired over the number of troops available to take on Lee's army. Hooker estimated his 105,000 men to be inadequate, so that it "may not be expected of me more than I have material to do with."[22]

On his way to Frederick, Maryland, Hooker stopped at Harper's Ferry, where he found 10,000 men that could take the field. He asked Halleck that they be added to his army, as "they cannot defend a ford of the river, and as far as Harper's Ferry is concerned, there is nothing of it." Harper's Ferry should be abandoned. Halleck was firm in his reply: "Maryland Heights have always been regarded as an important point to be held by us....I cannot approve their abandonment, except in case of absolute necessity."[23]

Exasperated, Hooker replied that his original instructions were to cover both Harper's Ferry and Washington, and now he had to contend with an enemy force in front of him, which he believed outnumbered his own army. "I am unable to comply with this condition with the means at my disposal, and earnestly request that I may at once be relieved from the position I occupy." Halleck and Lincoln were only too happy to comply.[24]

Marching through Maryland

Battles and Leaders of the Civil War

Some additional troops were added to Hooker's army, but they were small in numbers. They included the Pennsylvania Reserve division, two brigades from John Abercrombie's division (Hays's and George Stannard's), Henry Lockwood's brigade, and some cavalry units. General Couch received about 7,200 militia from New York for his Department of the Susquehanna. The practice of the Federal Government not to issue uniforms to the Pennsylvania militia became an impediment to filling the ranks, so Governor Curtin asked Lincoln to reverse the policy. Secretary of War Stanton wired Curtin a short time later with an affirmative answer.[25]

When the VI Corps crossed the Potomac River, the entire Army of the Potomac was now in Maryland. Unfortunately, the rebels were already well inside Pennsylvania. General Jenkins's cavalry brigade in Carlisle demanded 1,500 meals. If not met, the hungry troopers would be released on the town to secure their own provisions. A small mountain of supplies suddenly materialized. Soon after the troopers left the town, two large Confederate infantry divisions arrived from two directions. General Ewell levied his own demands on the town, including 1,500 barrels of flour. The problem was that only 200 barrels were present.[26]

I Corps

The day was an easy one for the men. Not on the road until 8:30 a.m., the corps went into camp just beyond Middletown, Maryland, about five hours later, after the eight-mile march. The soldiers received a warm welcome as they marched through each town, particularly Jefferson, which had a preponderance of flags. Some of the regiments brought their drum corps and bands up to the front of their units to add to the grand entrance. Colonel Rufus Dawes of the 6th Wisconsin summarized the life of the men during this part of the campaign: "trudging along all day in a soaking rain, getting as wet as a drowned rat, taking supper on hard tack and salt pork, and then wrapping up in a wet woolen blanket and lying down for a sleep, but waken up during the night three or four times to receive orders."[27]

II Corps

The column was on the road by mid-afternoon. Cherry trees laden with fruit lined the road, making the trip more pleasurable. The column passed through Poolesville and Barnesville. James Favill of the 52nd New York (Samuel Zook's brigade) explained that as the men entered each town, they "usually resume the regular step, with the bands playing and colors flying make a stunning appearance." The column camped in the late evening at the base of Sugar Loaf Mountain near Monocacy Junction on the Baltimore and Ohio Railroad after the 16-mile march.[28]

III Corps

The men expected an early start to their march but were not on the road again until noon. The column halted outside of Jefferson to grab a fast meal, and then with flags unfurled, the men marched through the small town. General Birney ordered the bands to play at prominent intersections, presumably to reduce straggling. The women were plentiful, and all were dressed in their Sunday best. Some of the men questioned their sincerity, but all appreciated their welcome. "Flags were waving across the streets and from many windows[, and] white handkerchiefs held by fair hands fluttered welcomes from porches, windows and doorways," recalled Thomas Marbaker of the 11th New Jersey (Carr's brigade). The corps went into camp a few miles beyond the town near Burkittsville at about 9:00 p.m. after the 15-mile march. The campsite was far enough away, according to John Halsey (17th Maine, de Trobriand's brigade), so "the men won't go back [to Jefferson] to bask in the sunlight of the smiling females." Not a man complained about the short, easy marches they had made the last two days. The march today was about 15 miles.[29]

V Corps

The V Corps was on the march at 6:00 a.m. The rainy conditions made the roads muddy and difficult to navigate. The column forded the Monocacy River in waist-deep water and passed through Buckystown, before going into bivouac at about 6:00 p.m.

at Ballinger's Creek, a few miles from Frederick. The corps had marched about 19 miles.[30]

The Pennsylvania Reserve division was on the march from Goose Creek at 6:00 a.m. and crossed the Potomac River at Edward's Ferry. Continuing their march, they finally camped for the night at the mouth of the Monocacy River after the 15-mile march.[31]

VI Corps

The VI Corps was on the road again at first light. Reaching Edward's Ferry at about noon, the men waited their turn to cross the Potomac River on the two pontoon bridges. Sgt. John Hartwell of the 121st New York (Bartlett's brigade) estimated that each was composed of 75 boats. Some of the units sang "Home Again," and the bands struck up the tune "Maryland, My Maryland." Eustis's brigade crossed about 4:30 p.m. and joined its comrades, who were camped between the river and Poolsville. In all, the men marched about ten miles that day. Officers issued strict orders against molesting private property, but wood was scarce, so the officers relented and permitted the men to remove the *top* rails of the fences. These were quickly depleted, and then the men took the next top rail, until all of the fence rails were gone.[32]

XI Corps

While the rest of the XI Corps settled in at Middletown, von Gilsa's brigade remained near Burkittsville. Calvin Heller of the 153rd Pennsylvania recorded in his diary that "we live good[,] we can git [*sic*] what we want to eat in the town[;] we can say for the first time that the privates can go whare [*sic*] they please[,] but it soon got stopt [*sic*] for us."[33]

XII Corps

Up at 4:30 a.m., the men crossed the stone Monocacy Aqueduct and continued along the canal path to Point of Rocks, and then to Petersville/Petonville, which they reached at 4:00 p.m. The march continued to Knoxville, about five miles from Harper's Ferry, where the column halted for the night at about 9:30 p.m. The march was made more bearable by the four-hour midday halt. General Hooker rode by on his large black horse during the corps's 18-mile march, and was loudly cheered by the men.[34]

June 28

CONFEDERATE

This was a quiet day for Lee's dispersed army. The First Corps remained near Chambersburg, Johnson's and Rodes's divisions (Second Corps) occupied Carlisle, while Early's division captured York, and the Third Corps camped near Fayetteville.

Jacob Hoke, a Chambersburg resident, looked upon the Confederate army with wonderment. He noted that most of the wagons bore the inscription "U.S.," and that no two regimental or brigade flags were identical. "This diversity...was typical of the cause for which the Confederates fought," he wrote. The infantry was dressed in a wild array of colors, with butternut predominating. While calling many "ragged, shoeless, and filthy," he marveled at their demeanor. The columns were tight during the march, and he never heard laughing, talking, or singing. He was especially impressed by the officers, who, along with the cavalrymen, seemed to be of a higher class. Hoke noted that a few Confederates deserted from the army and actually settled in Chambersburg.[1]

Stuart was still riding around the Federal army. His troopers cut the telegraph lines at Rockville and captured 125 new wagons, which stretched for eight miles. Now only 10 miles from Washington, and between it and the Army of the Potomac, Stuart briefly considered a dash into the capital. His command was, however, strung out because of the capture of the wagon train, so he decided against this bold venture. The wagons soon became an albatross hanging around Stuart's neck. The mule teams were unruly when underfed and thirsty, and the four hundred prisoners further slowed his progress. Stuart decided to parole the latter, but the process ate up precious time. Raiding parties were active in the meantime, tearing up railroad tracks and cutting communication lines.[2]

Meanwhile, Jenkins's cavalry brigade rode through Mechanicsburg, about eight miles from Harrisburg. General Jenkins stopped here to read Northern newspapers, which contained accurate information about Federal troop movements and positions. His men were also busy "shopping" at local stores. The Confederate raiders were described as being poorly dressed with the majority wearing no uniforms at all. One citizen called them a "pitiful sight." Their horses were fine, however, having been recently captured. Satisfied with the information, Jenkins remounted and rode toward Harrisburg with his brigade. A detachment riding up ahead encountered Federal militia at Sporting Hill, about four miles outside of Harrisburg. Information about the defenses was sent back to Ewell, who ultimately ordered Rodes to march on Harrisburg the next day.[3]

That night, Lee issued the following orders for June 29 from his tent in Messersmith's Woods outside of Chambersburg: Ewell was to take Harrisburg with Longstreet in support, and Hill was to cross the Susquehanna River downstream, behind Early's division, and seize the railroad between Harrisburg and Philadelphia. Lee was only partially confident of his plans, as he still did not know the exact location of the Army of the Potomac. A staff officer from Longstreet's Corps visited Lee at 10:00 p.m. with news that a spy named "Harrison" had arrived with information that Meade had relieved Hooker, and the Federal army was now at Frederick, Maryland—within striking distance of the army. Initially skeptical of the report, Lee interrogated Harrison and ultimately believed his story.[4]

First Corps

While Pickett's and Hood's divisions rested north of Chambersburg, McLaws's men passed through the town on the

Stuart's cavalry captures a Federal wagon train

Battles and Leaders of the Civil War

final leg of the march to rejoin them. Surgeon William Shine of Phillips's Legion (William Wofford's brigade) was most impressed with Chambersburg, but not its citizens, writing, "the people all look very <u>sour</u> at us as we passed through. A great many <u>sharp</u> things were said to them by the troops, who seemed to be in fine humor....Some of the soldiers would ask them the distance to Philadelphia, Baltimore, and Washington DC, and saying, it will only take us so many days to march there, at which the 'Yanks' would seem perfectly infuriated." Always on the lookout for a well-turned ankle, Tally Simpson wrote home, "I have seen a great many young ladies, but not very pretty. In fact I have not seen a really pretty girl since I have been in Penn." He did grudgingly admit that the women were always clean, neat and industrious. He also noted another oddity—he didn't see any "negros" in Pennsylvania.[5]

The time spent north of Chambersburg by Hood's men was heaven on earth. According to Thomas Ware, half of his 15th Georgia received passes and were out foraging. The men found they could get just about anything they cared for at a reasonable price, and noted that the Pennsylvania Dutch "seem to think more of their gardens and & barns than any thing else."[6]

Pickett's men were ordered to clean their guns and wash their clothes on this Sabbath. Some of the men wanted to go into Chambersburg to purchase goods, but were prevented from doing so. There was still plenty of food to be had. Private James Booker of the 38th Virginia (Lewis Armistead's brigade) wrote home that the local citizens "treat us verry [*sic*] kind though I believe it is done through fear....Thare [*sic*] is but verry [*sic*] few people that charges us eney [*sic*] thing for milk or butter." Harold Walthall·of the 1st Virginia (Kemper's brigade) noted that the men did not engage in "aggravated vandalism," although he couldn't "vouch for the fate of any pig or rooster who wouldn't get out of the way." David Johnson (Kemper's brigade) noted that the men's morale was never higher. "Officers and men were alike inspired with the greatest confidence in our ability to defeat the enemy anywhere he might choose to meet us, and never did an army move into an enemy's country in better fighting trim and spirit."[7]

Second Corps

Rodes's and Johnson's divisions remained at Carlisle. Because the townspeople were unable or unwilling to comply with Ewell's demands for supplies, he ordered his men to search the houses. The men scooped up large quantities of cattle, horses, flour, and other goods. The barracks' stables also yielded large quantities of grain. Unfortunately, most of the government supplies had already been removed by the time Rodes's men arrived. Large quantities of whiskey were found, and with ice, made wonderful mint juleps for the officers. Unfortunately, the enlisted men also helped themselves, and a fight almost erupted between the 23rd North Carolina (Iverson's brigade) and a Georgia regiment of Doles's brigade.[8]

General Ewell, who was stationed in Carlisle earlier in his career, conducted a flag-raising ceremony at the Barracks. This was a special occasion because the newly designed Confederate battleflag was hoisted up the pole. Bands played and Ewell gave a speech.[9]

Steuart's brigade marched through Springfield in the early morning and finally rejoined Johnson's division at Carlisle at about 3:00 p.m. During the march, Lieutenant Randolph McKim stopped at a store to purchase seven copies of the New Testament. "The surprise of the storekeeper when an officer of the terrible Rebel Army desired to purchase copies...may be imagined." McKim also noted the poor condition of his men: "broken down, many of them having marched barefooted." Upon their arrival at Carlisle, the men were ordered to cook several days' rations.[10]

A contingent of community leaders emerged from York to confer with General Gordon. They offered to surrender the town, but in return, asked that citizens and property not be molested. Gordon agreed, and by 10:00 a.m., Gordon's brigade entered the town in three columns. A large Federal flag flying over the town square was pulled down, as the brigade merely marched through the town, stopping about two miles east of it. Meanwhile, the rest of Early's division proceeded to Weigelstown. Here Early dispatched the 17th Virginia Cavalry under Colonel William French to burn two railroad bridges at the mouth of the Conewago Creek, and all of the others between there and York. Early marched with the remainder of his division to York.[11]

William Smith's brigade led Early's column as it approached York. Smith halted his men just outside of the town and moved his bands to the head of the column. "Go back and look up those tooting fellows, and tell them to make sure their drums and horns are all right, and then to come up here to the front," he told his aide. The brigade entered the town with bands playing "Dixie" and then "Yankee Doodle." General Smith could be seen, bowing and saluting to everyone in sight, particularly the pretty young women. Cheers and applause broke out when the citizens realized that they were not to be butchered by the dreaded rebels. An ex-governor of Virginia, Smith halted his brigade at the town square, and launched into a "rattling and humorous speech." Artilleryman Robert Stiles recalled what happened next: "A volley of very heated profanity poured forth in a piping, querulous treble, coming up from the rear." Suddenly, no-nonsense General Early pushed through the crowd, cursing all the while, only to find Smith's small brigade drawn up around the square, with its commander giving a speech. Demanding an explanation for why he had delayed the march, Smith could only mutter that he was "having a little fun" and trying to win the confidence of the citizens. Realizing that he could not embarrass his men, Early turned his back on the scene and walked away, leaving Smith to finish his speech.[12]

One North Carolinian in Hoke's brigade noted that the citizens "stopped and gazed at the troops as they passed with something like stupefaction." Although the citizens did not seem alarmed, they "seemed to give up the idea of going to church that day." The brigade finally settled into the extensive hospital buildings. From here they roamed around the town, often conversing with the male citizens. Meanwhile Hays's and Smith's brigades continued to Lauck's Mills at 2:00 p.m., where they went into camp. Early had another conference with General Gordon, reiterating his orders to capture the bridge over the Susquehanna River. They were not really Ewell's orders, as he had been told to destroy the bridge. However, Early believed that it might be worthwhile to have a column of troops marching on Harrisburg from a different direction.[13]

Returning to York, General Early requisitioned a number of supplies from the town, including 2,000 pairs of shoes, 1,000 hats, 1,000 pairs of socks, $100,000, and three-days' rations. The rations requested were: 165 barrels of flour or 28,000 pounds of bread, 3,500 pounds of sugar, 1,650 pounds of coffee, 300 gallons of molasses, 1,200 pounds of salt, and 32,000 pounds of beef or 21,000 pounds of bacon or pork. The town was able to supply between 1,200 and 1,500 pairs of shoes, and the requested hats, socks, and rations, but could only scrape together $28,600 in greenbacks. The mayor explained that most of the money had already been moved, and Early accepted this explanation. Early's modern biographer believed that these actions constituted widely acceptable "relatively humane rules of war" and did not violate Lee's General Orders No. 72. In fact, he believed that General

Lee probably "had little trouble reconciling his conscience" about this approach. We will never know for sure.[14]

Feeling good that the expedition was going as planned, Early rode toward Wrightsville and Gordon's brigade. He had not gotten far when he saw ominous clouds of smoke in the distance, and learned that Gordon had encountered the 20th and 27th Pennsylvania Militia. Gordon initially tried to move around their flank with three regiments to get into their rear. Finding this impractical, he opened fire with his artillery. The third shell caused the militia to flee their defenses and cross the bridge. Not to be denied, Gordon immediately ordered his men after them. Stepping onto the bridge, the men realized that its center was aflame. Gordon sent a detachment into the town of Wrightsville for buckets, but none were to be had. None that is, until errant sparks hit a lumberyard on the edge of the town, setting it ablaze. Before long, the fire spread to some nearby houses, and suddenly buckets miraculously appeared. Gordon's men formed a fire line from the river to the town, and soon the blaze was under control. Gordon later wrote that "notwithstanding the excessive fatigue of the men from the 20 miles and the skirmish with the enemy, I formed my brigade in line around the burning buildings, and resisted the progress of the flames until they were checked." When they turned to the bridge, however, they realized that it was a lost cause.[15]

Early was bitterly disappointed about the loss of the bridge, as it destroyed his plans to capture and ransom Lancaster, and then march on Harrisburg. He had hoped to come upon the capital from the rear, while the rest of the corps attacked from the opposite side. Realizing he had lost his opportunity, Early ordered Gordon's men back to the division at York the following day. Early returned to his command that night.[16]

Upon reaching his headquarters, Early learned that his cavalry was only modestly successful. Colonel White reported that his command reached Hanover Junction and destroyed the depot and two nearby bridges, but he was not able to destroy additional ones because Federal infantry defended them. Colonel

French was more successful in destroying a larger number of railroad bridges, though.[17]

Third Corps

The corps remained near Fayetteville, where the men rested, cleaned their weapons, and in some cases, were inspected. Looking around them, the men were impressed by the region's bounty. George Hall of the 14th Georgia (Thomas's brigade) estimated that "there is enough wheat here to supply the world."[18]

Guards were placed around the town to prevent pillaging. Horses were collected by the score, which George Hall noted were the "finest...I ever saw." While looting occurred, most of the citizens were only too happy to give their goods to the invaders out of fear. John Turner of the 7th North Carolina (Lane's brigade) wrote that "the North American Indian could not have been more surprised or frightened when Columbus landed than these people. They agree to any proposition—grant any request." Iowa Royster of the same brigade added, "they know how their soldiers have behaved in Virginia and they fear that ours will retaliate."[19]

Most of the men had lingering doubts about the enemy's location. "We hear nothing of Hooker's army at all, but General Lee knows what he is about," noted Spencer Welch of Perrin's brigade. Despite the many miles the men had marched, Surgeon Welch felt that they were therapeutic. "Troops have so much better health when on the march," he noted.[20]

UNION

Asleep in his tent, V Corps commander, General George Meade, was awoken by Colonel James Hardie of Halleck's staff. Thinking he was relieved of his command, he rubbed the sleep from his eyes and read the dispatch from General Halleck. He probably read the first line several times before it sunk in: "you will receive with this the order of the President placing you in command of the Army of the Potomac." As to his orders, Halleck wrote, "you will not be hampered by any minute instructions from these headquarters. Your army is free to act as you may deem proper under the circumstances as they arise." He did remind him that he was to operate against Lee's army and protect both Washington and Baltimore. In addition, Harper's Ferry was placed directly under his orders, and ultimately, "you are intrusted with all the power and authority which the President, the Secretary of War, or the General-in-Chief can confer on you."[21]

Meade accompanied Hardie to Hooker's tent, where the news was conveyed to "Fighting Joe." Because he had requested his removal from the army, he was probably not surprised by the visit. His demeanor was apparently positive and supportive, probably because he realized that he was in a "no-win" situation with Washington.[22]

After allowing the news to sink in, Meade sent the following reply to Halleck at 7:00 a.m.: "as a soldier, I obey it, and to the utmost of my ability will execute it." He admitted that he did not even know the disposition of his own army, let alone Lee's. Halleck was probably reassured when Meade wrote that "it appears to me that I must move toward the Susquehanna, keeping Washington and Baltimore well covered, and if the enemy is checked in his attempt to cross the Susquehanna, or if he turns toward Baltimore, to give him battle."[23]

Hooker was gracious about his removal in his last General Orders (#66). He noted that the army was transferred to George Meade, "a brave and accomplished officer, who has nobly earned the confidence and esteem of this army on many a well-fought field." The army's next General Order was from Meade. It was short and to the point. "As a soldier, in obeying this order—an order totally unexpected and unsolicited—I have no promises or pledges to make," he wrote. Although he did not use Hooker's name, he referred to him as an "eminent and accomplished soldier, whose name must ever appear conspicuous in the history of its achievements."[24]

Before returning to Washington, Colonel Hardie tried to judge the mood of the army after the announcement and found "there is cause for satisfaction with it." In actuality, it was a "mixed bag," as some respected and liked Meade, and an equal number probably did not.[25]

By the end of the day, the Union army was stretched along a 30-mile arc, from the Potomac River to the south, northeast to Middletown and Frederick. The I, II, V, XI, and XII Corps, along with the Artillery Reserve, were near Frederick, the III Corps was near Walkersville and Woodsboro, and the VI Corps was near Hyattstown. The four thousand wagons were 10 miles to the east at Westminster, along the Baltimore Road. Only the ammunition wagons remained with the troops.[26]

The news from Pennsylvania was not encouraging. The enemy had captured York and Carlisle and were poised to cross the Susquehanna River. Breastworks were built at the vital 5,620-foot-long wood bridge over the river at Wrightsville as early as June 18, and were defended by the 20th Pennsylvania Militia and the 27th Pennsylvania Militia. The latter had been in the service for less than a week when Gordon's Confederate infantry brigade approached the bridge at about 5:30 p.m. After the Confederate artillery opened fire, Colonel Jacob Frick pulled his troops across the river and ordered the bridge blown up. The explosion rocked the structure, but it did not destroy it, forcing the troops to set it on fire. Unfortunately, the fire jumped into the town, setting part of it on fire as well.[27]

I Corps

The men were given another reprieve during the morning and afternoon hours, and were not on the road again until after 5:00 p.m. Rain fell throughout the day. The new destination was Frederick, eight miles away, where the army was massing. The march took the men over the Catoctin Mountains again, giving them a beautiful view of Pennsylvania. They heard that Meade had replaced Hooker, but many were not pleased because they were averse to "swapping horses in the middle of a stream." Rufus Dawes of the Iron Brigade admitted that "few of our men knew him by sight. He was sometimes seen riding by the marching columns of troops at a fast trot, his hat brim turned down and a poncho over his shoulders. The only sign of rank was a gold cord on his hat."[28]

Rumors were rampant that General George McClellan had replaced Hooker. "The soldiers almost worship him as a god, he is their idol," wrote Henry Clare (83rd New York, Baxter's brigade).[29]

II Corps

The head of the column was on the road at 6:00 a.m. Fording the Monocacy River, the corps went into camp at Monocacy Junction, within sight of Frederick, in the mid-afternoon. The day was an important one for the Philadelphia Brigade, as its commander, General Joshua Owen, was replaced by one of Meade's proteges, General Alexander Webb. Rumors abounded that Owen was drunk again.[30]

III Corps

The corps was on the road by 5:00 a.m. As the men marched through Burkittsville in the early morning, they heard the church bells summoning the faithful to worship services, but the soldiers would do no praying, as they continued to Middletown. As the men approached the town, scores of African Americans lined the roads, distributing fruit and encouragement. In the town, the troops were welcomed by young women dressed in white, carrying small flags, and singing patriotic songs. Citizens also lined the road between towns, providing food to those who wanted it. "This act of generosity and kindness brought forth repeated and hearty cheers from the ranks," recalled Thomas Marbaker (Carr's brigade). A few of the men actually worried that "some of these loyal people did not keep enough for themselves to eat." The corps crossed the Catoctin Mountains and entered Frederick at about 3:00 p.m., where they were given a patriotic welcome. One old man waving a flag from a second-story window yelled incredulously, "Still they come! Still they come!" at the seemingly endless column of troops. A pretty young girl ran over to Colonel Regis de Trobriand with a bouquet of flowers. He called the march through the town "triumphal." The corps finally went into camp about six miles from Frederick, near Walkersville, after the easy 15-mile march. The men were aware of the change in command of the army. Charles Bardeen (Carr's brigade) merely entered in his diary, "Army doesn't like it."[31]

V Corps

The V Corps remained in camp near Frederick. Many of the enlisted men were out and about purchasing food to augment their boring diet. They were most impressed with their surroundings. "What a delightful country this is," wrote Corporal John Read of Tilton's brigade, "the farms are in a high state of cultivation, the soil good and the houses neat and comfortable and many of them beautiful." The men learned that their own corps commander, George Meade, had replaced General Hooker. One soldier referred to Meade as a "grumpy, stern, severe, and admirable soldier." Surgeon Joshua Wilbur of the 18th Massachusetts (Tilton's brigade) had hoped that General George McClellan would be restored to command, and noted that "there is only one consolation to draw from it and that is that we have got rid of him as a corps commander." General George Sykes was now in command of the V Corps, and General Romeyn Ayres took over the Second Division.[32]

On the final leg of its journey to join the V Corps, Crawford's Pennsylvania Reserve division took up the march at 6:00 a.m. After fording the Monocacy River, the two brigades marched through Buckytown. The men were relieved when they finally reached Frederick at about 1:00 p.m., where they finally reunited with the V Corps after their 15-mile march.[33]

VI Corps

The VI Corps marched through Poolsville and Barnsville, along the base of Sugar Loaf Mountain, to one mile north of Hyattsville—a march of about 18 miles. The men were especially pleased by their reception at Barnsville, where for the first time since moving north they were "greeted by smiling faces and words of sympathy" by the townspeople. Some men's feet were so badly blistered that they could not wear their shoes and therefore marched along barefooted.[34]

Tongue in cheek, Wilbur Fiske wrote home that to appreciate a beautiful state like Maryland, one had to "march through it with from sixty to eighty pounds of luggage strapped to his back." The abundant supply of cherries did brighten the march and augmented the dreary army rations.[35]

XI Corps

The march from the vital mountain gaps began at around 4:00 p.m. The column crossed the Catoctin Mountains and reached Frederick, Maryland, between 10:00 and 11:00 p.m., where the men went into camp. The march was slow because other troops and wagons clogged the road. The men had learned earlier in the day that they had a new commander. Most did not know anything about General Meade, but one professed confidence in President Lincoln. "I felt assured that the President would not place in command a person, in whom he had not the utmost confidence of his ability as a leader, and especially at a time when we were so near the enemy and in daily expectation of coming in contact with him," he wrote. The march was about 22 miles.[36]

Von Gilsa's brigade was also on the march. Because of a miscommunication, the brigade marched toward Middletown where it was to rejoin the corps. It arrived in the afternoon to find Union flags flying on almost every house, but the corps gone. Although he received a directive from his new commanding officer, General Barlow, to rejoin the division in Frederick, von Gilsa decided to wait until he received orders from General Howard. General Barlow promptly arrested von Gilsa for disobeying his orders. The men, who had pitched their tents and were preparing their evening meal, were dismayed when bugles rang out "assembly." They could not believe that their march was to continue to Frederick. The men were furious because their officers added unnecessary miles by marching them around the town, rather than through it. "They had a notion to lay down and not go any further," wrote Private Wallace.[37]

XII Corps

The men broke camp and were on the road at 4:30 a.m. Backtracking about three miles, the men struck the road toward Frederick, passing again through Petersville, Centerville, and Jefferson along the way. They reached the latter town at about 10:00 a.m. The head of the column finally reached its destination at about noon, but it took several hours for the entire corps to assemble after its 12-mile march. One soldier from Candy's brigade described the march as a "go-as-you-please manner" with the only requirement being that the men "keep well closed up." It was during this leg of the march that the men began to feel like they were "home," as the local citizens were friendly and generous with their food. The heavy rains falling in the afternoon did not dissuade the citizens of Frederick from lining the streets and distributing good will and more tangible items. One of the latter was whiskey, which was freely distributed while the supply lasted.[38]

The news of the change in command of the Army of the Potomac was received "in a very quiet, undemonstrative way," according to Edmund Brown of the 27th Indiana. He further explained that "there was no strong feeling one way or the other as to him [Meade] personally," but admitted that most of the men did appreciate the change as they had lost confidence in Hooker. The division commander, Alpheus Williams, shared the enlisted men's view, describing Hooker's behavior at the battle of Chancellorsville with the words "imbecility and weakness." This view was not universally held, however. George Collins of the 149th New York (George Greene's brigade) noted that "the men had great confidence in Gen. Hooker, and believed if untrammeled by his superiors in Washington, he would lead them to victory." Part of the problem with Meade was that the men did not really know him.[39]

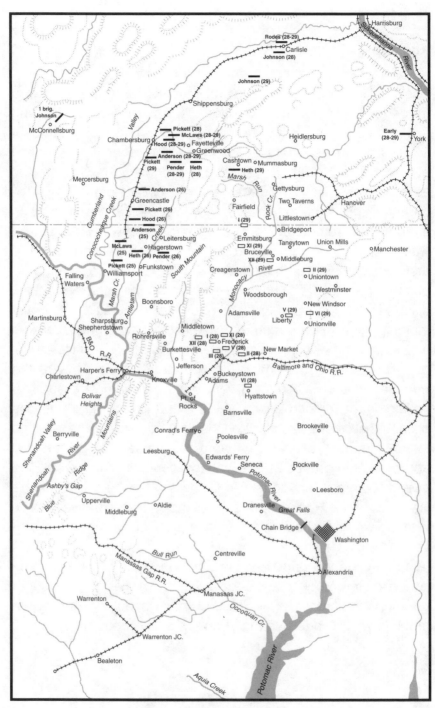

Operations June 28–June 29, 1863
(Dates in June in parentheses)

June 29

CONFEDERATE

With the knowledge of Meade's location, Lee issued new orders to Ewell, whose corps was well to the north. Instead of marching on Harrisburg, Ewell was to march down to Chambersburg and rejoin the army. Lee had a change of heart soon after and wrote to General Ewell, "I desire you to move in the direction of Gettysburg, via Heidlersburg, where you will have turnpike most of the way, and you can thus join your other divisions to Early's, which is east of the mountains. I think it preferable to keep on the east side of the mountains. When you come to Heidlersburg, you can either move directly on Gettysburg or turn down to Cashtown." Hill's Corps was to march from Fayetteville to Cashtown, and Longstreet's Corps was to follow it.[1]

Stuart was unable to provide Lee with reports about the enemy's whereabouts because he was between the Federal army and his own. Lee reported that "the march toward Gettysburg was conducted more slowly than it would have been had the movements of the Federal Army been known."[2]

After completing the task of paroling hundreds of additional prisoners, Stuart re-formed his column and pushed on to Westminster, Maryland, which he reached at 5:00 p.m. He had not intended to ride so far north, but Federal troops in the vicinity of Frederick necessitated it. About 95 members of the 1st Delaware

191

Cavalry blocked the approach to Westminster. Foolheartedly, they attempted to defend the town, only to be driven off after losing two-thirds of their men. Stuart next pushed on to Union Mills, only five miles from the Mason-Dixon Line.[3]

Jenkins's cavalry brigade left Mechanicsburg and rode toward Harrisburg. A skirmish occurred at Oyster Point (about four miles from the capital), which was accompanied by great noise, but no casualties. Meanwhile, a portion of General Imboden's cavalry brigade got into a tussle with part of the 12th Pennsylvania Cavalry at McConnellsburg. Imboden lost several men in this skirmish. An unsympathetic General Lee wrote, "it appears to have been the result of want of proper caution on his part. I hope it will have the effect of teaching proper circumspection in future."[4]

First Corps

Pickett's men were ordered to be ready to march by 8:00 a.m. These orders were subsequently changed to 3:00 p.m., when the division marched back toward Chambersburg. The citizens were excited to see the column, thinking that the enemy was retreating to Virginia. The men camped about two miles south of town in a grove of trees. The move was apparently to guard against a possible cavalry attack and to defend the trains until Imboden's cavalry brigade could relieve them.[5]

After a day where passes were freely distributed, the officers of Hood's and McLaws's divisions denied all requests. The men did not starve though. Robert Moore of the 17th Mississippi noted in his journal that the men dined on chicken pie, molasses, buttermilk, and pork, to mention just a few. An abundant supply of cherries was also brought into camp for the men to enjoy. It was a quiet period for most of the soldiers. After cooking three-days' rations, several regiments were ordered to tear up the railroad and burn bridges. The mission completed, the men returned to their camps after dark.[6]

Second Corps

General Ewell was just about to depart on his march on Harrisburg when a courier arrived from General Lee. The Army of the

Potomac was moving north, and Ewell was to reunite with Hill's and Longstreet's Corps at Chambersburg. Ewell was bitterly disappointed by the news, but reluctantly complied.[7]

Rodes's men, who had been preparing to march on Harrisburg at noon, were told to stand down and remain in camp at Carlisle. General Johnson's division, with the corps's trains and reserve artillery, marched for Chambersburg at 3:00 p.m. Ewell received another message from Lee with orders to march on Cashtown or Gettysburg, instead of Chambersburg. It was too late to recall Johnson's division, so Ewell told him to turn south at Green Village and march to Fayetteville, and then cross the mountains to Cashtown. It being so late, Rodes's division delayed its march until the following morning.[8]

Not content with the bounty he had procured at York, General Early ordered all the railroad cars destroyed. He was about to fire some of the buildings, but on closer examination, realized that the flames would jeopardize the remainder of the town. According to Early, "notwithstanding the barbarous policy pursued by the enemy in similar cases, I determined to forbear in this case, hoping that it might not be without its effect even upon our cruel enemy. This example has been lost upon the Yankees, however." Indeed, Early was furious when he read in the Northern papers that his men had intentionally tried to destroy Wrightsville. The men couldn't care less. Most were drunk on "Dutch" whiskey. Gordon's brigade rejoined the division at about 4:00 p.m.[9]

That night Early received Lee's communication to fall back and rejoin the rest of the corps on the western side of South Mountain. Early met with Generals Ewell and Rodes to discuss the order, which had the corps marching back to Gettysburg or Cashtown, "according to circumstances." The orders were too vague for the new corps commander, and he reread them several times. He was accustomed to serving under Stonewall Jackson, who gave explicit, not discretionary orders. He decided to wait until morning to make a decision. His men could hear Ewell grumbling, "Why can't a Commanding General have some one on his staff who can write an intelligible order?"[10]

Third Corps

Heth's division was on the road by 4:30 a.m., heading toward Cashtown on the opposite side of the South Mountains. Rain pelted the men in the morning. During this leg of the march the men passed "notorious abolitionist's" Thaddeus Stevens's Iron Works, which had been destroyed by Early's division.[11]

Pender's and Anderson's divisions remained behind near Fayetteville. Private Holt of the 16th Mississippi (Posey's brigade) reported that morale was high, but the condition of the men's shoes was a concern. Many were even barefooted.[12]

J. Caldwell summed up the bounty of the land when he wrote, "we are now in a beautiful country. In every direction yellow fields of grain extended themselves; on every farm were droves of the largest, fattest cattle; gardens thronged with inviting vegetables; orchards gave promise of a bounteous fruit-yield...full dairies, flocks of sheep, and poultry were almost monotonously frequent."[13]

UNION

After concentrating his forces near Frederick, Meade informed Halleck that the army would march on the following towns: the I Corps to Emmitsburg via Lewistown and Mechanicstown (Thurmont); the XI Corps to Emmitsburg via Utica and Creagerstown; the III Corps to Taneytown via Woodsboro and Middleburg; the XII Corps to Taneytown via Ceresville, Walkerville, and Woodsboro; the V Corps to follow the II Corps to Frizzleburg via Johnsville, Liberty, and Union; the VI Corps to New Windsor via New Market and Ridgeville. The cavalry was guarding the flanks and rear. Meade hoped that some part of his army would fall on Lee's dispersed forces.[14]

Several corps commanders informed Meade by the end of the day that they had not made the kind of progress that had been expected of them. The VI Corps had not reached New Windsor, and the XII Corps would not get beyond Double Pipe Creek. Meade was especially unhappy with the III Corps, whose wagons blocked the road at Middleburg, and delayed the troops behind them.[15]

General Julius Stahel's timidity was finally rewarded with his removal from command of his cavalry division. General Hugh Kilpatrick was promoted and took his place. While Gregg's cavalry division was riding through Westminster and Manchester, protecting the army's right flank, Buford's division protected the left flank along the Emmitsburg-Gettysburg axis. Kilpatrick's division advanced before the center of the army. His orders were to ride toward York to ascertain the location of Early's Confederate infantry division.[16]

General Couch wired Meade that the bridge over the Susquehanna River at Columbia was burned to prevent the rebels from crossing. He complained that he had only 15,000 men to face Lee's army, which was almost entirely in his district. In a wire to the secretary of war, Couch expressed his dissatisfaction that General Napoleon Dana, the military commander of Philadelphia, was mustering militia into service for only three months.[17]

Secretary of State Simon Cameron informed Lincoln that Lee would cross the Susquehanna River within 48 hours. This would have catastrophic consequences and could only be avoided if Meade quickly attacked Lee. Expressing concerns that his state would be invaded next, the governor of New Jersey requested that General George McClellan be installed as commander of the Army of the Potomac. Stanton would have none of it, especially since Meade had just been appointed. He did order General Dana to remove machinery from the Alfred Jenks Company in Philadelphia, which manufactured arms for the Federal forces.[18]

Raiders from Imboden's cavalry brigade rode into Mercersburg, Pennsylvania, demanding supplies and rounding up horses. These were not the courteous men of other Confederate commands who had visited the town during earlier raids.[19]

Halleck could not have been pleased when he received a dispatch from General Dix on the Virginia peninsula, informing him that a council of war unanimously agreed to halt the movement toward Richmond.[20]

I Corps

Reveille sounded at 5:00 a.m., and the men broke camp at Frederick. The intermittent rains did not dampen the men's spirits, as local citizens lined the roads providing refreshments and encouragement. Many men marched barefooted because their shoes had given out. When the soldiers traveled through the towns, "the colors were unfurled, the bands and drum-corps struck up, and quickly taking the step, with muskets at a shoulder, the regiments treated the delighted citizens to an exhibition scarcely less stately and impressive than a grand review," noted one soldier. At Mechanicsville, a farmer and his wife sat in a wagon, throwing bread to the soldiers. The men yelled out, "God bless you, old lady!" The march ended at Emmitsburg, about 25 miles from Frederick. The enlisted men noted subtle changes in their officers. Avery Harris of the 149th Pennsylvania (Stone's brigade) recalled that "the expressions in [their] faces have changed....[they have become] grave and quiet and very reticent and apparently

Maryland hospitality

Bardeen, *A Little Fifer's War Diary*

more thoughtful." Changes could also be discerned in the citizens. According to A. P. Smith of the 76th New York (Cutler's brigade), "the people grew more intensely and heartily loyal. The road sides became lined with ladies, old and young...as each with a pail and dipper or cup, dealt out cooling draughts of water."[21]

II Corps

The long, hard march from near Frederick to Frizzelburg was to begin at 4:00 a.m., but a clerk failed to deliver the orders to General Hancock, so the corps did not start out until 8:00 a.m. Meade's headquarters shot back that the clerk should be punished, and Hancock promised that he would. The 14-hour march took the men through Liberty, Johnsville, Union Bridge, and one mile beyond Uniontown, where the head of the column finally halted at about 10:00 p.m. Hancock admitted that he did not reach Frizzelburg that night, because it was "considerably farther from Monocacy Junction than indicated by the maps." According to Jacob Cole of the 57th New York (Zook's brigade), "there was complaining, grumbling, growling and worse." Part of the problem was that General Hancock drove his men unmercifully. For example, Hancock would not permit the men to halt and remove their shoes and socks before fording bodies of water. According to Captain Benjamin Thompson of the 111th New York (Willard's brigade), "it is an invariable rule after troops have forded a stream, unless under the enemy's fire, to halt them long enough to take off their shoes, wring out their stockings and wipe their feet. But Hancock marched us several miles at a rapid pace before he allowed us a breath. By that time the feet of nearly [every] man and officer were blistered and many could just hobble." Upon approaching a knee-deep stream, some of the men of the 1st Minnesota scurried across on fallen logs. Seeing this, II Corps inspector general, Colonel Charles Morgan, arrested the regiment's commander, Colonel William Colvill.[22]

Gilbert Frederick of the 57th New York noted that "straggling began early and rapidly increased towards evening and was fearful by midnight" when the march ended. Upon returning to their unit, a small detachment of men from the 14th Indiana (Carroll's brigade) noted that "we would not have known whether it was the brigade or a squad of stragglers had not the flag been waving in the breeze." The provost guards initially drove the stragglers back into the column, but eventually the numbers simply overwhelmed them. The soldiers recalled that "the day began with route march and ended with go as you please." A bystander watching the end of the column would see an army of "the lame, the halt...and last of all the born tired." The men were appreciative of the support they received from the citizens who lined the road, even in the dead of night.[23]

III Corps

The corps broke camp at about 6:00 a.m. in the pouring rain. Many of the men did not have a chance to prepare breakfast before marching through Walkersville. The column halted at Woodboro (Woodbury), where the men were given a short rest. Some were frustrated by their inability to purchase sweets. Others wanted no part of food, as they were suffering from intestinal distress brought on by the large quantities of fruit they had consumed the day before. The column moved on to Taneytown. Looking for something to break their continued loneliness, some of the men wrote their names and units on newspapers with a plea for letters and tossed them at the pretty young women they passed. The column briefly halted just beyond Taneytown after 4:00 p.m., where some men received shoes and mail. They were also visited by several townspeople who wished to see how soldiers lived. The march continued until about 6:00 p.m. In all, the troops marched about 20 miles that day. The men were happy to welcome back their corps commander, General Daniel Sickles, who had been away on leave. "The wild cheering that followed his passage through the ranks showed the great esteem in which he was held by the men under him," noted Thomas Marbaker (Carr's brigade).[24]

The new army commander, George Meade, was not happy with the III Corps's pace. Although it had covered 20 miles that day, Meade wrote to General Sickles that his men's slow marching was delaying the movements of units behind it. Sickles's wagon train, now at a standstill at Middleburg, especially concerned Meade.[25]

V Corps

Barnes's and Ayres's divisions were on the road at 7:00 a.m. The column first marched three miles back to Frederick, where wild celebrations erupted. The column turned onto the macadamized Baltimore Pike after leaving the town. The weather was cool and wet, making the march more bearable. The countryside bore a bounty of cherry trees. One 1st Michigan (Tilton's brigade) soldier wrote that the "boys break off the limbs instead of picking the cherries. Spoilt all the trees." The column marched through Ceresville, Mount Pleasant, and halted for the night at Liberty at about 8:00 p.m., after the 15-mile march. Most of the men ignored orders to leave the fence rails alone, as there was no other firewood available.[26]

Crawford's division, which had rejoined the corps the day before, was to march with the rest of the troops. However, it did not begin until 1:00 p.m. because of a long wagon train moving through the area. Falling in behind it, the division made very slow time. The other V Corps troops, which had arrived hours earlier, listened with disdain as the Reserves trudged by at 11:00 p.m. Colonel M. Hardin of the 12th Pennsylvania Reserves noted that "most of us were so hot and tired we dropped down and went to sleep without even making coffee. A bad beginning to a long march."[27]

VI Corps

The VI Corps was up at 3:00 a.m. and broke camp near Hyattsville an hour later. The 28-mile march that day took them through Monrovia, New Market, Ridgeville, Mount Airy, and finally to near New Windsor after midnight, where they halted for the night. While they may have been satisfied with their progress that day, General Slocum was not, as his men had not actually reached their destination of New Windsor.[28]

The soldiers encountered small knots of citizens, usually waving flags, along the way. They were too often empty-handed. The men tried to purchase food, but the prices were often exorbitant, which dissuaded even the hungriest. Gristmills proved to be more reasonable, and the men purchased supplies of flour and cornmeal.[29]

XI Corps

The men were awoken at 3:00 a.m. and on the road 90 minutes later. It was a long march that began badly, as they were not permitted to eat breakfast. The constant rain did not help the men's spirits as it made the roads muddy and the marching difficult. According to Private Muenzenberger of the 26th Wisconsin (Krzyzanowski's brigade), "we must march like dogs, and now that the rainy weather has started, the road is pretty bad." The first stop for a meal occurred at 4:00 p.m. The 25-mile march took the column past Utica, across the Catoctin Mountains to Creagerstown, and finally to camp near Emmitsburg.[30]

XII Corps

The corps was on the road by 5:30 a.m. and soon passed through Frederick. The citizens lined the streets despite the early hour, and the XII Corps rewarded their loyalty with quite a show. The men assumed their best military demeanors, while bands played and the flags fluttered in the breeze. After marching a short distance beyond Frederick, the column halted for a few hours to let a wagon train pass. The march continued to Woodsboro, and it finally ended near Bruceville/Ladiesburg, after 20 miles. Much of it was through fields along the side of the road, permitting the artillery and trains to move unhindered on the road surface. Pioneers moved ahead of the column, quickly removing obstructions. The men actually preferred this route, as it meant an end to the constant stopping and starting so common when infantry shared the road with wheeled vehicles. The soft ground was also easier on the men's feet.[31]

June 30

CONFEDERATE

Lee's army was now concentrating at the Cashtown-Gettysburg region of Pennsylvania. While Ewell's troops were moving south, General Heth sent Pettigrew's brigade to Gettysburg in search of supplies. The brigade returned with news of Federal cavalry in the town.[1]

As Stuart's troopers moved north from Union Mills, the units became strung out. Spotting a Federal cavalry brigade outside of Hanover, John R. Chambliss's brigade pitched into it. A lively fight ensued, which ended when the Confederates were driven from the town. Stuart could only helplessly watch, as relief was too far away. When reinforcements arrived, Stuart positioned them about two miles south of the town. Here he contemplated the best route to take to reunite with Lee's army.[2]

Stuart withdrew his men after dark and rode to Jefferson. He was again hampered by hundreds of prisoners, including farmers whom he retained because he did not want them to divulge his whereabouts. Reaching York Pike, Stuart was dismayed to learn that Early's division had moved west from York, and believed that he had marched to Carlisle or Shippensburg. His men were so exhausted that they were falling asleep in their saddles. Stuart conferred with his officers and decided to ride for Carlisle.[3]

To deal with the growing threat from Dix's raid on Richmond, a number of men were mobilized, including 1,112 convalescents from hospitals, 600 exchanged prisoners, and one company of approximately 60 men. About 560 convalescents were already organized and awaiting arms.[4]

First Corps

McLaws's division was on the road by 7:00 a.m. Hood's men were not formed into ranks until 8:00 a.m., and their march began about an hour later. The pace through the drizzling rain was slow, and frequent stops were permitted. A two-mile march brought them to Fayetteville. Leaving Chambersburg Road, the column took a country road for two miles and halted for the day between 1:00 p.m. and 2:00 p.m. near Greenwood at the foot of South Mountain. In all, the men had marched about 11 miles. Thomas Ware of the 15th Georgia noted in his journal that "we made fences fly." Rumors abounded about the location of the enemy, but Robert Moore of the 17th Mississippi (Barksdale's brigade) was most accurate when he apprehensively recorded in his diary, "know not the whereabouts of the enemy."[5]

Prior to Hood's division beginning its march, Law's brigade was put on the road to New Guilford, where it was to guard against a Federal thrust from Emmitsburg.[6]

South of Chambersburg, a detachment of Pickett's division again ripped up the Cumberland Valley Railroad tracks. Henry Owen of the 18th Virginia (Garnett's brigade) noted his men's appearance with a tinge of sadness. "The bright uniforms and braided caps of earlier days were gone and had given place to the slouched hat, the faded threadbare jacket and patched pantaloons. Their faces were tanned by summers' heat and winters' storms and covered with unkempt beards. Boys who enlisted in their teens appeared changed now into men of middle age." In the last two months, these men had marched over 430 miles.[7]

Second Corps

Reveille sounded in Johnson's camps at 3:00 a.m., and two hours later the men were on the road. The division marched south through Shippensburg, Green Village, and Scotland, where it bivouacked. John Garibaldi of the 27th Virginia (Walker's brigade) wrote home that "the people of Pennsylvania treated us very kindly, but I think it was only from their teeth out. When we went to their houses they gave us plenty to eat."[8]

Rodes's men broke camp at Carlisle at 5:00 a.m. and marched south along York Pike through Papertown (now York Springs, where Ewell and his officers toured a paper plant), Petersburg, and Heidlersburg. The division camped at the latter town after the 22-mile march. The men were disappointed that they had changed direction and were now marching away from Harrisburg. Exhausted by the long march along the muddy roads, they were soaked to the skin by the frequent showers. This did not stop them from collecting the delicious ripe cherries. Not permitted to stop to harvest them, the men merely ran from the ranks, swung their camp hatchets against the trees and returned with whole branches laden with cherries, which they ate as they marched.[9]

Early's division left York at daylight and retraced its steps west toward Heidlersburg, marching through Weigelstown and East Berlin. Early finally camped about three miles from Heidlersburg, where he met General Ewell, and was told that the army was concentrating at Cashtown, and the corps could move directly there or through Gettysburg. Early was especially annoyed about the ambiguity of Lee's orders. After much consideration, Ewell decided to follow the pattern that had served him so well in the Shenandoah Valley: to march along parallel roads. Early would travel to Gettysburg via Hunterstown and Mummasburg, while Rodes's route was through Middletown to Gettysburg.[10]

Third Corps

While the rest of his division rested near Cashtown, General Heth ordered Pettigrew to take three regiments from his brigade and march to Gettysburg for needed supplies. The men were on the road by 6:30 a.m. and reached the vicinity of Seminary Ridge between 9:30 and 10:00 a.m. The approach of Buford's Federal cavalry at about 10:30 a.m. caused Pettigrew to abort the mission. Pettigrew reported that some of his men heard the beat of drums on the other side of the town. If he entered it in search of shoes, his command would have become scattered, and this could have proved disastrous if a large Federal force was nearby.[11]

As Pettigrew was reporting to Heth, A. P. Hill rode up. After listening for a while, Hill remarked that "the only force at Gettysburg is cavalry, probably a detachment of observation. I am just from General Lee, and the information he has from his scouts corroborates that I have received from mine—that is, the enemy are still at Middleburg, and have not yet struck their tents." Heth told Hill, "If there is no objection, I will take my division tomorrow and go to Gettysburg and get those shoes!" Hill replied, "None in the world," as Pettigrew listened in disgust.[12]

Despite orders to be ready to continue the march at 7:00 a.m., Anderson's division remained in Fayetteville. Pender's division was not so fortunate, as it hit the road early toward Cashtown. Colonel Francis Fleming of the 2nd Florida (Perry's brigade) was incredulous about the price of goods. He was able to secure butter for $.12 a pound, chickens at $.15 apiece, and milk at $.05 a quart. Despite these low prices, some of the men resorted to pillaging. Fleming rationalized that these "poor fellows...whose houses and property have been entirely destroyed by the brutes whose country we are now invading and who have driven their families from their homes in a destitute condition." Fleming was surprised that these men did not commit greater atrocities.[13]

UNION

Meade reported to Halleck during the late afternoon that his army was dispersed in a manner that anticipated a collision at Gettysburg. The I and XI Corps were between Gettysburg and Emmitsburg, and most of the other corps were within supporting distance. The XII Corps was at Littlestown; the II Corps was resting at Uniontown; the VI Corps was at Manchester; the V Corps was at Union Mills; and the III Corps was between Taneytown and Emmitsburg.[14]

Realizing that it was just a matter of time before the two armies collided, Meade ordered his commanders to tell the men about the gravity of the situation, and how they were fighting for their homes. He also gave blanket permission to execute any soldier who "fails in his duty at this hour." It was payday for the Army of the Potomac, so the men marched toward Gettysburg with full pockets.[15]

Meade deemed it advisable to retain Reynolds in command of his own I Corps, plus the III and XI Corps, forming the left wing. Meade sent a wire to this effect, with the notation that "he [Reynolds] will make such dispositions and give such orders as circumstances may require."[16]

Entering Hanover, Pennsylvania, at about 8:00 a.m., Kilpatrick's cavalrymen were served a hearty breakfast by the local citizens. As the last of Kilpatrick's brigades, Farnsworth's, approached Hanover at about 10:00 a.m., it was attacked by advance units of Stuart's cavalry and driven back. A counterattack was ordered and Stuart's troopers were routed.[17]

A skirmish broke out between Couch's militia and Jenkins's cavalry at Sporting Hill, just outside of Harrisburg. It didn't amount to much, and the rebel cavalry, who were reconnoitering the capital's defenses, rode back to Carlisle.[18]

The strain of the long weeks of dealing with Lee's invasion was beginning to show. For example, Secretary of War Stanton asked Halleck to position batteries at the streets leading to Washington. Halleck politely demurred, saying that it was best leaving them in the defenses. Military authorities declared martial law in Baltimore, and the same was being considered in Philadelphia. This meant the suspension of civil government and cessation of a number of the citizens' personal rights.[19]

I Corps

The men were up by 5:00 a.m., but not on the road until after 8:00 a.m. Because the enemy was thought to be nearby, skirmishers were on the flanks and the column was closed up. Stragglers were scarce, as no one wanted to be left behind and possibly captured by the enemy. The men felt energized as they crossed into Pennsylvania. The 56th Pennsylvania (Cutler's brigade) "sent up cheer upon cheer, showing their appreciation of 'Home, sweet, sweet, home.' " The six-mile march took Wadsworth's division to the banks of Marsh Creek, about five miles south of Gettysburg; Robinson's and Doubleday's camped three miles away, near Moritz Tavern. The ongoing intermittent rains made the roads muddy. Many of the men enjoyed the march because of the cheers of the well-wishing civilians, and the good food they provided. Their spirits were lagging as they neared their encampment, for "not a man can hardly drag one blistered, bleeding foot after the other," according to Edwin Palmer (Stannard's brigade).[20]

II Corps

The men were pleased to be given a day's rest near Uniontown. Steady streams of soldiers who had straggled the day before now returned to their units. "A motely, dirty crowd they were, for having fallen in their tracks and slept, they had made an early start to find their corps, not waiting to wash or clean themselves," noted Jacob Cole (Zook's brigade). The camps were also visited by local civilians, who sold food.[21]

III Corps

The morning was a quiet one for the men at Taneytown. They watched as the XI Corps passed, but they stayed put until early afternoon when they took to the road. After marching approximately nine miles, the column halted for the night at about 6:00 p.m. beyond Bridgeport and near Emmitsburg. A number of soldiers commented on the less than enthusiastic welcome they received in comparison with the other towns. Some of the units occupied the grounds of St. Mary's College. A shower soaked the men in the evening, but few minded it because it relieved the horribly hot weather. In addition to being paid, some men received shoes to replace those that had given out. Local citizens also arrived by the score to see the soldiers' camps.[22]

Meade was again unhappy with the progress of the III Corps. His aide noted to General Sickles that the corps was to have marched at an early hour, but had not. As a result, it had marched only half the distance of the II Corps the day before. The correspondence ended with the phrase, "the commanding general looks for rapid movement of the troops."[23]

V Corps

Reveille sounded at 3:00 a.m. and the men of Barnes's and Ayres's divisions were on the march an hour later. General Ayres, now commanding the Second Division, received the following message from General Sykes: "A long march is before us, and every effort must be made to keep the command together and well closed up, as the enemy is not far from us. Strong exertions must be made to prevent straggling and to make the men keep in ranks." The march took them through Liberty (7:00 a.m.), Johnstown (8:30 a.m.), Union Bridge (10:00 a.m.), Uniontown (1:30 p.m.), and Frizzelburg. A hundred children stood on their school's steps at the latter community, waving small flags and singing the "Star-Spangled Banner." Church bells rang wildy, and flags hung from the houses as the men marched through Liberty. Perhaps even more uplifting was the fact that three or four buckets of cool water stood in front of each house. The continuing rain made the roads muddy and slippery. The men finally completed their 25-mile march at 5:30 p.m. at Union Mills, a mere three miles from the Pennsylvania border. A surgeon in Weed's brigade sadly noted, "our brave boys are so wasted and worn...that in their emaciated forms, I can hardly recognize the hale and hearty lads who started in such good cheer, with such elastic steps and buoyant spirits." [24]

Crawford's Pennsylvania Reserves brought up the rear, not hitting the road until 7:00 a.m. The division again made slow progress in the morning hours, but the pace quickened in the afternoon. The men were chagrined, however, when they heard that Meade had received a report that the Pennsylvania Reserves were unable to march as fast as the corps's other divisions.[25]

VI Corps

It rained all night, so the men were even stiffer than normal. They were somewhat relieved to learn that they would not march until after 6:00 a.m. The additional time was provided to allow them to dry their wet blankets and other personal items. It really didn't matter because additional rains fell, again soaking the men and their belongings. The march took the men through Westminster, which they reached at about noon. Earlier, Gregg's cavalry had tangled with Stuart's horsemen here. The column camped for the night near Manchester after the 20-mile march.[26]

XI Corps

The march began at 6:00 a.m. and the men passed through Emmitsburg. Continuing only one mile beyond it to near St. Joseph's Academy, they halted and were told to await further orders. It turned out to be only a change of campsite. The men were excited when the mail wagons arrived in the afternoon—the first they had received in weeks. Later, many wrote letters home. They had been told that a fight with the invaders was imminent, so many wanted to get what might be their last words home. Even the rain could not dampen the men's spirits. That evening, the Third Division commander, Carl Schurz, ordered the 45th New York's band to play for the priests and nuns.[27]

XII Corps

The men were on the march by 7:00 a.m. and passed through Middleburg and then Taneytown, which they reached at about 9:00 a.m. Here they passed the III Corps, still in camp. The men reached the Pennsylvania State line at about noon. After some celebrations, the men marched rapidly toward Littletown. These long marches were different from others, as the hilarity and noise were missing. The soldiers halted two miles shy of the town in the evening, and were told to check their guns and ammunition. They learned that their cavalry had run into a rebel cavalry picket line, causing a short skirmish. Generals Slocum and John Geary dashed ahead, as did a battery, and soon the infantry was double-quicking toward the town. The enemy was gone by the time the infantry arrived, but that didn't stop the grateful citizens from laying out their larders. "On every doorstep and on the walks in front of the houses were stationed men, women and children, each holding a pan or basket of cakes, pails of water, cold meats....on the upper piazza of the small hotel was congregated a crowd of ladies and gentlemen, singing that grand old tune, 'Hail Columbia,'" recalled Sgt. Henry Morhous of the 123rd New York (McDougall's brigade). Morhous also recalled that many ladies waved white handkerchiefs as tears streamed down their faces. The corps went into camp about one mile north of the town after the 30-mile march, much to the relief of the people of Littletown.[28]

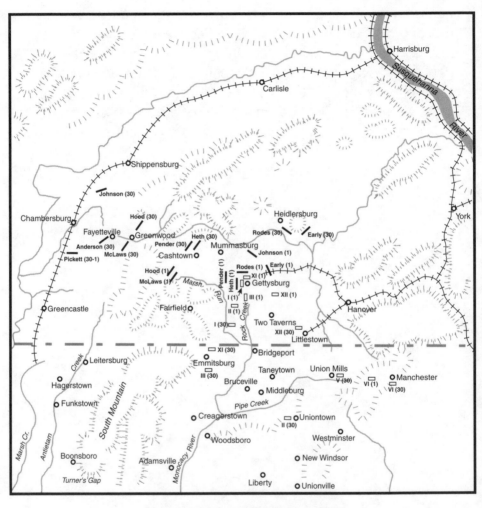

Operations June 30–July 1, 1863
(Dates in June/July in parentheses)

July 1

CONFEDERATE

Marching down Chambersburg Pike, A. P. Hill's Third Corps collided with Federal infantry outside of Gettysburg in the morning. Ewell's Second Corps began arriving from the north in the early afternoon, and pitched into the Federal right flank. Longstreet's Corps was still to the south, as was Johnson's division (Second Corps).

Stuart and his long wagon train rested at Dover before starting again for Carlisle, where they believed the Second Corps to be. Several more prisoners were paroled here. The militia they encountered at Carlisle refused to surrender or retreat until Stuart's artillery opened fire on the town. Now they fled in all directions. Learning that Lee was fighting a pitched battle at Gettysburg, Stuart pulled his dispersed troops together and quickly moved in that direction.[1]

First Corps

Because Johnson's division and Ewell's wagon train occupied the road in front of them, Hood's and McLaws's men waited near Greenwood until about 4:00 p.m. to begin their march. They spent the time cooking three days' rations. When the march finally began, Hood tried to make up for the lost time by unmercifully pushing his men. The march seemed endless. In growing desperation, some of the men yelled out "Rest, Rest," but their pleas were ignored. Some slept while they marched, and in many instances, bumped into the soldier in front of them, resulting in being "cussed for tramping on his heals [*sic*]." Midnight passed, and still they marched.[2]

Pickett's division was to the west, near Chambersburg, where the men diligently tore up railroad tracks. According to David Johnson of the 7th Virginia (Kemper's brigade), the task was accomplished by "piling up the ties, firing them, and then laying the rails on the fire, and when heated, bending them around trees." These were called "Sherman's Bowties" later in the war. Other men destroyed the shops of the Cumberland Valley Railroad. Using the heavy iron rails as battering rams, the men punched holes through the walls, yelling "Remember Haymarket" every time contact was made. This was in reference to the Virginia town that had been looted and burned by General Louis Blenker in 1862.[3]

Second Corps

After learning that no Federal infantry was in Gettysburg, and that Hill's Corps was marching on Cashtown, Ewell decided to march on that town as well. Early was ordered to march there via Hunterstown and Mummasburg, while Rodes marched via Middletown (Biglerville). Hearing that Hill was now marching on Gettysburg, Ewell also turned his two divisions in that direction.[4]

Rodes's men broke camp at 6:30 a.m. and marched seven miles to Middletown, arriving there at about 10:00 a.m. Prior to reaching the town, Ewell received a dispatch from General A. P. Hill, informing him that Federal cavalry was in Gettysburg and he was taking his Third Corps there. Ewell decided to support him, and turned Rodes's men to the left (south), on Middletown Road to Gettysburg. The men could hear the sounds of battle when about two miles north of Gettysburg and formed line of battle after the 15-mile march. The soldiers would never forget what happened next.[5]

Realizing that the road to Hunterstown was rough and circuitous, Early decided to march his division by way of Heidlersburg. A short distance beyond it, Early received a message from Ewell with information that A. P. Hill's Third Corps was marching from Cashtown to Gettysburg, and that Rodes had turned off at

Middletown. He was instructed to also march on Gettysburg. "I therefore continued to move on the road I was then on [Harrisburg Road] toward Gettysburg," he wrote. The rest is history.[6]

Johnson's division heard reveille at 5:00 a.m., and the men were on the road before 7:00 a.m. Reaching Fayetteville, Johnson's division turned onto Chambersburg Pike and marched toward Gettysburg. The day was fearfully hot, and the division took a leisurely pace. The men could hear the sounds of battle when they were about eight miles from Gettysburg, and soon a courier arrived with orders to "hurry up." The division arrived on the battlefield during the late afternoon—too late to participate in the first day's battle.[7]

Third Corps

Rain continued to fall during the early morning hours, and Heth's and Pender's divisions were on the road at 7:00 a.m., marching toward their rendezvous with fate at Gettysburg. Anderson's division finally left Fayetteville soon after daylight and made good progress toward Cashtown, arriving there in the afternoon. Earlier, the men were led to believe that their destination was Harrisburg. They halted at Cashtown, where they could clearly hear the sounds of battle up ahead. Rumors flew, as the men were told that it was a cavalry fight, then it was a fight with militia. Either way, they were anxious to enter the fray. The division reached the outskirts of Gettysburg as the light faded. They would not become engaged until the following afternoon.[8]

UNION

Meade unveiled his "Pipe Creek" defensive plan. Facing north behind the creek, the left of the line was to rest around Middleburg and the right at Manchester. Reynolds's three corps (I, III, XI) were to be on the left and Sedgwick's VI Corps on the right. In between was to be Slocum's XII Corps. General Slocum was to take charge of the V Corps and keep it near his own men. Finally, the II Corps was to be kept in reserve near Uniontown and Frizzelburg. All wagons were to be sent to the rear.[9]

The battle of Gettysburg precluded these movements from occurring. When Meade learned that the I and XI Corps were engaged, he quickly sent dispatches to his other corps commanders. With the death of General Reynolds, General Hancock was ordered to Gettysburg ahead of his corps to ascertain the situation and take command of the I and XI Corps already there. Sickles marched his III Corps toward Gettysburg from Emmitsburg, and Slocum was ordered to march his XII Corps to Two Taverns, and then on to Gettysburg. The V Corps was to march from Hanover to Gettysburg, and the II Corps was ordered to march to Taneytown.[10]

I Corps

The men awoke at 7:00 a.m., not by drums or bugles, but by the morning guard. This was a precaution to avoid excessive noise because the enemy was nearby. Three-days' rations were prepared and carefully placed in the men's haversacks. Because it had rained during the night, the men had to put their muskets back into working order as well. The final march to Gettysburg began at 9:00 a.m. It was made at "quick time," or 110 steps per minute.[11]

II Corps

The head of the II Corps broke camp at Uniontown, Maryland, between 7:00 and 8:00 a.m., and marched to Taneytown, arriving there at about 11:00 a.m. The rearguard did not reach the town until several hours later. The men were given the impression that they would remain here the rest of the day, so after preparing their noon meal, many washed their clothes. Bugles sounded in the early afternoon, and the men were soon back on the march. The column crossed the Pennsylvania State line at about sunset. As the soldiers trudged northward they passed citizens slowly walking past them who told of the deadly battle being waged ahead. Other civilians remained in their homes, providing food and encouragement. Not all of the homeowners along the march were generous. One man would not permit the troops to use his well. Hearing this, General Hays rode over and had the man arrested, who then marched with the troops into the night, until he was finally released.[12]

The men received orders to halt at about 9:00 p.m.; they were about three miles from Gettysburg. Although some of the units were ordered to build breastworks, most of the men ignored the order and fell asleep.[13]

III Corps

The final leg of the march to Gettysburg began shortly after noon. Because of the concern about Confederates coming through Fairfield Gap in the Blue Ridge Mountains, de Trobriand's and George Burling's brigades with two batteries were left behind at Emmitsburg.[14]

The rest of the III Corps marched toward Gettysburg on Emmitsburg Road. Early rains made the roads muddy. One U.S. sharpshooter yelled out, "G-D your Pennsylvania. The rebels ought to destroy the whole state if you can't afford better roads. This road is worse than Virginia roads." The pace quickened, causing many to stagger from the ranks. Yet, the continual booming of distant cannon told the men that they were needed, and this provided them with added endurance. Those accouterments that had not been discarded earlier in the campaign now found their way to the side of the road, as men struggled to keep up. A steady column of citizens moved in the opposite direction, providing information about the desperate fight at Gettysburg.

Birney's division finally reached the battlefield at about 5:30 p.m. Humphreys's division's final approach to the battlefield was much more exciting. Upon approaching Marsh Run that evening, Humphreys was ordered to take position "on the left of Gettysburg." He planned to take Emmitsburg Road, but one of Sickles's aides, Lieutenant Colonel Julius Hayden, told him to march by way of Black Horse Tavern. Lieutenant Colonel Clark Baldwin wrote later that Hayden "was more noted for frouth [*sic*] and foam than for common sence [*sic*]." As the column marched along in the darkness, its head unknowingly approached a Confederate picket post. Fortunately for Humphreys, he realized his mistake before the rebels and quickly "about-faced" his men. As a result of this misstep, the division did not arrive in the vicinity of Gettysburg until 1:00 a.m. on July 2.[15]

V Corps

The V Corps broke camp at Union Mills between 8:00 a.m. and 10:00 a.m. The orders were strict: "under no pretext whatever should a man be permitted to leave the column. Disobedience of this order...would be followed by instant death. Officers were instructed to march in rear of their companies and rigidly enforce the execution of the order," according to the historian of the 118th Pennsylvania (Tilton's brigade). The soldier went on to write that "such a cruel and unusual measure was scarcely justifiable. As soon as the men understood the situation, they needed no stimulant or threat of punishment, to muster all the energy they possessed."[16]

The head of the column reached the Pennsylvania border by late morning. Some of the commands halted at the state line and stacked arms. According to James Houghton of the 4th Michigan (Sweitzer's brigade), Colonel Harrison Jeffords then said, "Men[,] you are now standing on free soil once more, now give three cheers for the free States." Houghton recalled that he never heard louder or more enthusiastic cheering. Some of the troops did not know that they had crossed the state line until they had marched another half a mile. According to Chilion Lukens of the 118th Pennsylvania (Tilton's brigade), "somebody inquired what state it was and a little dutch woman sung out 'Adams Co. Pennsylvania.' Getting the drum and fife corps together, we had music for the next 3 miles. The Colonel riding down the column ordered the flags to be unfurled and 3 cheers for Penn., which were given with a will." Local citizens lined the roads, and according to Daniel MacNamara of the 9th Massachusetts (Sweitzer's brigade), "gazed at our ranks in open-mouthed silence. Here and there we received a word of welcome, and grins of satisfaction were visible as they viewed our seemingly interminable columns of infantry."[17]

The fact that some of the citizens were selling food at exorbitant prices infuriated the men. John Porter of the 155th Pennsylvania (Weed's brigade) noted that "these mercenary people so engaged were in many cases young athletic farmer boys, who, many soldiers thought, were capable and should have been willing to take guns and to harrass [sic] the invading columns of Lee, instead...[of] making money from the unfortunate footsore and over-marched Union soldiers." The men encountered citizens later in the march who provided food without any thought of compensation. The column reached Hanover, Pennsylvania, at about 3:00 p.m. after the eight-mile march. The men could see the aftermath of the cavalry battle that had been waged here the day before. After resting until sunset, they saw a courier on a foaming horse approach with orders to immediately march to the battlefield. The exhausted men packed up their belongings and reluctantly fell into line. Citizens rushed from their homes as the column approached in the moonlit night. "Bands played, the soldiers and the people cheered, banners waved, and white handkerchiefs fluttered from doors and windows, as the blue, dusty column surged on." As the long march continued, some of the officers ordered their drum corps to strike up tunes to invigorate the men. Many men were buoyed by the rumor that George McClellan was again in charge of the army. "Instantly the space above was filled with the hats and caps of the gratified soldiers. They shouted and hollered, and kicked up their heels, and were frisky with the supposed good news," noted one soldier. Midnight passed, and the column continued onward.[18]

VI Corps

The men were relieved to remain in camp all day, despite the ominous sounds of battle to the northwest. The time was spent resting, cleaning weapons, and repairing clothing. At about 6:00 p.m., they could see that something was up. "The clatter of hoofs, the hurried dash of staff officers, the bustle of preparation at headquarters, and the vigorous command to 'pack up and fall in!' drove away in a moment all hope of a refreshing night's sleep," recalled

James Bowen (Eustis's brigade). The men did not know it, but General Meade had sent a courier to General Sedgwick, who said, "General, you must be at Gettysburg by afternoon of to-morrow." Sedgwick's replied, "Say to General Meade that I will be at Gettysburg with my Corps at 2 o'clock tomorrow afternoon." The men were soon on the road, and marching at a rapid clip. The direction was back toward Westminster. A farmer distributing milk told the men that a battle was being waged at Gettysburg.[19]

The night was dark, and halts were not permitted, as the officers knew that some of the men would fall into deep slumber and be left behind. After toiling for several miles, an aide appeared, yelling, "Make way here, make way, for God's sake; you are all wrong!" As he reached the head of the column, the officer yelled, "Halt your men, colonel; you are on the wrong road!" The column therefore had to countermarch three to four miles, wasting six to eight miles and almost three hours in the process. The march continued through the night. It rained, making the roads muddy. Colonel Elisha Rhodes of the 2nd Rhode Island (Eustis's brigade) summed up the situation when he wrote, "we struggle on through the night, the men almost dead for lack of sleep and falling over their own shadows....little is said by any one, for we were too weary to talk, only now and then an officer sharply orders the men to close up." The men fell into a stupor that bordered on sleep. This was especially hazardous for the officers. Major F. W. Morse of the 121st New York (Bartlett's brigade) admitted falling off his horse twice that night.[20]

XI Corps

The march to Gettysburg began between 6:30 and 7:30 a.m. The corps marched on two different roads. Barlow's First Division followed the I Corps's route, while the other two divisions marched along Taneytown Road. The 13-mile march began at "common time," or about 90 steps per minute (70 yards). No rests were permitted. Rain fell, making the roads muddy, and those men who still had shoes, lost them to the sticky slop. The column reached Horner's Mill at about 10:30 a.m., just as the sun broke through the clouds, creating a bright, humid day. When about halfway to Gettysburg, the men could hear gunfire in the distance. Soon a courier appeared with orders to quicken the pace, and the column broke into "quick step," or 110 paces per minutes (86 yards). The slippery mud made this pace difficult. The head of the column approached Gettysburg shortly after noon.[21]

XII Corps

The march began at 7:00 a.m. for Williams's division. John Geary's division started earlier, at 5 a.m., as it had moved from Littletown toward Hanover the day before. The corps now retraced its steps for about a mile and struck the Baltimore Pike leading to Gettysburg. It halted at Two Taverns, about eight miles from Gettysburg, at around 11:00 a.m., where the men rested, ate, and wrote letters home. Despite his close proximity to the battlefield, Slocum insisted that he never heard the sounds of battle, although many rank and file soldiers clearly remember hearing gunfire in the distance. Soon the men saw a courier dash up, then a second, followed by a third. The veterans knew that something was up, and bugles sounded a short time later. The couriers carried pleas from General Howard for assistance. The march began again around 2:30 p.m. and continued until the corps reached Wolf Hill on the battlefield at about 4:00 p.m.[22]

July 2

CONFEDERATE

Only Longstreet's First Corps was still on the road to Gettysburg—the remainder of Lee's army had already arrived, and most of the units had already been committed to battle.

First Corps

Hood's and McLaws's divisions' long march that began on July 1 continued. McLaws's division halted at Marsh Creek at about midnight of July 1, while Hood's division, marching behind it, stopped around 2:00 a.m. The exhausted men simply fell by the side of the road, approximately four miles from Gettysburg. The rest was a relatively short one, and the men were back on the road at about 4:00 a.m.[1]

Shortly after Hood's division had halted for the night, Law's brigade was beginning its 28-mile forced march to the battlefield from New Guilford. The morning brought a blistering sun, and water was scarce, but General Law refused to reduce the rapid pace. General Longstreet later called this march "the best marching done in either army to reach the field of Gettysburg."[2]

Relieved by Imboden's cavalry brigade, Pickett's division began its march to the battlefield at 2:00 a.m. Marching through a darkened Chambersburg, the men could see many heads sticking out of windows. The march took the men over the South Mountains, where they rested for about an hour, then through Cashtown.

It was a hot, dusty march, but the men were fairly rested. The division finally reached the vicinity of Marsh Creek by about 2:30 p.m., after the 23-mile march.[3]

UNION

The I, III, XI, and XII Corps had reached the battlefield, while the remainder of the army moved toward Gettysburg, where they took their positions on the Federal line.

II Corps

Up between 3:00 and 4:00 a.m., the men were permitted to fix coffee before making the final march to the battlefield.[4]

III Corps

Bugles in Burling's and de Trobriand's brigades' camps at Emmitsburg blew at 3:00 a.m. The men were told to immediately break camp, but because it took time to pull in their dispersed units, the two brigades were not on the road until 5:00 a.m. The men grumbled that they hadn't even had a chance for breakfast. The column finally halted and the soldiers were told to quickly prepare their coffee. Before the water was hot, a courier from General Birney arrived with orders to get to Gettysburg quickly. Fires were extinguished, and the men were back on the road. As they approached Gettysburg, they passed a steady stream of civilians loaded down with their belongings. The two brigades finally reached the battlefield at about 10:00 a.m., where they rejoined the rest of the corps.[5]

V Corps

The march of the V Corps, which had begun near Union Mills, ended at Bonaughtown (Bonneville) at about 1:00 a.m., after the men had marched about nine miles. A moon shining through a cloudless night lit the way, and citizens rushed from their houses to see the men pass. The final four-mile march began at about 3:00 a.m., and the head of the column reached the battlefield about two hours later.[6]

VI Corps

A halt was permitted at about dawn, and a nearby stream provided water for coffee. Some of the men were in the process of removing their shoes so that they could bathe their blistered feet in the cool stream, when bugles sounded assembly. Oaths filled the air, as the men gulped down their half-cooked coffee and rejoined the ranks. With empty haversacks, they looked forward to a grim day of hard marching.[7]

The column crossed the Pennsylvania State Line in the morning, where the bands played the "Star Spangled Banner" and the men gave three cheers. Continuing on, the corps finally reached Littlestown, about 10 miles from Gettysburg. The soldiers were pleased by the townspeople's response, when they seemed "actuated by a common impulse to empty their larders for the benefit of the soldiers." Unfortunately, their supplies lasted for only the first two brigades of the eight-brigade corps. The citizens all along the way did, however, have enough water to provide to the thirsty men.[8]

Another halt was permitted around midday. As the men broke ranks, they were told that the halt was to be a short one, so they should not build fires. The few-minute rest probably did more harm than good, as it accentuated how tired and sore the men were.[9]

James Bowen of the 37th Massachusetts accurately described the misery of the march when he wrote:

> It was a hot, breathless July day. The sun poured down with merciless, unbroken heat, and the dust that rose in great lazy clouds from the highway enveloped man and horse...in its all-embracing mantle of torture. How the exhausted lungs panted for one full breath of pure, cool fresh air! Panted only to be mocked by the bitter, burning, dust-laden blast that seemed to come from the mouth of a furnace...strong men gasped and staggered and fell, while the thick blood burst forth from mouth and nostrils and the tortured frame was placed tenderly in some shaded nook....[10]

The men passed wounded soldiers as they approached the battlefield. Some yelled out, "You fellows will catch it; the whole army is smashed to pieces!" The column finally reached Rock Creek at 3:00 p.m., and the men were permitted to rest after the epic 18-hour, 36-mile march. Some of the men still had enough of their wits about them to refill their canteens with water. The corps was now ready to enter the fray, which it did by being broken up, with the various brigades being sent to different parts of the field.[11]

So ended the "Roads to Gettysburg."

Appendix 1

TROOPS' MOVEMENTS

Hood's Division (First Corps)

June

3—Old Verdiersville

4—Culpeper Court House

5—Brandy Station

6—Stevensburg

7—Culpeper Court House

8—Brandy Station

9—Culpeper Court House

15—Between Hazel River and Gaines' Crossroads

16—Marcum Station (Manassas Gap Railroad)

17—Piedmont Station and Upperville

18—Paris, Ashby's Gap, and Shenandoah River

19—Snicker's Gap (two brigades) and Snickersville (two brigades)

20—Snicker's Gap

22—Snicker's Ford, Shenandoah River, near Millwood

23—Millwood

24—Berryville and Summit Point

25—Smithfield, Clarksburg, Martinsburg, near Potomac River

26—Crossed Potomac River

27—Greencastle (Pa.) and Chambersburg

28—Chambersburg

30—Fayetteville and Greenwood

July

1—Near Gettysburg

McLaws's Division (First Corps)

June

3—Spotsylvania Court House

4—Raccoon Ford

6—Stevensburg

7—Culpeper Court House

16—Between Hazel River and Gaines' Crossroads

17—Little Washington and Gaines' Crossroads

18—Piedmont Station

19—Paris and Ashby's Gap

20—Shenandoah River and Ashby's Gap

24—Berryville and Summit Point

25—Smithfield, Clarksburg, Martinsburg, near Potomac River

26—Crossed Potomac River

27—Hagerstown, Middleburg, Greencastle, and Chambersburg

28—Chambersburg

30—Fayetteville and Greenwood

July

1—Near Gettysburg

Pickett's Division (First Corps)

June

3—Hanover Court House

8—New Market

10—Between Somerville Ford and Culpeper Court House

11—Culpeper Court House

16—Beyond the Hazel River, near Gaines' Crossroads

17—Brice's Crossroads

18—Piedmont Station

19—Between Snicker's Gap and Ashby's Gap

24—Berryville to near Darksville (W.Va.)

25—Martinsburg, Falling Waters, crossed Potomac River
26—Hagerstown, Middleburg, Greencastle
27—Greencastle to within three miles of Chambersburg
28—Chambersburg

July

1—March toward Gettysburg

Rodes's Division (Second Corps)

June

4—Spotsylvania Court House
5—Verdiersville
6—Between Verdiersville and Culpeper Court House
7—Culpeper Court House
9—Brandy Station
10—Culpeper Court House and Gourd Vine Church
11—Flint Hill
12—Chester Gap, Front Royal, and Stone Bridge
13—Millwood, Berryville, and Summit Point
14—Smithfield, Bunker Hill, and Martinsburg
15—Astride the Potomac River at Williamsport
19—Funkstown
22—Middletown (Pa.) and Greencastle
23—Greencastle
24—Chambersburg
26—Shippensburg and Dykeman Springs
27—Carlisle
30—Papertown, Petersburg, to three miles from Heidlersburg

July

1—Middletown and Gettysburg

Early's Division (Second Corps)

June

5—Verdiersville
6—Where Plank and Spotsylvania Roads intersect
7—Near Culpeper Court House
8—Culpeper Court House

9—Brandy Station

10—Culpeper Court House and Woodville

11—Sperryville and Washington

12—Chester Gap, Front Royal, crossed Shenandoah River, to near Cedarville

13—Ninevel, Newton, Kernstown, and just south of Winchester

14—Winchester

18—Leestown and two miles from Kearneysville

19—Shepherdstown

22—Crossed Potomac River at Boteler's Ford, to Sharpsburg and Boonsborough

23—Cavetown (Md.), Smithburg, Ringgold, and Waynesboro (Pa.)

24—Waynesboro, Quincy, Altodale, and Greenwood

25—Greenwood

26—Mummasburg/Gettysburg

27—Hunterstown, New Chester, Hampton, and East Berlin

28—York

30—Weigelstown, East Berlin, and Heidlersburg

July

1—Heidlersburg to Gettysburg

Johnson's Division (Second Corps)

June

5—Verdiersville

6—Where Plank and Spotsylvania Roads intersect

7—Near Culpeper Court House

8—Culpeper Court House

9—Brandy Station

10—Culpeper Court House and Woodville

11—Sperryville and Washington

12—Chester Gap, Front Royal, crossed Shenandoah River, to near Cedarville

13—Ninevel, Newton, Kernstown, and just south of Winchester

14—Winchester

15—Stephenson's Depot

16—Smithfield
17—Three miles from Shepherdstown
18—Crossed Potomac River at Boteler's Ford, to Sharpsburg
19—Antietam Battlefield (Md.)
23—Hagerstown to near Pennsylvania border
24—Greencastle (Pa.) to within three miles of Chambersburg
25—Chambersburg
26—Shippensburg and Dykeman Springs
27—Carlisle
29—Green Village
30—Shippensburg, Greencastle, and Scotland

July

1—Fayetteville, Cashtown, and Gettysburg

Heth's Division (Third Corps)

June

3—Fredericksburg
15—Chancellorsville
16—12 miles from Chancellorsville
17—Culpeper Court House
18—Crossed Hazel River, Sperryville to near Gaines' Crossroads
19—Chester Gap
20—Front Royal, crossed Shenandoah River, White Oak
21—Berryville
23—Charlestown
24—Charlestown to close to the Potomac River
25—Shepherdstown, crossed Potomac River at Blackford Ford, to within 8 miles of Hagerstown
26—Hagerstown
27—Hagerstown, Waynesboro, to within a mile of Fayetteville (Pa.)
28—Fayetteville
29—Toward Cashtown
30—Cashtown

July

 1—To Gettysburg

Pender's Division (Third Corps)

June

 3—Fredericksburg
 16—Ely's Ford (Rapidan River)
 17—Twelve-mile march toward Culpeper Court House
 18—Culpeper Court House
 19—Hazel River, and Gaines' Crossroads
 20—Flint Hill and through Chester Gap
 21—Front Royal and White Post
 22—Near Berryville
 23—Beyond Berryville
 24—Charlestown to within two miles of the Potomac River
 25—Shepherdstown, crossed Potomac River at Blackford
   Ford and toward Hagerstown
 26—Hagerstown
 27—Hagerstown to within a mile of Fayetteville (Pa.)
 28—Fayetteville
 30—Cashtown

July

 1—To Gettysburg

Anderson's Division (Third Corps)

June

 3—Fredericksburg
 14—Chancellorsville
 15—Germanna Ford (Rapidan) to near Stevensburg
 16—Culpeper Court House
 17—Hazel River
 18—Flint Hill
 19—Chester Gap to Front Royal and crossed Shenandoah River
 20—Two miles beyond White Post
 21—Berryville
 22—Near Charlestown

23—Charlestown and Shepherdstown
24—Crossed Potomac River to Antietam Battlefield
25—Hagerstown and Middleburg
26—Greencastle
27—Chambersburg and Fayetteville
28—Fayetteville
30—Cashtown

July

1—To Gettysburg

Federal I Corps

June

3—White Oak Church
7—Franklin's Crossing (Wadsworth's division)
8—Wadsworth's division returns to White Oak Church
12—Stoneman's Switch and Deep Run
13—Bealton Station (Orange and Alexandria Railroad)
14—Warrington and toward Manassas Junction
15—Manassas Junction and Centreville
16—Centreville
17—Herndon Station (Alexandria and Loudoun Railroad)
18—Guilford Station
25—Crossed Potomac to Poolsville and Barnsville
26—Jefferson
27—Middletown
28—Frederick
29—Lewistown, Mechanicstown, and Emmitsburg
30—Five miles from Gettysburg

July

1—Gettysburg

Federal II Corps

June

3—Falmouth
14—Four miles north of Rappahannock River
15—Stafford Court House and one mile beyond Aquia Creek

16—Wolf Run Shoals

17—Sangster's Station (Orange and Alexandria Railroad)

19—Centreville

20—Gainesville (one division) and Thoroughfare Gap (two divisions)

25—Haymarket and Gum Springs

26—Farmwell Station, Frankville, and crossed the Potomac River

27—Poolsville and Barnsville

28—Crossed Monocacy River to Monocacy Junction

29—Johnsville, Liberty, Union Bridge, and Uniontown

30—Uniontown

July

1—To within three miles of Gettysburg

Federal III Corps

June

3—Boscobel

11—Hartwood Church

12—Bealton Station (Orange and Alexandria Railroad)

14—Licking Creek, Kettle Run, Warrenton Junction, and Catlett's Station

15—Crossed Bull Run near Manassas Junction

16—Near Manassas Junction

17—Centreville

19—Gum Springs

25—Mount Hope, Farmwell, Edward's Ferry, and Monocacy Aqueduct

26—Near Point of Rocks

27—Jefferson to near Burkettsville

28—Burkettsville, Middletown, and Frederick

29—Woodsboro, Middleburg, Taneytown

30—Bridgeport to close to Emmitsburg

July

1—Emmitsburg to Gettysburg

Federal V Corps

June

3—Stoneman's Switch
4—Banks' Ford
13—Hartwood Church
14—Catlett's Station
15—Manassas Junction and Centreville
16—Centreville
17—Gum Springs
19—Aldie
21—Aldie (one division), Middleburg (two brigades), and Ashby's Gap (one brigade)
22—Aldie
26—Crossed Potomac to Poolesville
27—Buckystown to near Frederick
28—Frederick
29—Ceresville, Mt. Pleasant, Johnsville, and near Liberty
30—Liberty, Union Bridge, Frizzelburg, and Union Mills

July

1—Bonaughtown

Federal VI Corps

June

3—White Oak Church
7—Rappahannock River crossing (one division)
12—Pulled back from River
13—Toward Brooke Station
14—Just beyond Stafford Court House
15—Dumfries
16—Wolf Run Shoals and Fairfax Court House
17—Fairfax Court House
20—Fairfax Court House and Bristoe Station (one division)
25—Reassembles at Fairfax Court House
26—Chantilly, Herndon Station, and Dranesville
27—Crossed Potomac River
28—Poolesville, Barnsville, and Hyattstown

29—New Market, Ridgeville, Manchester

30—Manchester

July

1—Manchester toward Gettysburg

2—Littlestown

Federal XI Corps

June

3—Brooke's Station

12—Hartwood Church

13—Weaverville (near Catlett Station on Orange and Alexandria Railroad)

14—Three miles from Centreville

15—Centreville

17—Goose Creek near Leesburg

24—To Edward's Ferry

25—Crossed Potomac River to Poolesville

26—Jefferson and Middletown

27—Middletown

28—Frederick and Utica

29—Creagerstown and Emmitsburg

30—Emmitsburg

July

1—Gettysburg

Federal XII Corps

June

3—Near Stafford Court House and Aquia Landing

14—Dumfries

15—Fairfax Court House

17—Two miles from Dranesville

18—Dranesville, crossed Goose Creek, to Leesburg

26—Crossed Potomac to Poolesville and Monocacy Aqueduct

27—Point of Rocks, Petersville, and Knoxville

28—Petersville, Jefferson, and Frederick

29—Frederick, Woodsboro, Bruceville, and Ladiesburg

30—Middleburg, Taneytown, and Littlestown

July

1—Two Taverns to Gettysburg

Appendix 2

Army of the Potomac

I Corps: Maj. Gen. John Reynolds

1st Division: Brig. Gen. James Wadsworth
- 1st Brigade: Brig. Gen. Solomon Meredith
  19th Ind.; 24th Mich.; 2nd, 6th, 7th Wisc.
- 2nd Brigade: Brig. Gen. Lysander Cutler
  7th Ind.; 76th, 84th, 95th, 147th N.Y.; 56th Pa.

2nd Division: Brig. Gen. John Robinson
- 1st Brigade: Brig. Gen. Gabriel Paul
  13th Mass.; 16th Maine; 94th, 104th N.Y.; 107th Pa.
- 2nd Brigade: Brig. Gen. Henry Baxter
  12th Mass.; 83rd, 97th N.Y.; 11th, 88th, 90th Pa.

3rd Division: Maj. Gen. Abner Doubleday
- 1st Brigade: Brig. Gen. Thomas Rowley
  80th N.Y.; 121st, 142nd, 151st Pa.
- 2nd Brigade: Col. Roy Stone
  43rd, 149th, 150th Pa.
- 3rd Brigade: Brig. Gen. George Stannard
  12th, 13th, 14th, 15th, 16th Vt.

Artillery Brigade: Col. Charles Wainwright—guns: 28
  2nd Maine Battery; 5th Maine Battery; 1st N.Y. Battery L; 1st Pa. Battery B; 4th U.S. Battery B

II Corps: Maj. Gen. Winfield Hancock

1st Division: Brig. Gen. John Caldwell
- 1st Brigade: Col. Edward Cross
  5th N.H.; 1st N.Y.; 81st, 148th Pa.
- 2nd Brigade: Col. Patrick Kelly
  28th Mass.; 63rd, 69th, 88th N.Y.; 116th Pa.
- 3rd Brigade: Brig. Gen. Samuel Zook
  52nd, 57th, 66th N.Y.; 140th Pa.
- 4th Brigade: Col. John Brooke
  27th Conn.; 2nd Del.; 64th N.Y.; 53rd, 145th Pa.

2nd Division: Brig. Gen. John Gibbon
- 1st Brigade: Brig. Gen. William Harrow
  15th Mass.; 19th Maine; 1st Minn.; 82nd N.Y.
- 2nd Brigade: Brig. Gen. Alexander Webb
  69th, 71st, 72nd, 106th Pa.
- 3rd Brigade: Col. Norman Hall
  19th, 20th Mass.; 7th Mich.; 42nd, 59th N.Y.

3rd Division: Brig. Gen. Alexander Hays
- 1st Brigade: Col. Samuel Carroll
  14th Ind.; 4th, 8th Ohio; 7th W.Va.
- 2nd Brigade: Col. Thomas Smyth
  14th Conn.; 1st Del.; 12th N.J.; 10th, 108th N.Y.
- 3rd Brigade: Col. George Willard
  39th, 111th, 125th, 126th N.Y.

Artillery Brigade: Capt. John Hazard—guns: 28
   1st N.Y. Lt. Battery B; 14th N.Y. Battery; 1st R.I. Battery A,
   Battery B; 1st U.S. Battery I; 4th U.S. Battery A

III Corps: Maj. Gen. Daniel Sickles

1st Division: Maj. Gen. David Birney
- 1st Brigade: Brig. Gen. Charles Graham
  57th, 63rd, 68th, 105th, 114th, 141st Pa.
- 2nd Brigade: Brig. Gen. Hobart Ward
  20th Ind.; 3rd, 4th Maine; 86th, 124th N.Y.; 99th Pa.;
  1st, 2nd U.S. Sharpshooters

- 3rd Brigade: Col. Regis De Trobriand
  17th Maine; 3rd, 5th Mich.; 40th N.Y.; 110th Pa.

2nd Division: Brig. Gen. Andrew Humphreys
- 1st Brigade: Brig. Gen. Joseph Carr
  1st, 11th, 16th Mass.; 12th N.H.; 11th N.J.; 26th Pa.
- 2nd ("Excelsior") Brigade: Col. William Brewster
  70th, 71st, 72nd, 73rd, 74th, 120th N.Y.
- 3rd Brigade: Col. George Burling
  2nd N.H.; 5th, 6th, 7th, 8th N.J.; 115th Pa.

Artillery Brigade: Capt. George Randolph—guns: 30
  2nd N.J. Battery B; 1st N.Y. Battery D; 1st R.I. Battery E; 4th U.S. Battery K; 4th N.Y. Battery

V Corps: Maj. Gen. George Sykes

1st Division: Brig. Gen. James Barnes
- 1st Brigade: Col. William Tilton
  18th, 22nd Mass.; 1st Mich.; 118th Pa.
- 2nd Brigade: Col. Jacob Sweitzer
  9th, 32nd Mass.; 4th Mich.; 62nd Pa.
- 3rd Brigade: Col. Strong Vincent
  20th Maine; 16th Mich.; 44th N.Y.; 83d Pa.

2nd Division: Brig. Gen. Romeyn Ayres
- 1st Brigade: Col. Hannibal Day
  3rd, 4th, 6th, 12th, 14th U.S. Regulars
- 2nd Brigade: Col. Sidney Burbank
  2nd, 7th, 10th, 11th, 17th U.S. Regulars
- 3rd Brigade: Brig. Gen. Stephen Weed
  140th, 146th N.Y.; 91st, 155th Pa.

3rd Division: Brig. Gen. Samuel Crawford
- 1st Brigade: Col. William McCandless
  1st, 2nd, 6th, 13th Pa. Reserves
- 2nd Brigade (detached duty)
- 3rd Brigade: Col. Joseph Fisher
  5th, 9th, 10th, 11th, 12th Pa. Reserves

Artillery Brigade: Capt. Augustus Martin—guns: 26
   5th U.S. Battery D, Battery I; 1st Ohio Battery L; 3rd Mass.
   Battery; 1st N.Y. Battery C

VI Corps: Maj. Gen. John Sedgwick

1st Division: Brig. Gen. Horatio Wright
• 1st ("Jersey") Brigade: Brig. Gen. Alfred Torbert
   1st, 2nd, 3rd, 4th, 15th N.J.
• 2nd Brigade: Brig. Gen. Joseph Bartlett
   5th Maine; 121st N.Y.; 95th, 96th Pa.
• 3rd Brigade: Brig. Gen. David Russell
   6th Maine; 49th, 119th Pa.; 5th Wisc.

2nd Division: Brig. Gen. Albion Howe
• 2nd ("1st Vermont") Brigade: Col. Lewis Grant
   2nd, 3rd, 4th, 5th, 6th Vt.
• 3rd Brigade: Brig. Gen. Thomas Neill
   7th Maine; 33rd, 43rd, 49th, 77th N.Y.; 61st Pa.

3rd Division: Maj. Gen. John Newton
• 1st Brigade: Brig. Gen. Alexander Shaler
   65th, 67th, 122nd N.Y.; 23rd, 82nd Pa.
• 2nd Brigade: Col. Henry Eustis
   7th, 10th, 37th Mass.; 2nd R.I.
• 3rd Brigade: Brig. Gen. Frank Wheaton
   62nd N.Y.; 93rd, 98th, 139th Pa.

Artillery Brigade: Col. Charles Tompkins—guns: 48
   1st Mass. Battery A; 1st, 3rd N.Y.; 1st R.I. Battery C; 1st R.I.
   Battery G; 2nd U.S. Battery D, Battery G; 5th U.S. Battery F

XI Corps: Maj. Gen. Oliver Howard

1st Division: Brig. Gen. Francis Barlow
• 1st Brigade: Col. Leopold von Gilsa
   41st, 54th, 68th N.Y.; 153rd Pa.
• 2nd Brigade: Brig. Gen. Adelbert Ames
   17th Conn.; 25th, 75th, 107th Ohio

2nd Division: Brig. Gen. Adolph von Steinwehr
- 1st Brigade: Col. Charles Coster
  134th, 154th N.Y.; 27th, 73rd Pa.
- 2nd Brigade: Col. Orlando Smith
  33rd Mass.; 136th N.Y.; 55th, 73rd Ohio

3rd Division: Maj. Gen. Carl Schurz
- 1st Brigade: Brig. Gen. Alexander Schimmelfennig
  82nd Ill.; 45th, 157th N.Y.; 61st Ohio; 74th Pa.
- 2nd Brigade: Col. Wladimir Krzyzanowski
  58th, 119th N.Y.; 82nd Ohio; 75th Pa.; 26th Wisc.

Artillery Brigade: Maj. Thomas Osborn—guns: 26
  13th N.Y., 1st N.Y. Battery I; 1st Ohio Battery I, 1st Ohio
  Battery K, 4th U.S. Battery G

XII Corps: Maj. Gen. Henry Slocum

1st Division: Brig. Gen. Alpheus Williams
- 1st Brigade: Col. Archibald McDougall
  5th, 20th Conn.; 3rd Md.; 123rd, 145th N.Y.; 46th Pa.
- 2nd Brigade: Brig. Gen. Henry Lockwood
  1st Md. Eastern Shore, 1st Md. Potomac Home Brigade; 150th N.Y.
- 3rd Brigade: Brig. Gen. Thomas H. Ruger
  27th Ind.; 2nd Mass.; 13th N.J.; 107th N.Y.; 3rd Wisc.

2nd Division: Brig. Gen. John Geary
- 1st Brigade: Col. Charles Candy
  5th, 7th, 29th, 66th Ohio; 28th, 147th Pa.
- 2nd Brigade: Brig. Gen. Thomas Kane
  29th, 109th, 111th Pa.
- 3rd Brigade: Brig. Gen. George Greene
  60th, 78th, 102nd, 137th, 149th N.Y.

Artillery Brigade: Lt. Edward Muhlenberg—guns: 20
  1st N.Y. Battery M; Pa. Lt. Battery E; 4th U.S. Battery F; 5th
  U.S. Battery K

Artillery Reserve: Brig. Gen. Robert Tyler
- 1st Regular Brigade: Capt. Dunbar Ransom—guns: 24
  1st U.S. Battery H; 3rd U.S. Battery F, K; 4th U.S. Battery C; 5th
  U.S. Battery C

- 1st Volunteer Brigade: Lt. Col. Freeman McGilvery—guns: 22
  5th Mass., 9th Mass.; 10th, 15th N.Y.; Pa. Lt. Battery C, F
- 2nd Volunteer Brigade: Capt. Elijah Taft—guns: 12
  2nd Conn.; 5th N.Y.
- 3rd Volunteer Brigade: Capt. James Huntington—guns: 20
  1st N.H.; 1st Ohio Battery H; 1st Pa. Battery F, G, C; 1st W.Va.
  Battery C
- 4th Volunteer Brigade: Capt. Robert Fitzhugh—guns: 24
  6th Maine; Md. Battery A; 1st N.J.; 1st N.Y. Battery K, 11th N.Y.
  Battery, 1st N.Y. Battery G

Cavalry Corps: Maj. Gen. Alfred Pleasonton

<u>1st Division: Brig. Gen. John Buford</u>
- 1st Brigade: Col. William Gamble
  12th Ill.; 3rd Ind.; 8th N.Y.; 8th Ill.
- 2nd Brigade: Col. Thomas Devin
  6th, 9th N.Y.; 17th Pa.; 3rd W.Va.
- Reserve Brigade: Brig. Gen. Wesley Merritt
  6th Pa.; 1st, 2nd, 5th, 6th U.S.

<u>2nd Division: Brig. Gen. David Gregg</u>
- 1st Brigade: Col. John McIntosh
  1st Mass.; 1st Md.; 1st N.J.; 1st, 3rd Pa.
- 2nd Brigade (detached duty)
- 3rd Brigade: Col. Irwin Gregg
  1st Maine; 10th N.Y.; 4th, 16th Pa.

<u>3rd Division: Brig. Gen. Judson Kilpatrick</u>
- 1st Brigade: Brig. Gen. Elon Farnsworth
  5th N.Y.; 18th Pa.; 1st Vt.; 1st W.Va.
- 2nd Brigade: Brig. Gen. George Custer
  1st, 5th, 6th, 7th Mich.

<u>Horse Artillery</u>
- 1st Brigade: Capt. James Robertson—guns: 28
  2nd U.S. Battery B, L, M; 4th U.S. Battery E, 6th N.Y. Battery;
  9th Mich. Battery
- 2nd Brigade: Capt. John Tidball—guns: 20
  1st U.S. Battery E, G, K; 2nd U.S. Battery A

The Army of Northern Virginia

First Corps: Lt. Gen. James Longstreet

Maj. Gen. John Bell Hood's Division
- Brig. Gen. Evander Law's Brigade
  4th, 15th, 44th, 47th, 48th Ala.
- Brig. Gen. Jerome Robertson's Brigade
  1st, 4th, 5th Tex.; 3rd Ark.
- Brig. Gen. George Anderson's Brigade
  7th, 8th, 9th, 11th, 59th Ga.
- Brig. Gen. Henry Benning's Brigade
  2nd, 15th, 17th, 20th Ga.
- Maj. Mathis Henry's Artillery Battalion—guns: 19
  Latham's, Bachman's, Garden's, and Reilly's Batteries

Maj. Gen. Lafayette McLaws's Division
- Brig. Gen. Joseph Kershaw's Brigade
  2nd, 3rd, 7th, 8th, 15th S.C.; 3rd S.C. Battalion
- Brig. Gen. Paul Semmes's Brigade
  10th, 50th, 51st, 53rd Ga.
- Brig. Gen. William Barksdale's Brigade
  13th, 17th, 18th, 21st Miss.
- Brig. Gen. William Wofford's Brigade
  16th, 18th, 24th Ga., Cobb's Legion, Phillips's Legion
- Col. Henry Cabell's Artillery Battalion—guns: 16
  Manly's, Carlton's, Fraser's, McCarthy's

Maj. Gen. George Pickett's Division
- Brig. Gen. James Kemper's Brigade
  1st, 3rd, 11th, 24th Va.
- Brig. Gen. Richard Garnett's Brigade
  8th, 18th, 19th, 28th, 56th Va.
- Brig. Gen. Lewis Armistead's Brigade
  9th, 14th, 38th, 53rd, 57th Va.
- Maj. James Dearing's Artillery Battalion—guns: 18
  Stribling's, Caskie's, Macon's, Blount's Batteries

Artillery Reserve for I Corps
- Col. E. Porter Alexander's Artillery Battalion—guns: 24
  Moody's, Gilbert's, Woolfolk's, Jordan's, Parker's, Taylor's
  Batteries
- Maj. Benjamin Eshleman's Battalion
  Washington Artillery of Louisiana: 4 batteries
  Squires's, Richardson's, Miller's, Norcom's

Second Corps: Lt. Gen. Richard Ewell

Maj. Gen. Robert Rodes's Division
- Brig. Gen. George Doles's Brigade
  4th, 12th, 21st, 44th Ga.
- Brig. Gen. Junius Daniel's Brigade
  32nd, 43rd, 45th, 53rd, N.C. & 2nd N.C. Battalion
- Brig. Gen. Alfred Iverson's Brigade
  5th, 12th, 20th, 23rd N.C.
- Brig. Gen. Stephen Ramseur's Brigade
  2nd, 4th, 14th, 30th N.C.
- Col. Edward O'Neal's Brigade
  3rd, 5th, 6th, 12th, 26th Ala.
- Lt. Col. Thomas Carter's Artillery Battalion—guns: 16
  Reese's, W. Carter's, Page's, Fry's Batteries

Maj. Gen. Jubal Early's Division
- Brig. Gen. John Gordon's Brigade
  13th, 26th, 31st, 38th, 60th, 61st Ga.
- Brig. Gen. Harry Hays's Brigade
  5th, 6th, 7th, 8th, 9th La.
- Col. Isaac Avery's Brigade
  6th, 21st, 57th N.C.
- Brig. Gen. William Smith's Brigade
  31st, 49th, 52nd Va.
- Lt. Col. Hilary Jones' Artillery Battalion—guns: 16
  Carrington's, Tanner's, Green's, Garber's Batteries

Maj. Gen. Edward Johnson's Division
- Brig. Gen. George Steuart's Brigade
  1st Md.; 1st, 3rd N.C.; 10th, 23rd, 37th Va.

- Col. Jesse Williams's Brigade
  1st, 2nd, 10th, 14th, 15th La.
- Brig. Gen. James Walker ("Stonewall") Brigade
  2nd, 4th, 5th, 27th, 33rd Va.
- Brig. Gen. John Jones's Brigade
  21st, 25th, 42nd, 44th, 48th, 50th Va.
- Maj. James Latimer's Artillery Battalion—guns: 16
  Dement's, Carpenter's, Brown's, Raine's Batteries

Artillery Reserve for Second Corps
- Dance's Battalion—guns: 20
  Watson's, Smith's, Cunningham's, A. Graham's, G. Griffin's
  Batteries
- Nelson's Battalion—guns: 10
  Kirkpatrick's, Milledge's, Massie's Batteries

Third Corps: Lt. Gen. Ambrose Powell Hill

Maj. Gen. Henry Heth's Division
- Brig. Gen. James Archer's Brigade
  1st, 7th, 14th Tenn.; 13th Ala., 5th Ala. Battalion
- Brig. Gen. Joseph Davis's Brigade
  2nd, 11th, 42nd Miss.; 55th N.C.
- Brig. Gen. James J. Pettigrew's Brigade
  11th, 26th, 47th, 52nd N.C.
- Col. John Brockenbrough's Brigade
  40th, 47th, 55th Va.; 22nd Va. Battalion
- Lt. Col. John Garnett's Artillery Battalion—guns: 15
  Maurin's, Moore's, Lewis's, Grandy's Batteries

Maj. Gen. W. Dorsey Pender's Division
- Col. Abner Perrin's Brigade
  1st, 12th, 13th, 14th S.C.; 1st S.C. Rifles
- Brig. Gen. James Lane's Brigade
  7th, 18th, 28th, 33rd, 37th N.C.
- Brig. Gen. Alfred Scales's Brigade
  13th, 16th, 22nd, 34th, 38th N.C.
- Brig. Gen. Edward Thomas's Brigade
  14th, 35th, 45th, 49th Ga.

- Maj. William Pogue's Artillery Battalion—guns: 16
Wyatt's, J. Graham's, Ward's, Brooke's Batteries

Maj. Gen. Richard Anderson's Division
- Brig. Gen. Cadmus Wilcox's Brigade
8th, 9th, 10th, 11th, 14th Ala.
- Brig. Gen. Edward Perry's Brigade
2nd, 5th, 8th Fla.
- Brig. Gen. Ambrose Wright's Brigade
3rd, 22nd, 48th Ga.; 2nd Ga. Battalion
- Brig. Gen. Carnot Posey's Brigade
12th, 16th, 19th, 48th Miss.
- Brig. Gen. William Mahone's Brigade
6th, 12th, 16th, 41st, 61st Va.
- Maj. John Lane's Artillery Battalion—17 guns
(Three batteries of Sumter-Georgia Artillery) Ross's, Patterson's,
Wingfield's

Artillery Reserve for Third Corps
- McIntosh's Battalion—guns: 16
Rice's, Hurt's, Wallace's, Johnson's Batteries
- Pegram's Battalion—guns: 20
Crenshaw's, Marve's, Brander's, Zimmerman's, McGraw's
Batteries

Cavalry Division: Maj. Gen. J.E.B. Stuart
- Brig. Gen. Wade Hampton's Brigade
1st, 2nd S.C.; 1st N.C.; Cobb's Ga. Legion Cavalry; Phillips's
Ga. Legion; Jeff Miss. Davis Legion
- Brig. Gen. Fitzhugh Lee's Brigade
1st, 2nd, 3rd, 4th, 5th Va.; 1st Md. Battalion
- Col. John Chambliss's Brigade
9th, 10th, 13th Va.; 2nd N.C.
- Brig. Gen. Albert Jenkins's Brigade
14th, 16th, 17th Va.; 34th, 36th Va. Battalion
- Horse Artillery: Maj. Robert Beckham—guns: 15
Breathed's, W. Griffin's, Hart's, McGregor's Batteries

Notes

BACKGROUND

1. United States War Department. *The War of the Rebellion: A Compilation of the Official Records of the Union and Confederate Armies.* 128 volumes (Washington: U.S. Government Printing Office, 1880–1901; (Hereafter, "OR,"), vol. 25, pt. 2, 570, 713–14, 715.
2. Douglas S. Freeman, *R. E. Lee* (New York: Scribners, 1935), vol. 3, 19, 23.
3. Wilbur Sturtevant Nye, *Here Come the Rebels!* (Baton Rouge, La.: Louisiana State University Press, 1965), 4–5; John W. Schildt, *Roads to Gettysburg* (Parsons, W.Va.: McClain Print. Co., 1978), 18.

   Lee would ultimately invade Pennsylvania via the Shenandoah and Cumberland Valleys—two of the richest agricultural areas in the East (Edwin B. Coddington, *The Gettysburg Campaign: A Study in Command* [New York: Charles Scribner's Sons, 1968], 23).
4. Nye, *Here Come the Rebels,* 5.
5. Coddington, *Gettysburg Campaign,* 4–5.
6. Schildt, *Roads to Gettysburg,* 17–18.
7. Jeffry D. Wert, *General James Longstreet: The Confederacy's Most Controversial Soldier* (New York: Simon & Schuster, 1993), 250; Coddington, *Gettysburg Campaign,* 24.

   After the war, General Hooker characterized Lee's attacks as "vigorous" and "vehement." They were "blows...and the shock seemed to make the earth tremble on which we stood." Hooker felt that the "bitterness of feeling toward their adversaries" was the reason for this intensity (Joseph Hooker letter, Samuel Bates Collection, Pennsylvania State Archives).
8. OR, vol. 27, pt. 3, 858; Nye, *Here Come the Rebels,* 42.

   Jeb Stuart's cavalry was already at Culpeper Court House with orders to "better observe the enemy" (OR, vol. 25, pt. 2, 792).
9. Coddington, *Gettysburg Campaign,* 50–51.
10. Nye, *Here Come the Rebels,* 42; OR, vol. 27, pt. 2, 293.
11. Nye, *Here Come the Rebels,* p. 27.
12. Gideon Welles, *The Diary of Gideon Welles* (Boston: Houghton Mifflin Company, 1911), vol. 1, 329.
13. Coddington, *Gettysburg Campaign,* 36.

245

Shortly after the Chancellorsville campaign, several officers visited Lincoln with a plea for Hooker's removal, and one, II Corps commander General Darius Couch, actually resigned rather than continue to serve under Hooker. Lincoln offered the Army of the Potomac to John Reynolds, but he turned it down because he would not have the full autonomy that he demanded (Coddington, *Gettysburg Campaign*, 36–37).

14. Coddington, *Gettysburg Campaign*, 39; Nye, *Here Come the Rebels*, 30–31.

The army dwindled from 111,650 infantry on April 30 (just before Chancellorsville) to 80,000 about two weeks later. Most distressing was the cavalry's attrition, which went from a strength of 11,542 on June 30 to 4,677, or almost 60%, a month later (OR, vol. 25, pt. 1, 804; OR, vol. 25, pt. 2, 476–77; Coddington, *Gettysburg Campaign*, 40).

15. Jacob Hoke, *The Great Invasion* (New York: Thomas Yoseloff, 1959), 66.

16. Coddington, *Gettysburg Campaign*, 50–51.

17. OR, vol. 27, pt. 2, 278; Nye, *Here Come the Rebels*, 22.

JUNE 3

1. OR, vol. 27, pt. 2, 293; Schildt, *Roads to Gettysburg*, 30.

2. Journal of Private T. M. Mitchell, Copy in Phillips's Legion Folder, Gettysburg National Military Park Library (Hereafter, GNMP); James W. Silver, ed. *A Life for the Confederacy* (Wilmington, N.C.: Broadfoot Publishing Company, 1991), 148–49; Thomas Ware Journal, Southern Historical Collection, University of North Carolina.

3. John Edward Dooley, *John Dooley, Confederate Soldier, His War Journal* (Washington, D.C.: Georgetown University Press, 1945), 95; Lee A. Wallace, *First Virginia Infantry* (Lynchburg, Va.: H. E. Howard, 1985), 41; Edwin Loving Journal, copy in 1st Virginia folder, GNMP.

4. Gregory C. White, *A History of the 31st Georgia Volunteer Infantry* (Baltimore: Butternut and Blue, 1997), 79; Laura V. Hale and Stanley S. Phillips, *History of the Forty-Ninth Virginia Infantry* (Lanham, Md.: S. S. Phillips, 1981), 67.

JUNE 4

1. OR, vol. 27, pt. 2, 293, 545–46, 564, 591; OR, vol. 27, pt. 3, 858–59.

2. Ware Journal; R. T. Coles, From Huntsville to Appomattox : R. T. Coles's History of 4th Regiment, Alabama Volunteer Infantry (Knoxville, Tenn.: University of Tennessee Press, 1996), 97.

The Confederate soldiers probably suffered less than their Union counterparts during the marches to Gettysburg because they were less encumbered with equipment. A typical Confederate infantryman carried a woolen blanket, haversack, and cartridge box, which weighed less than 14 pounds (Coddington, *Gettysburg Campaign*, 22).

3. Silver, *A Life for the Confederacy*, 149; John W. Lynch, *The Dorman-Masbourne Letters* (Senoia, Ga.: Down South Publishing Company, 1995), 49.

4. Hale and Phillips, *Forty-Ninth Virginia Infantry*, 67; OR, vol. 27, pt. 2, 545; Samuel Pickens Diary, copy in Brake Collection, USAMHI; Gregory C. White, *A History of the 31st Georgia Volunteer Infantry: Lawton-Gordon-Evans Brigade Army of Northern Virginia Confederate States of America 1861–1865* (Baltimore: Butternut and Blue, 1997), 79.

5. OR, vol. 27, pt. 2, 859–60.

6. OR, vol. 27, pt. 1, 29.

7. OR, vol. 27, pt. 3, 3–4.

8. OR, vol. 27, pt. 3, 6–7.

9. Richard E. Matthews, *The 149th Pennsylvania Volunteer Infantry Unit in the Civil War* (Jefferson, N.C.: McFarland & Company, 1994), 67; William Perry Diary, copy in Brake Collection, United States Army Military History Institute (Hereafter, USAMHI).

10. OR, vol. 27, pt. 3, 3–4.

11. John M. Priest, *John T. McMahon's Diary of the 136th New York* (Shippensburg, Pa.: White Mane Publishing Co., Inc., 1993), 49; Calvin S. Heller Diary, Civil War Miscellaneous Collection, USAMHI.

JUNE 5

1. OR, vol. 27, pt. 2, 293, 499.

2. OR, vol. 27, pt. 2, 293; OR, vol. 27, pt. 3, 863.

3. OR, vol. 27, pt. 3, 861.

4. Nye, *Here Come the Rebels,* 49.

5. Mitchell journal; Coles, *Fourth Alabama,* 98.

6. Louis Leon, *Diary of a Tar Heel* (Charlotte, N.C.: Stone Publishing Company, 1913), 29; OR, vol. 27, pt. 2, 546; Samuel Pickens Diary.

7. Dayton, ed., *Diary of a Confederate Soldier,* 80; Jubal A. Early, *Autobiographical Sketch and Narrative of the War Between the States* (Philadelphia: J. B. Lippincott Company, 1912), 237; White, *History of the 31st Georgia,* 79; Randolph McKim, *A Soldier's Recollections* (New York: Longmans Green, 1911), 138.

8. J. F. J. Caldwell, *The History of a Brigade of South Carolinians* (Marietta, Ga.: Continental Book Company, 1951), 90.

9. OR, vol. 27, pt. 3, 11.

10. OR, vol. 27, pt. 1, 30.

11. OR, vol. 27, pt. 1, 31.

12. OR, vol. 27, pt. 1, 31.

13. OR, vol. 27, pt. 1, 32.

14. William Perry Diary.

15. OR, vol. 27, pt. 1, 7.

JUNE 6

1. OR, vol. 27, pt. 2, 293.

2. Ware journal.

3. Silver, *A Life for the Confederacy,* 149; Mitchell journal.

4. OR, vol. 27, pt. 2, 546; Samuel Pickens Diary; McKim, *A Soldier's Recollections,* 138; Early, *Autobiographical Sketch,* 237; Dayton, *Diary of a Confederate,* 80; Hale and Phillips, *Forty-Ninth Virginia Infantry,* 68.

5. William K. McDaid, *Four Years of Arduous Service* (Ph.D. Dissertation, Michigan State University, 1987), 200–201; Franklin L. Riley, *Grandfather's Journal* (Dayton, Ohio: Morningside, 1988), 144.

6. OR, vol. 27, pt. 1, 33.

7. OR, vol. 27, pt. 3, 12; 17–18.

8. OR, vol. 27, pt. 3, 14, 17, 24.

9. OR, vol. 27, pt. 3, 17; Nye, *Here Come the Rebels,* 47.

10. OR, vol. 27, pt. 3, 20.

11. Allen T. Nolan, *The Iron Brigade* (New York: McMillan Company, 1961), 225.

12. OR, vol. 27, pt. 3, 17–18.

13. OR, vol. 27, pt. 3, 12, 13.

14. Emil and Ruth Rosenblatt, *Hard Marching Every Day* (Lawrence, Kans.: University Press of Kansas, 1992), 99, 100.

15. Rosenblatt, *Hard Marching Every Day,* 100.

16. OR, vol. 27, pt. 3, 13.

JUNE 7

1. Nye, *Here Come the Rebels,* 45; OR, vol. 27, pt. 3, 865–66.
2. OR, vol. 27, pt. 2, 293.
   At least three of Lee's veteran brigades were to the south. General D. H. Hill, commanding the troops in North Carolina, suggested that Lee accept large brigades composed of raw recruits, in exchange for his old brigades. Three of Lee's newest brigades, Pettigrew's, Daniel's, and Davis's, fell into this category (OR, vol. 18, 1063; OR, vol. 51, 720; Coddington, *Gettysburg Campaign,* 19, 21).
3. Ware journal; Mitchell journal.
4. Howard G. Gregory, *Thirty-eighth Virginia* (Lynchburg, Va.: H. E. Howard, 1988), 35.
5. Hale and Phillips, *Forty-Ninth Virginia,* 68; Bartlett Y. Malone, *Whipt 'Em Everytime* (Jackson, Tenn.: McCowat-Mercer Press, 1960), 80; Leon, *Diary of a Tar Heel,* 29; McKim, *A Soldier's Recollections,*139; OR, vol. 27, pt. 2, 546.
6. OR, vol. 27, pt. 3, 27–28, 29.
7. OR, vol. 27, pt. 3, 31.
8. OR, vol. 27, pt. 3, 32.
9. OR, vol. 27, pt. 3, 24.
10. OR, vol. 27, pt. 3, 26.
11. Rosenblatt, *Hard Marching Every Day,* 101.

JUNE 8

1. OR, vol. 27, pt. 3, 873; Dabney H. Maury, *Recollections of a Virginian in the Mexican, Indian, and Civil Wars* (New York: C. Scribner's Sons, 1894), 239.
2. OR, vol. 27, pt. 2, 294; OR, vol. 27, pt. 3, 869.
3. OR, vol. 27, pt. 3, 868–69.
4. Silver, *A Life for the Confederacy,* 149; Ware journal.
5. Edwin Loving journal; Gregory, *Thirty-Eighth Virginia,* 35.
6. McKim, *A Soldier's Recollections,*139; Hale and Phillips, *Forty-Ninth Virginia ,* 68; OR, vol. 27, pt. 2, 546.
   General Rodes explained in his report that the men had access to nine days' rations. Three days' rations were transported in each brigade's commissary trains, another three were in the division's wagons, and each man carried three-days' in his haversack (OR, vol. 27, pt. 2, 546).
7. Walter Clark, ed. *Histories of the Several Regiments and Battalions from North Carolina, in the Great War, 1861–'65* (Raleigh, N.C.: E. M. Uzzell, printer, 1901), vol. 3, p. 235; John W. Busey and David G. Martin, *Regimental Strengths and Losses at Gettysburg* (Hightstown, N.J.: Longstreet House, 1994), 174.
8. Hoke, *The Great Invasion,* 70.
9. OR, vol. 27, pt. 3, 36.
10. Nolan, *The Iron Brigade,* 226.

JUNE 9

1. OR, vol. 27, pt. 3, 874, 876; Schildt, *Roads to Gettysburg,* 39.
2. Mitchell journal; Ware journal.
3. Gregory, *Thirty-Eighth Virginia,* 35.
4. OR, vol. 27, pt. 2, 546; Donald C. Pfanz, *Richard S. Ewell—A Soldier's Life* (Chapel Hill, N.C.: University of North Carolina Press, 1998), 281.

5. OR, vol. 27, pt. 2, 439–40; Hale and Phillips, *Forty-Ninth Virginia*, 68; Dayton, *Diary of a Confederate*, 81.
6. Schildt, *Roads to Gettysburg*, 37–39.
7. OR, vol. 27, pt. 1, 33–34.
8. OR, vol. 27, pt. 1, 35; Nye, *The Rebels are Coming*, 37.
9. Joseph Newell, *"Ours," Annals of the Tenth Regiment Massachusetts Volunteers* (Springfield, Mass.: C. A. Nichols & Co., 1875), 216.

JUNE 10

1. Nye, *Here Come the Rebels*, 70–71.
2. Ware journal; Silver, *A Life for the Confederacy*, 150; Gregory, *Thirty-Eighth Virginia*, 35.
3. Malone, *Whipt 'Em*, 80–81; Hale and Phillips, *Forty-Ninth Virginia Infantry*, 68; McKim, *A Soldier's Recollections*, 143; Leon, *Diary of a Tar Heel*, 30; Nye, *Here Come the Rebels*, 71.
4. OR, vol. 27, pt. 1, 33–34.
5. OR, vol. 27, pt. 3, 47–48, 54; Hoke, *The Great Invasion*, 75.
6. OR, vol. 27, pt. 3, 50–51, 233.
7. OR, vol. 27, pt. 3, 54, 55.
8. Rosenblatt, *Hard Marching Every Day*, 101; Newell, *Ours*, 216.

JUNE 11

1. OR, vol. 27, pt. 3, 882.
2. Silver, *A Life for the Confederacy*, 150; Ware journal; Gregory, *Thirty-Eighth Virginia*, 35.
   Robert Moore of the 17th Mississippi admitted that it was the first time he had done so in nearly six months.
3. Pfanz, *Ewell*, 281; Hale and Phillips, *Forty-Ninth Virginia*, 68–69; Samuel Pickens Diary; OR, vol. 27, pt. 2, 546.
4. McKim, *A Soldier's Recollections*, 143; Dayton, *Diary of a Confederate*, 81; Leon, *Diary of a Tar Heel*, 30; Samuel Pickens Diary; Nye, *Here Come the Rebels*, 73.
5. McDaid, *Four Years of Arduous Service*, 201.
6. OR, vol. 27, pt. 1, 36; OR, vol. 27, pt. 3, 58, 59, 60, 61, 67; Hoke, *The Great Invasion*, 76.
7. OR, vol. 27, pt. 1, 41; OR, vol. 27, pt. 2, 92, 188.
   Modern historian Edwin Coddington questioned why Schenck, whose orders were to protect the vital Baltimore and Ohio Railroad in Maryland, Virginia, and West Virginia, had stationed Milroy's division at Winchester, 20 miles to the south. Schenck did not heed these orders from Halleck because he thought they were merely suggestions (Coddington, *Gettysburg Campaign*, 86–87).
8. OR, vol. 27, pt. 2, 189.
9. OR, vol. 27, pt. 3, 66.
10. Charles W. Bardeen, *A Little Fifer's War Diary* (Syracuse, N.Y.: C. W. Bardeen, Publisher, 1910), 204; Frank Rauscher, *Music on the March: 1861–'65 with the Army of the Potomac, 114th Regiment* (Philadelphia: Fell, 1892), 75–76.
11. Newell, *Ours*, 216.

JUNE 12

1. OR, vol. 27, pt. 3, 885.

2. Mitchell journal; Ware journal.

3. Malone, *Whipt 'Em,* 81; Samuel Pickens Diary; Leon, *Diary of a Tar Heel,* 30; McKim, *A Soldier's Recollections,* 143; Robert J. Driver, *Fifty-second Virginia Infantry* (Lynchburg, Va.: H. E. Howard, Inc., 1986), 37.

4. OR, vol. 27, pt. 2, 440, 546–47; Clifford Dowdey, and Louis H. Manarin, *The Wartime Papers of R. E. Lee* (New York: Bramhall House, 1961), 510; Pfanz, *Ewell,* 282.

5. Johnson, "A Limited Review of What One Man Saw of the Battle of Gettysburg," Copy in the GNMP.

6. OR, vol. 27, pt. 3, 69, 72.

7. OR, vol. 27, pt. 3, 78–79.

8. OR, vol. 27, pt. 3, 70, 75, 77.

   General Pleasonton entertained a bizarre idea—that the services of Colonel John Mosby, whose Confederate irregulars tormented the Federal army and who regularly collected valuable information, could be purchased. In this way, Mosby would begin providing information to the Federals. As expected, this idea went nowhere (OR, vol. 27, pt. 3, 72).

9. OR, vol. 27, pt. 2, 42–43, 69; Nye, *Here Come the Rebels,* 74–77.

10. OR, vol. 27, pt. 3, 76, 77.

11. OR, vol. 27, pt. 3, 79–80.

12. Hoke, *The Great Invasion,* 76; Matthews, *149th Pennsylvania,* 68; William Perry Diary; O. B. Curtis, *History of the Twenty-Fourth Michigan of the Iron Brigade* (Detroit, Mich.: Winn and Hammond, 1891), 144; C. V. Tervis, *The History of the Fighting Fourteenth* (Brooklyn, N.Y.: Brooklyn Eagle Press, 1911), 76; Charles E. Davis, *Three Years in the Army: The Story of the Thirteenth Massachusetts Volunteers* (Boston: Estes & Lownat, 1864), 213.

   Craig L. Dunn, *Iron Men, Iron Will* (Indianapolis, Ind.: Guild Press, 1995), 180.

13. William B. Jordan, *Red Diamond Regiment: The 17th Maine Infantry, 1862–1865* (Shippensburg, Pa.: White Mane Publishing Co., Inc., 1996), 63; Bardeen, *Little Fifer's War Diary,* 205; Rauscher, *Music on the March,* 76; Henry N. Blake, *Three Years in the Army of the Potomac* (Boston: Lee and Shepard, 1865), 195; Thomas B. Marbaker, *History of the Eleventh New Jersey Volunteers* (Hightstown, N.J.: Longstreet House, 1990), 80.

   Blake purported that a general ordered the provost guard to set the dry tracts of land on fire to rouse out the stragglers.

14. OR, vol. 27, pt. 3, 73; Rosenblatt, *Hard Marching Every Day,* 101; Martin A. Haynes, *History of the Second New Hampshire Regiment: Its Camps, Marches, and Battles* (Manchester, N.H.: Charles F. Livingston Printer, 1865), 70–71.

15. Jacob Smith, *Camps and Campaigns of the 107th Regiment Ohio Volunteer Infantry* (n.p., n.d.), 79; Priest, *John McMahon's Diary,* 49.

JUNE 13

1. OR, vol. 27, pt. 3, 886.

2. Ware journal; Silver, *A Life for the Confederacy,* 150.

3. OR, vol. 27, pt. 2, 547.

4. OR, vol. 27, pt. 2, 83, 547–48; Leon, *Diary of a Tar Heel,* 30–31.

5. OR, vol. 27, pt. 2, 440; Pfanz, *Ewell,* 283.

6. OR, vol. 27, pt. 2, 460, 491; Charles S. Grunder and Brandon H. Beck, *The Second Battle of Winchester* (Lynchburg, Va.: H. E. Howard, Inc., 1989), 29–30.

7. OR, vol. 27, pt. 2, 499–500, 520, 524; Dennis Frye, *Second Virginia Infantry* (Lynchburg, Va.: H. E. Howard, Inc, 1984), 52–53.

8. OR, vol. 27, pt. 1, 38; OR, vol. 27, pt. 3, 88–89.
9. OR, vol. 27, pt. 3, 82, 91.
10. OR, vol. 27, pt. 2, 165.
11. OR, vol. 27, pt. 2, 109; OR, vol. 27, pt. 3, 96–97.
12. Nye, *Here Come the Rebels,* 88.
13. OR, vol. 27, pt. 3, 97.
14. Matthews, *149th Pennsylvania,* 69; Curtis, *History of the 24th Michigan,* 147; Davis, *Three Years in the Army,* 214.
15. OR, vol. 27, pt. 3, 88.
16. Bardeen, *Little Fifer's War Diary,* 205.
17. OR, vol. 27, pt. 1, 637; OR, vol. 3, pt. 3, 88; Timothy Reese, *Sykes' Regular Infantry Division, 1861–1864* (Jefferson, N.C.: McFarland, 1990), 230; Ira S. Pettit, *Diary of a Dead Man* (New York: Eastern Acorn Press, 1976), p. 146; True Blue letter, *Evening Express,* June 19, 1863.
18. Martin A. Haynes, *History of the Second New Hampshire Regiment: Its Camps, Marches, and Battles* (Manchester, N.H.: Charles F. Livingston Printer, 1865), 70–71.
19. Rosenblatt, *Hard Marching Every Day,* 101.
20. OR, vol. 27, pt. 3, 88; Rosenblatt, *Hard Marching Every Day,* 104–5.
21. Priest, *John McMahon's Diary,* 49; Heller Diary; Smith, *107th Ohio,* 79.
22. OR, vol. 27, pt. 1, 797; *Pennsylvania at Gettysburg—Ceremonies at the Dedication of the Monuments* (Harrisburg, Pa.: Wm. Stanley Ray, State Printer, 1904), vol. 2, 568; Edmund R. Brown, *The Twenty-Seventh Indiana Volunteer Infantry in the War of the Rebellion* (Monticello, Ind.: n.p., 1899), 356, 357; Alpheus Williams, *From the Cannon's Mouth* (Detroit, Mich.: Wayne State University Press, 1959), 212.

JUNE 14

1. Hoke, *The Great Invasion,* 87.

   Despite the fact that Hooker had pulled his men from Falmouth, Lee was still concerned about the threat to Richmond from the south, so he hesitated in pulling out Hill's remaining two divisions until June 16 (Freeman, *Lee,* vol. 3, 36).

2. Silver, *A Life for the Confederacy,* 150; Coles, *Fourth Alabama,* 99; Charles T. Loehr, *War History of the Old First Virginia Infantry Regiment, Army of Northern Virginia* (Richmond, Va.: William Ellis Jones, Printer, 1884), 35.

3. OR, vol. 27, pt. 2, 548; Samuel Pickens Diary; Leon, *Diary of a Tar Heel,* 31.

4. OR, vol. 27, pt. 2, 548–49.

   According to General Lee's report, Rodes's men captured 700 prisoners, 5 pieces of artillery, and a considerable quantity of stores (OR, vol. 27, pt. 2, 306).

5. OR, vol. 27, pt. 2, 440–41, 500.

6. OR, vol. 27, pt. 2, 462; Grunder and Beck, *Second Battle of Winchester,* 36; *Richmond Daily Enquirer,* June 22, 1863.

7. OR, vol. 27, pt. 2, 463, 477–78; Grunder and Beck, *Second Battle of Winchester,* 40–41; Nye, *Here Come the Rebels,* 100.

8. Terry L. Jones, *Lee's Tigers* (Baton Rouge, La.: Louisiana State University Press, 1987), 159; OR, vol. 27, pt. 2, 463, 477–78; Percy Gatling Hamlin, *Old Bald Head—The Portrait of a Soldier* (Strasburg, Va.: Shenandoah Publishing House, 1940), 139; Jones, "Going Back Into the Union at Last," *Civil War Times Illustrated,* January/February, 1991, 55.

9. Harry Gilmor, *Four Years in the Saddle* (New York: Harper & Brothers, 1866), 89–90.

10. McKim, *A Soldier's Recollections,* 146.

11. OR, vol. 27, pt. 2, 463.

12. OR, vol. 27, pt. 2, 500.

13. OR, vol. 27, pt. 2, 500–501.

14. OR, vol. 27, pt. 2, 613; Johnson, "What One Man Saw of the Battle of Gettysburg."

15. OR, vol. 27, pt. 2, 54; Nye, *Here Come the Rebels,* 91–92.

    Milroy had been in command at Winchester since Christmas of 1862 (Schildt, *Roads to Gettysburg,* 65).

16. OR, vol. 27, pt. 2, 46; Nye, *Here Come the Rebels,* 98.

17. OR, vol. 27, pt. 2, 36, 40, 109–10, 549, 592.

18. OR, vol. 27, pt. 1, 38, 39.

19. OR, vol. 27, pt. 1, 39.

20. OR, vol. 27, pt. 3, 111.

21. OR, vol. 27, pt. 3, 111, 112, 113.

22. Nye, *Here Come the Rebels,* 156–57.

23. OR, vol. 27, pt. 3, 129; Nye, *Here Come the Rebels,* 223–24.

24. OR, vol. 27, pt. 3, 101; A. R. Small, *The Sixteenth Maine Regiment in the War of the Rebellion 1861–1865* (Portland, Maine: Thurston & Co., 1886), 111; Matthews, *149th Pennsylvania,* 69; George A. Hussey, *History of the Ninth Regiment N.Y.S.M.* (New York: J. S. Ogilvie, 1889), 260; George Soult Diary, Civil War Miscellaneous Collection, USAMHI.

25. Edward Longacre, *To Gettysburg and Beyond: The Twelfth New Jersey Volunteer Infantry, II Corps, Army of the Potomac, 1862–1865* (Hightstown, N.J.: Longstreet House, 1988), 109; Fuller, *Personal Recollections of the War,* 89–90; Joseph Ward, *History of the One Hundred and Sixth Pennsylvania Volunteers, 2d Brigade, 2d Division, 2d Corps, 1861–1865* (Philadelphia: Grant, Faires & Rodgers, 1883), 170–71; R. I. Holcombe, *History of the First Regiment Minnesota Volunteer Infantry, 1861–1864* (Gaithersburg, Md.: VanSickle, 1987), 312; Joseph W. Muffly, ed. *The Story of Our Regiment: A History of the 148th Pennsylvania Volunteers* (Des Moines, Iowa: Kenyon Printing and Manufacturing Company, 1904), 455; George A. Bowen, "The Diary of Captain George D. Bowen, *The Valley Forge Journal,* vol. 2 (June 1984), 127.

26. Ruth L. Silliken, *The Rebel Yell & Yankee Hurrah* (Camden, Maine: Down East Books, 1985), 90; Jordan, *Red Diamond Regiment,* 63; Charles Mattocks, *Unspoiled Heart, The Journal of Charles Mattocks of the 17th Maine* (Knoxville, Tenn.: University of Tennessee Press, 1994), 38; Bardeen, *Little Fifer's War Diary,* 205.

27. Reese, *Sykes' Regular Infantry,* 230; Pettit, *Diary of a Dead Man,* 146; Diary of Sgt. Charles Bowen, copy in 12th U.S. folder, GNMP.

28. George W. Parsons, *Put the Vermonters Ahead: The First Vermont Brigade in the Civil War* (Shippensburg, Pa.: White Mane Publising Co., Inc., 1996), 58; Ann H. Britton and Thomas Reed, *To My Beloved Wife and Boy at Home* (Madison, N.J.: Fairleigh Dickinson University Press, 1997), 102; Joseph G. Bilby, *Remember Fontenoy! The 69th New York and the Irish Brigade in the Civil War* (Hightstown, N.J.: Longstreet House, 1995), 81; Alfred S. Roe, *The Tenth Regiment, Massachusetts Volunteer Infantry, 1861–1864* (Springfield, Mass.: Tenth Regiment Veteran Association, 1909); Roe, *The Tenth Massachusetts,* 198; Haines, *History of the 15th New Jersey,* 72.

29. Newell, *Ours,* 217–18; Rosenblatt, *Hard Marching Every Day,* 105; Bowen, *History of the Thirty-Seventh Massachusetts,* 163–64.

30. OR, vol. 27, pt. 3, 101; Smith, *107th Ohio,* 79; Priest, *John McMahon's Diary,* 49.

31. OR, vol. 27, pt. 1, 797; Williams, *From the Cannon's Mouth,* 213.

JUNE 15

1. OR, vol. 27, pt. 2, 295.

2. Ware journal; John C. West, *A Texan in Search of a Fight* (Waco, Tex.: Press of J. S. Hill and Company, 1901), 89.

3. Mitchell journal; Silver, *A Life for the Confederacy*, 150; Charles Lippitt Journal, Southern Historical Collection, University of North Carolina; Dooley, *John Dooley*, 95.

4. OR, vol. 27, pt. 2, 501.

5. OR, vol. 27, pt. 2, 501–2, 508, 512; Ted Barclay, *Ted Barclay, Liberty Hall Volunteers:Letters from the Stonewall Brigade* (Natural Bridge Station, Va.: Rockbridge Publishing Co., 1992), 88; Lowell Reidenbaugh, *Twenty-Seventh Virginia* (Lynchburg, Va.: H. E. Howard, Inc., 1993), 85.

   An exuberant General Johnson rode after the fleeing Federals and soon outdistanced his infantry. Jumping into Opequon Creek, the general was briefly submerged. When he surfaced, Federal troops retrieved his hat before surrendering to him (Henry Kyd Douglas, *I Rode with Stonewall* (Chapel Hill, N.C.: University of North Carolina Press, 1940, 242).

6. Grunder and Beck, *Second Battle of Winchester*, 43; OR, vol. 27, pt. 2, 464, 491; Hale and Phillips, *Forty-Ninth Virginia*, 70.

7. Reidenbaugh, *Twenty-seventh Virginia*, 85.

   General Ewell issued General Orders Number 44, which read, "the lieutenant-general commanding asks the men and officers of the corps to unite with him in returning thanks to our Heavenly Father for the signal success which has crowned the valor of this command. In acknowledgment of Divine favor, chaplains will hold religious services in the respective regiments at such times as may be most convenient" (OR, vol. 27, pt. 3, 894).

8. OR, vol. 27, 549–50; Leon, *Diary of a Tar Heel*, 32.

9. Douglas S. Freeman, *Lee's Lieutenants* (New York: Charles Scribner's Sons, 1949–51), vol. 3, 74; OR, vol. 27, pt. 2, 613; Archie K. Davis, *The Boy Colonel: The Life and Times of Henry King Burgwyn, Jr.* (Chapel Hill, N.C.: University of North Carolina Press, 1985), 270; Frank Foote, "Marching In Clover," *Philadelphia Weekly Times*, October 8, 1881; Riley, *Grandfather's Journal*, 145.

10. OR, vol. 27, pt. 1, 40–41, 42.

11. Coddington, *Gettysburg Campaign*, 83–84.

12. OR, vol. 27, pt. 3, 133, 134, 135, 136–37, 145; Nye, *Here Come the Rebels*, 158.

13. OR, vol. 27, pt. 3, 137, 138, 142, 144.

14. OR, vol. 27, pt. 3, 129, 130, 131.

15. OR, vol. 27, pt. 2, 48, 119, 130, 136–37, 148.

16. Nye, *Here Come the Rebels*, 115–18, 122.

   Despite the fact that General Milroy outranked General Tyler when both arrived at Harper's Ferry, the latter was ordered to take command of the facility. He energetically put his men to work rebuilding the town's fortifications (Coddington, *Gettysburg Campaign*, 92).

17. OR, vol. 27, pt. 3, 124.

18. OR, vol. 27, pt. 1, 43, 44.

19. OR, vol. 27, pt. 1, 44.

20. OR, vol. 27, pt. 3, 131.

21. Frank Moore, ed. *Rebellion Record: A Diary of American Events with Documents and Narratives, Illustrative Incidents, Poetry, etc.* (New York, 1864), vol. 7, 194, 196–97; Hoke, *Great Invasion*,108.

22. Davis, *Three Years in the Army*, 214; Smith, *The Seventy-Sixth New York*, 226; Chronicles of Francis Bacon Jones, copy in Brake Collection, USAMHI.

23. Davis, *Three Years in the Army*, 214; Tervis, *Fighting Fourteenth*, 77; H. P. Clare letter, William Keating Clare Papers, USAMHI.

24. Holcombe, *History of the First Minnesota*, 312–13; Muffly, *The Story of Our Regiment*, 455; Gerry H. Poriss and Ralph G. Poriss, *While My Country is in Danger: The Life and Letters of Lieutenant Colonel Richard S. Thompson* (Hamilton, N.Y.: Edmonston Publishing, 1994), 64; George Walters Diary, copy in 148th Pennsylvania folder, GNMP; Andrew Ford, *Story of the Fifteenth Regiment Massachusetts Volunteers Infantry* (Clinton, Mass.: Press of W. J. Coulter, 1898), 256, 257.

25. Cowtan, *Services of the Tenth New York*, 199.

26. Silliken, *Rebel Yell and Yankee Hurrah*, 91–92; Bardeen, *Little Fifer's War Diary*, 205; Davis, Oliver Wilson, *Life of David Bell Birney, Major General United States Volunteers* (Philadelphia: King & Baird, 1867), 178; Jordan, *Red Diamond Regiment*, 64; Frederick C. Floyd, *History of the Fortieth (Mozart) Regiment, New York Volunteers* (Boston : F. H. Gilson Company, 1909), 199.

27. Pettit, *Diary of a Dead Man*, 146; Alfred Apted Diary, copy in 16th Michigan folder, GNMP; Timothy Brooks, "Memories of the War: Jacob Shenkel's Gettysburg Diary," copy in the 62nd Pennsylvania folder, GNMP; Charles Bowen Diary.

28. Newell, *Ours*, 218; Rosenblatt, *Hard Marching Every Day*, 105, 106; Bowen, *History of the 37th Massachusetts*, 164; OR, vol. 27, pt. 3, 118; Haines, *History of the 15th New Jersey*, 72.

29. Heller Diary; Hartwell Osborn, *Trials and Triumphs: The Record of the Fifty-fifth Ohio Volunteer Infantry* (Chicago: A. C. McClurg, 1904), p. 88; Priest, *John McMahon's Diary*, 50; Smith, *107th Ohio*, 79.

30. Nathaniel Parmeter diary, Ohio Historical Center; Henry C. Morhous, *Reminiscences of the 123rd Regiment, New York State Volunteers* (Greenwich, N.Y.: People's Journal Book and Job Office, 1879), 40–41.

31. Morhous, *Reminiscences of the 123rd New York*, 40, 41; Brown, *History of the Twenty-Seventh Indiana*, 359; OR, vol. 27, pt. 1, 797.

JUNE 16

1. Schildt, *Roads to Gettysburg*, 103.

2. Hoke, *The Great Invasion*, 105–7.

3. Ware journal.

4. Silver, *A Life for the Confederacy*, 150; Mitchell journal.

5. Lippitt journal.

6. J. G. de Roulhac Hamilton, ed. *Shotwell Papers*, vol. 1 (Raleigh N.C.: North Carolina Historical Commission, 1929–31), 479.

7. Samuel Firebaugh journal, SHC, University of North Carolina; anonymous diary, copy in the 1st Maryland folder, GNMP; Richard L. Armstrong, *Twenty-fifth Virginia Infantry and Ninth Virginia Infantry* (Lynchburg, Va.: H. E. Howard, Inc., 1990), 60; John Chapla, *The Forty-Eighth Virginia Infantry* (Lynchburg, Va.: H. E. Howard, 1989), 56.

8. Hale and Phillips, *Forty-Ninth Virginia*, 70–71.

9. OR, vol. 27, pt. 2, 550.

10. "The Civil War Diary and Letters of James Thomas McElvany," copy in 35th Georgia file, GNMP; Davis, *Boy Colonel*, 270; Caldwell, *History of a Brigade of South Carolinians*, 91.

11. Riley, *Grandfather's Journal*, 145.

12. OR, vol. 27, pt. 1, 45, 47.

13. OR, vol. 27, pt. 1, 47.

14. OR, vol. 27, pt. 1, 47–48.

15. OR, vol. 27, pt. 3, 169.

Many believed that Curtin would have had more luck raising "bushwhackers." Indeed Edwin Coddington believed that as many as 5,000 Pennsylvanians took up their rifles for this purpose, particularly in the Juniata River Valley, where they protected the mountain gaps leading to their homes (Coddington, *Gettysburg Campaign,* 143).

16. Nye, *Here Come the Rebels,* 259–65.
17. Coddington, *Gettysburg Campaign,* 147.
18. Hoke, *The Great Invasion,* 115–16.
19. Davis, *Three Years in the Army,* 215; Tervis, *Fighting Fourteenth,* 77; James M. Hart Diary, copy in Brake Collection, USAMHI; Thomas Chamberlin, *History of the One Hundred and Fiftieth Regiment Pennsylvania Volunteers, Second Regiment, Bucktail Brigade* (Philadelphia: J. B. Lippincott, Co., 1895), 113.
20. Ford, *Story of the Fifteenth Regiment Massachusetts,* 256; Bowen, "Diary of Captain George D. Bowen," 127.
21. Mattocks, *Unspoiled Heart,* 39; Jordan, *Red Diamond Regiment,* 64.
22. Pettit, *Diary of a Dead Man,* 146; Charles Bowen Diary; John T. Porter, *Under the Maltese Cross: Campaigns of the 155th Pennsylvania Regiment* (Pittsburgh, Pa.:155th Regimental Association, 1910), 147.
23. Bowen, *History of the 37th Massachusetts,* 164; Joseph Taper Diary, copy in the 23rd Pennsylvania folder, GNMP; Britton and Reed, *To My Beloved Wife,* 102.
24. OR, vol. 27, pt. 1, 797; Nathaniel Parmeter diary.

JUNE 17

1. OR, vol. 27, pt. 3, 900–901.
2. OR, vol. 27, pt. 2, 306; Nye, *Here Come the Rebels,* 169; Schildt, *Roads to Gettysburg,* 122.
3. Ware journal; Mark Nesbitt, *35 Days to Gettysburg* (Harrisburg, Pa.: Stackpole Books, 1992), 80.
4. Silver, *A Life for the Confederacy,* 151; Mitchell journal; Mac Wyckoff, *A History of the Third South Carolina Infantry, 1861–1865* (Fredericksburg, Va.: Sergeant Kirkland's Museum and Historical Society, 1995), 114.
5. Lippitt journal; William A. Young, *Fifty-Sixth Virginia Infantry* (Lynchburg, Va.: H. E. Howard, 1990), 77–78; Hamilton, *Shotwell Papers,* vol. 1, 477, 479.
   The men were treated to a Robert E. Lee sighting. One soldier in the 56th Virginia (Armistead's brigade) wrote to his wife, "we gave the old fellow a lusty cheer and, as he passed, he took off his hat and saluted us and rode on, and seemed as tranquil as the morning sun" (Young, *Fifty-Sixth Virginia,* 77–78).
6. George Buswell letter, copy in the 33rd Virginia folder, GNMP; Anonymous 1st Maryland journal; McKim, *A Soldier's Recollections,* 155.
7. OR, vol. 27, pt. 2, 464; Hale and Phillips, *Forty-Ninth Virginia,* 71.
8. Leon, *Diary of a Tar Heel,* 32; OR, vol. 27, pt. 2, 550.
9. OR, vol. 27, pt. 2, 613; Riley, *Grandfather's Journal,* 145.
10. "Diary James McElvany"; Davis, *Boy Colonel,* 270; Clark, *N.C. Regiments,* vol. 3, 235.
11. OR, vol. 27, pt. 1, 48; OR, vol. 27, pt. 3, 171, 181, 186, 191.
12. OR, vol. 27, pt. 3, 174–75.
13. OR, vol. 27, pt. 3, 171, 176; Nye, *Here Come the Rebels,* 181.
    These orders actually came from Halleck, who wrote to Hooker on June 16, "I want you to push out your cavalry, to ascertain something definite about the enemy (OR, vol. 27, pt. 1, 47).
14. Hoke, *The Great Invasion,* 109–11.
15. OR, vol. 27, pt. 3, 189–90.
16. OR, vol. 27, pt. 3, 185, 187.

17. Nye, *Here Come the Rebels*, 213, 216.

18. OR, vol. 27, pt. 3, 189.

19. OR, vol. 27, pt. 3, 190.

20. Chamberlin, *One Hundred and Fiftieth Pennsylvania*, 110; Matthews, *149th Pennsylvania*, 69; Smith, *The 76th New York*, 227–28; Tervis, *Fighting Fourteenth*, 78; Smith, *The Twenty-fourth Michigan*, 114.

21. Ford, *Story of the Fifteenth Regiment Massachusetts*, 313; Charles D. Page, *History of the Fourteenth Regiment, Connecticut Vol. Infantry* (Gaithersburg, Md.: Van Sickle, 1987), 130, 131.

22. Mattocks, *Unspoiled Heart*, 39; Sulliken, *Rebel Yell and Yankee Hurrah*, 92.

23. Diary of Samuel J. Keene, copy in 20th Maine folder, GNMP; Francis Charles Bowen Diary; John L. Parker, *Henry Wilson's Regiment: History of the Twenty-second Regiment, Massachusetts Infantry* (Boston: Press of Rand Avery Company, 1887), 324; Francis J. Parker, *The Story of the Thirty-Second Massachusetts Infantry* (Boston: C.W. Calkins & Company, 1887), 163.

24. Evan M. Woodward, Our Campaigns—The Second Regiment, Pennsylvania Reserve Volunteers (Philadelphia: J. E. Potter, 1865), 204–5.

25. Bowen, *History of the 37th Massachusetts*, 164; Britton and Reed, *To My Beloved Wife*, 102; Rosenblatt, *Hard Marching Every Day*, 103.

26. Priest, *John McMahon's Diary*, 50; William Simmers, *The Volunteers' Manual, or Ten Months with the One Hundred and Fifty-third Pennsylvania Volunteers* (Easton, Pa.: D. H. Neiman, 1863); Smith, *107th Ohio*, 80; Mark H. Dunkelman and Michael J. Winey, *The Hardtack Regiment: An Illustrated History of the 154th Regiment, New York State Infantry Volunteers* (East Brunswick, N.J.: Fairleigh Dickinson University Press, 1981), 68–69; Henry Henney Diary, copy in Brake Collection, USAMHI.

27. OR, vol. 27, pt. 1, 797; Williams, *From the Cannon's Mouth*, 214; Schildt, *Roads to Gettysburg*, 121.

JUNE 18

1. OR, vol. 27, pt. 2, 295.

2. OR, vol. 27, pt. 2, 306; OR, vol. 27, pt. 3, 905.

3. Ware journal; Harold B. Simpson, *Hood's Texas Brigade: Lee's Grenadier Guard* (Waco, Tex.: Texian Press, 1970), 248–49.

4. Lippitt journal; Hamilton, *Shotwell Papers*, vol. 1, 479–80.

5. Mitchell journal; Silver, *Life for the Confederacy*, 151.

6. Anonymous 1st Maryland journal; John Stone letter, Civil War Miscellaneous Collection, USAMHI; Firebaugh journal; McKim, *A Soldier's Recollections*, 155; Clark, *N.C. Regiments*, vol. 1, 148, 194.

7. OR, vol. 27, pt. 2, 464; Hale and Phillips, *Forty-Ninth Virginia*, 71.

8. OR, vol. 27, pt. 2, 550.

9. OR, vol. 27, pt. 2, 613; "Diary James McElvany"; James S. Harris, *Historical Sketches: Seventh Regiment, North Carolina Troops* (Ann Arbor, Mich.: University Microfilms, 1972), 33; Rod Gragg, *Covered with Glory* (New York: HarperCollins, 2000), 56–57.

10. OR, vol. 27, pt. 1, 50; OR, vol. 27, pt. 3, 198, 200–201.

11. OR, vol. 27, pt. 1, 50; OR, vol. 27, pt. 3, 197–98.

12. OR, vol. 27, pt. 1, 51.

13. OR, vol. 27, pt. 3, 198.

14. OR, vol. 27, pt. 3, 93.

15. OR, vol. 27, pt. 3, 194.

16. OR, vol. 27, pt. 3, 192.

17. OR, vol. 27, pt. 3, 203; Nye, *Here Come the Rebels*, 216–17.

18. Matthews, *149th Pennsylvania*, 69; Schildt, *Roads to Gettysburg*, 126.

19. Charles Bowen Diary; William Crennell Diary, copy in 140th New York folder, GNMP.

20. Newell, *Ours*, 218; Britton and Reed, *To My Beloved Wife*, 103; Haines, *The 15th New Jersey*, 73.

21. Osborn, *Trials and Triumphs*, 88; Heller Diary; Priest, *John McMahon's Diary*, 50; Heller Diary; Stephen Wallace Diary, Diaries and Journals Collections, Pennsylvania State Archives; James S. Pula, *The Sigel Regiment: A History of the Twenty-sixth Wisconsin Volunteer Infantry, 1862–1865* (Campbell, Calif.: Savas, 1998), 152.

22. OR, vol. 27, pt. 3, 178; OR, vol. 27, pt. 1, 797–98; Harlan Rugg Diary, Copy in 5th Connecticut folder, GNMP; Morhous, *Reminiscences of the 123rd New York*, 42; Williams, *From the Cannon's Mouth*, 215.

JUNE 19

1. OR, vol. 27, pt. 3, 904.

   Hooker apparently sent the corps to Leesburg when he heard that rebel cavalry was at Point of Rocks, Maryland (Coddington, *Gettysburg Campaign*, 95).

2. Schildt, *Roads to Gettysburg*, 155.

3. Coles, *Fourth Alabama*, 100–101; Ware journal.

4. Silver, *A Life for the Confederacy*, 151; Mitchell journal.

5. OR, vol. 27, pt. 2, 357; Lippitt journal.

6. Hale and Phillips, *Forty-Ninth Virginia*, 71; OR, vol. 27, pt. 2, 464; Firebaugh journal.

7. OR, vol. 27, pt. 2, 550–51; Samuel Pickens Diary; Leon, *Diary of a Tar Heel*, 32.

8. Douglas, *I Rode with Stonewall*, 244.

9. OR, vol. 27, pt. 2, 613; Riley, *Grandfather's Journal*, 146.

10. Davis, *Boy Colonel*, 283; Caldwell, *History of a Brigade of South Carolinians*, 92; "Diary James McElvany"; Spencer Glasgow Welch, *A Confederate Surgeon's Letters to His Wife* (New York: Neale Publishing Co., 1911), 55–57.

11. OR, vol. 27, pt. 1, 51–52; Coddington, *Gettysburg Campaign*, 96.

    Hooker was later told by Halleck that his orders could be "given direct to Heintzelman [commanding the Washington area], he reporting them to headquarters before executing them, where they conflict with his special instructions" (OR, vol. 27, pt. 1, 54).

12. OR, vol. 27, pt. 1, 53.

13. OR, vol. 27, pt. 3, 208–9; Schildt, *Roads to Gettysburg*, 144.

14. OR, vol. 27, pt. 1, 52.

15. Nye, *Here Come the Rebels*, 238–39.

16. Matthews, *149th Pennsylvania*, 71; Tervis, *Fighting Fourteenth*, 78.

17. Ford, *Story of the Fifteenth Regiment Massachusetts*, 257; Holcombe, *First Minnesota*, 313; Muffly, *The Story of Our Regiment*, 456, 457; Thomas F. Galway, *The Valiant Hours: Narrative of "Captain Brevet," An Irish-American in the Army of the Potomac* (Harrisburg, Pa.: Stackpole, 1961), 91.

18. Sulliken, *Rebel Yell and Yankee Hurrah*, 93; Mattocks, *Unspoiled Heart*, 39; Houghton, *Campaigns of the Seventeenth Maine*, 75; David Craft, *One Hundred and Forty-First Regiment Pennsylvania Volunteers* (Towanda, Pa.: Reporter-Journal Printing Company, 1885), 109; Jordan, *Red Diamond Regiment*, 64.

19. Charles Bowen Diary; Parker, *Story of the Thirty-Second Massachusetts*, 163; Pettit, *Diary of a Dead Man*, 147; Samuel Keene Diary; Daniel G. Macnamara, *The History of the Ninth Regiment, Massachusetts Volunteer Infantry* (Boston: E. B. Stillings, 1899), 310.

20. Newell, *Ours,* 218; Britton and Reed, *To My Beloved Wife,* 103; Rosenblatt, *Hard Marching Every Day,* 110.

21. Priest, *John McMahon's Diary,* 50; Heller Diary.

22. Morhous, *Reminiscences of the 123rd New York,* 43–44; Lawrence Wilson, *Itinerary of the Seventh Ohio Volunteer Infantry, 1861–1864, With Roster, Portraits, and Biographies* (New York: Neale Publishing Company, 1907), 252.

JUNE 20

1. OR, vol. 27, pt. 3, 905–6.

2. *Philadelphia Evening Bulletin,* June 20, 1863; Nye, *Here Come the Rebels,* 252.

3. OR, vol. 27, pt. 2, p. 357; Ware journal; Coles, *Fourth Alabama,* 101.

4. Loving journal; Lippitt journal; Lohr, *Old First Virginia,* 35; Hamilton, *Shotwell Papers,* vol. 1, 481–82.

5. OR, vol. 27, pt. 2, 366, 371; Mitchell journal; Silver, *A Life for the Confederacy,* 151; Guy R. Everson and Edward W. Simpson, Jr., *Far, Far From Home* (New York: Oxford University Press, 1994), 248.

6. Hale and Phillips, *Forty-Ninth Virginia,* 71; Firebaugh journal; Buswell letter; Samuel Pickens Diary.

7. OR, vol. 27, pt. 2, 613.

8. Davis, *Boy Colonel,* 283; "Diary James McElvany"; George Henry Mills, *History of the 16th North Carolina Regiment (originally 6th N.C. Regiment) in the Civil War* (Hamilton, N.Y: Edmonston Publishers, 1992), 35.

9. OR, vol. 27, pt. 1, 53; OR, vol. 27, pt. 3, 228.

10. Schildt, *Roads to Gettysburg,* 150.

11. OR, vol. 27, pt. 3, 203, 236, 237, 238.

12. OR, vol. 27, pt. 2, 230; Nye, *Here Come the Rebels,* 228, 231–32.

13. Smith, *The 76th New York,* 228; Tervis, *Fighting Fourteenth,* 78; Hussey-Todd, *The Ninth New York,* 262.

14. Ford, *Story of the Fifteenth Massachusetts,* 257; Ward, *One Hundred and Sixth Pennsylvania,* 172–73; John Gibbon, *Personal Recollections of the War* (New York: G. P. Putnam's Sons, 1928), 169.

15. Mattocks, *Unspoiled Heart,* 40; William H. Cudsworth, *History of the First Regiment Massachusetts Infantry* (Boston: Walker, Fuller and Company, 1866), 387.

16. Samuel Keene Diary.

17. Newell, *Ours,* 218; Britton and Reed, *To My Beloved Wife,* 103.

18. Priest, *John McMahon's Diary,* 51; Heller Diary; Osborn, *Trials and Triumphs,* 88.

JUNE 21

1. According to Douglas Freeman, Longstreet misunderstood his orders and pulled his troops from the vital Blue Ridge Mountain passes. This cleared the way for the Federal cavalry's successful incursion (Freeman, *Lee,* vol. 3, 41–44).

2. OR, vol. 27, pt. 3, 912–13.

While in the enemy's country, the following regulations for procuring supplies will be strictly observed, and any violation of them promptly and rigorously punished.

I. No private property shall be injured or destroyed by any person belonging to or connected with the army, or taken, excepting by the officers hereinafter designated.

II. The chiefs of the commissary, quartermaster's, ordnance, and medical departments of the army will make requisitions upon the local authorities or inhabitants for the necessary supplies for their respective departments, designating the places and times of delivery. All persons complying with such requisitions shall be paid the market price for the articles furnished, if they so desire, and the officer making such payment shall take duplicate receipts for the same, specifying the name of the person paid, and the quantity, kind, and price of the property, one of which receipts shall be at once forwarded to the chief of the department to which such officer is attached.

III. Should the authorities or inhabitants neglect or refuse to comply with such requisitions, the supplies required will be taken from the nearest inhabitants so refusing, by the order and under the directions of the respective chiefs of the departments named.

IV. When any command is detached from the main body, the chiefs of the several departments of such command will procure supplies for the same, and such other stores as they may be ordered to provide, in the manner and subject to the provisions herein prescribed, reporting their action to the heads of their respective departments, to whom they will forward duplicates of all vouchers given or received.

V. All persons who shall decline to receive payment for property furnished on requisitions, and all from whom it shall be necessary to take stores or supplies, shall be furnished by the officer receiving or taking the same with a receipt specifying the kind and quantity of the property received or taken, as the case may be, the name of the person from whom it was received or taken, the command for the use of which it is intended, and the market price. A duplicate of said receipt shall be at once forwarded to the chief of the department to which the officer by whom it was executed is attached.

VI. If any person shall remove or conceal property necessary for the use of the army, or attempt to do so, the officers hereinbefore mentioned will cause such property, and all other property belonging to such person that may be required by the army, to be seized, and the officer seizing the same will forthwith report to the chief of his department the kind, quantity, and market price of the property so seized, and the name of the owner.

3. John O. Casler, *Four Years in the Stonewall Brigade* (Marietta, Ga.: Continental Book Co., 1951), 168, 170.

4. OR, vol. 27, pt. 3, 912.

5. Ware journal.

6. Edwin Loving journal.

7. OR, vol. 27, pt. 2, 366; Mitchell journal; Silver, *A Life for the Confederacy,* 151; Everson and Simpson, *Far, Far From Home,* 248–49.

8. Hale and Phillips, *Forty-Ninth Virginia,* 71–72; Samuel Pickens Diary; OR, vol. 27, pt. 2, 551.

9. OR, vol. 27, pt. 2, 613; Riley, *Grandfather's Journal,* 146; Foote, "Marching in Clover."

10. McDaid, *Four Years of Arduous Service,* 202; Thomas M. Littlejohn, "Recollections of a Confederate Soldier," Copy in 1st South Carolina folder, GNMP.

11. OR, vol. 27, pt. 1, 54; OR, vol. 27, pt. 3, 248.

12. OR, vol. 27, pt. 3, 246, 249.

13. OR, vol. 27, pt. 3, 252.

14. Matthews, *149th Pennsylvania,* 72.

15. Holcombe, *First Minnesota,* 313.

16. Mattocks, *Unspoiled Heart,* 41; Sulliken, *Rebel Yell and Yankee Hurrah,* 94.

17. Samuel Keene Diary; Amos M. Judson, *History of the Eighty-Third Regiment, Pennsylvania Volunteers* (Erie, Pa.: B. F. H. Lynn, 1865), 118–19; Eugene A. Nash, *A History of the 44th New York Volunteer Infantry* (Chicago: R. R. Donnelley & Sons Company, 1911), 136; George Ervay Diary, copy in 16th Michigan folder, GNMP; Ellis Spear, *The Civil War Recollections of General Ellis Spear* (Orono, Maine: University of Maine Press, 1997), 214; Alfred Apted Diary; OR, vol. 27, pt. 1, 613–15.

18. OR, vol. 27, pt. 1, 615.
19. Parker, *History of the Twenty-Second Massachusetts,* 326–27.
20. OR, vol. 27, pt. 3, 255.
21. Newell, *Ours,* 218; Britton and Reed, *To My Beloved Wife,* 103; Rosenblatt, *Hard Marching Every Day,* 110.

JUNE 22

1. OR, vol. 27, pt. 3, 913.
2. OR, vol. 27, pt. 3, 914; Nye, *Here Come the Rebels,* 267.

    For some reason, Early's division did not take the road to Emmitsburg, instead opting to march through Greenwood and Cashtown.
3. Freeman, *Lee,* vol. 3, 42–43.
4. Coles, *Fourth Alabama,* 101; Ware journal.
5. Silver, *A Life for the Confederacy,* 151; OR, vol. 27, pt. 2, 371; Lohr, *Old First Virginia,* 35.
6. OR, vol. 27, pt. 2, 464, 491; Nye, *Here Come the Rebels,* 147; Early, *Autobiographical Sketch,* 254; Malone, *Whipt 'Em,* 83; Hale and Phillips, *Forty–ninth Virginia,* 72.
7. Samuel Pickens Diary; Leon, *Diary of a Tar Heel,* 32; OR, vol. 27, pt. 2, 551; Hoke, *The Great Invasion,* 124–26; Haskell Monroe, "The Road to Gettysburg" *North Carolina Historical Review,* (October 1959), 512.

    The movement north effectively ended Jenkins's cavalry raids through the area. The area's losses may have been between $100,000 and $250,000. Some of the losses were indirect, such as the crops not harvested when Jenkins removed the farm horses (Coddington, *Gettysburg Campaign,* 162).
8. Harry Lewis letter (June 22, 1863), SHC, UNC; OR, vol. 27, pt. 2, 613.
9. Davis, *Boy Colonel,* 283; James McElvany Diary.
10. OR, vol. 27, pt. 3, 254, 263.
11. OR, vol. 27, pt. 3, 264.
12. OR, vol. 27, pt. 3, 263.
13. OR, vol. 27, pt. 3, 258.
14. Hoke, *The Great Invasion,*130.

    Jacob Hoke insisted that a person dressed as a woman in mourning walking about Chambersburg was really a Confederate soldier gaining information about the Federal troops occupying the town (Hoke, *The Great Invasion,* 123).
15. Hoke, *The Great Invasion,* 127–29.

    Not all of Knipe's troops got on the train. In the confusion, half a battalion of the 71st New York Militia was left behind. They ultimately marched toward Carlisle, until another train arrived to take them the rest of the way.
16. OR, vol. 27, pt. 1, 55.
17. Mattocks, *Unspoiled Heart,* 41; Sulliken, *Rebel Yell and Yankee Hurrah,* 96.
18. OR, vol. 27, pt. 1, 616; Samuel Keene Diary.
19. Newell, *Ours,* 218; Britton and Reed, *To My Beloved Wife,* 104.
20. Heller Diary.

JUNE 23

1. OR, vol. 27, pt. 2, 297.
2. OR, vol. 27, pt. 3, 923.
3. OR, vol. 27, pt. 3, 924–25; OR, vol. 27, pt. 2, 297.

Lee also wanted Generals Bragg and Buckner to invade Kentucky and General Samuel Jones to attack the enemy in southwestern Virginia.

4. Ware journal.

5. OR, vol. 27, pt. 2, 366; Silver, *A Life for the Confederacy,* 151; OR, vol. 27, pt. 2, 358.

6. Anonymous 1st Maryland journal; Stone letter; McKim, *A Soldier's Recollections,* 163; Buswell letter.

   Marching north, they passed through Filmertown [Funkstown], which Samuel Firebaugh of the 10th Virginia (Steuart's brigade) noted was "renowned for its ugly women."

7. OR, vol. 27, pt. 2, 464; Hale and Phillips, *Forty-ninth Virginia,* 72.

8. Samuel Pickens Diary; Jacob Hoke, *The Great Invasion,* 134–35.

9. OR, vol. 27, pt. 2, 613; Riley, *Grandfather's Journal,* 146; Foote, "Marching In Clover"; Harry Lewis letter.

10. Davis, *Boy Colonel,* 283; Diary of George Washington Hall, Library of Congress.

11. OR, vol. 27, pt. 3, 269–70, 273, 277.

12. OR, vol. 27, pt. 3, 272, 275, 278.

13. Hoke, *The Great Invasion,* 132–34.

14. OR, vol. 27, pt. 3, 277, 278.

15. Mattocks, *Unspoiled Heart,* 41.

16. George Ervay Diary; Samuel Keene Diary.

17. OR, vol. 27, pt. 3, 273.

18. Louise W. Hitz, ed. *The Letters of Frederick C. Winkler* (Privately printed, 1963), 63.

JUNE 24

1. OR, vol. 27, pt. 3, p. 927.

   Despite these very clear orders, Robertson never stirred from Virginia to aid Lee's infantrymen in Pennsylvania.

2. OR, vol. 27, pt. 2, 358.

3. Lippitt journal; Gregory, *Thirty-eighth Virginia,* 35; Davis F. Riggs, *Seventh Virginia Infantry* (Lynchburg, Va.: H. E. Howard, 1982), 22.

4. Mitchell journal; OR, vol. 27, pt. 2, 366; Ware journal; Coles, *Fourth Alabama,* 101; Captain D. U. Barziza diary, Southern Historical Collection, University of North Carolina.

5. Reidenbaugh, *Thirty-third Virginia Infantry,* 69; Firebaugh journal; Sheeran, *Confederate Chaplain,* 24.

6. Charles Batchelor letter, copy in Brake Collection, USAMHI; Armstrong, *Twenty-fifth Virginia,* 61; Thomas Rankin, *Twenty-Third Virginia* (Lynchburg, Va.: H.E. Howard, Inc., 1985), 63.

7. OR, vol. 27, pt. 2, 464; Malone, *Whipt 'Em,* 83–84; Hale and Phillips, *Forty-ninth Virginia,* 72–73; Nye, *Here Come the Rebels,* 268.

8. OR, vol. 27, pt. 2, 551; Samuel Pickens Diary; Hoke, *The Great Invasion,* 135–43.

   Jacob Hoke observed a "thin, sallow-faced man, with strongly-marked Southern features, and a head and physiognomy which strongly indicated culture, refinement, and genius" emerging from a carriage. General Richard Ewell had arrived in Chambersburg. He immediately ordered all liquor secured to prevent it from falling into his troops' hands. This materially reduced the problems that the local citizens faced (Hoke, *The Great Invasion,* 136, 137–38).

9. OR, vol. 27, pt. 2, 565–66; Nye, *Here Come the Rebels,* 259.

10. OR, vol. 27, pt. 2, 613; Riley, *Grandfather's Journal,* 146.

11. George Hall Diary.

12. OR, vol. 27, pt. 1, 55.

13. OR, vol. 27, pt. 3, 285, 288, 296.

    This desperate measure was caused in part by the fact that Halleck had stripped the capital of troops—four brigades had been sent to Hooker and another 10,000 to Dix on the Virginia peninsula (Coddington, *Gettysburg Campaign,* 98–99).

14. Hoke, *The Great Invasion,* 148–49.

15. Hoke, *The Great Invasion,* 140–42.

16. OR, vol. 27, pt. 3, 291, 299.

17. Matthews, *149th Pennsylvania,* 72–73.

18. Holcombe, *First Minnesota,* 313; Cowtan, *Services of the Tenth New York Volunteers,* 201.

    General Alexander Hays eventually replaced French and commanded the division during the battle of Gettysburg.

19. George Ervay Diary; Samuel Keene Diary; William Crennell Diary; Alfred Apted Diary; Brooks, "Memories of War."

20. M. D. Hardin, *History of the Twelfth Regiment, Pennsylvania Reserve Volunteer Corps* (New York: M. D. Hardin, 1890), 140; Nesbitt, *35 Days to Gettysburg,* 103.

21. Rosenblatt, *Hard Marching Every Day,* 111; Roe, *Tenth Massachusetts,* 202.

22. OR, vol. 27, pt. 3, 285; Priest, *John McMahon's Diary,* 51; Schildt, *Roads to Gettysburg,* 180–81; Coddington, *Gettysburg Campaign,* 121.

    Private Stephen Wallace indicated in his diary that march orders arrived at noon, and the march of Barlow's division began at 1:30 p.m.

23. Robert Cruikshank Diary, copy in Brake Collection, USAHMI; Morhous, *Reminiscences of the 123rd New York,* 44–45.

JUNE 25

1. OR, vol. 27, pt. 3, 933, 938.

2. OR, pt. 1, 314; Nye, *Here Come the Rebels,* 314–15.

3. Schildt, *Roads to Gettysburg,* 232–33.

4. Ware journal; Mitchell journal; Coles, *Fourth Alabama,* 101–2; Everson and Simpson, *Far, Far From Home,* 249; Nesbitt, *35 Days to Gettysburg,* 114; Silver, *A Life for the Confederacy,* 152.

   The men marched through parts of Virginia that Lincoln had annexed into the Union as West Virginia on June 20.

5. Lippitt journal; Dooley, *John Dooley,* 96; Hamilton, *Shotwell Papers,* vol. 1, 488; Young, *Fifty-sixth Virginia,* 78; Richard Irby, *Historical Sketch of the Nottoway Grays* (Richmond: J. W. Ferguson and Son, 1878), 27; William N. Wood, *Reminiscences of Big I* (Charlottesville, Va.: Michie Company, 1909), 42.

6. Samuel Pickens Diary; Firebaugh journal; Anonymous 1st Maryland journal.

7. OR, vol. 27, pt. 2, 464–65; Early, *Autobiographical Sketch,* 255.

8. OR, vol. 27, pt. 2, 613; Johnson; Foote, "Marching in Clover."

9. George Hall Diary; James McElvany Diary; Littlejohn, "Recollections of a Confederate Soldier"; Caldwell, *Brigade of South Carolinians,* 92.

10. OR, vol. 27, pt. 3, 305–6, 307, 315–16; Coddington, *Gettysburg Campaign,* 122.

11. OR, vol. 27, pt. 1, 57.

12. OR, vol. 27, pt. 3, 324, 325.

13. OR, vol. 27, pt. 3, 327, 328.

14. OR, vol. 27, pt. 3, 330–31.

15. OR, vol. 27, pt. 3, 331–32.

16. John Irvin Diary, copy in Brake Collection, USAMHI; Small, *16th Maine*, 114; Smith, *The 76th New York*, 229; James Hart Diary; Davis, *Three Years in the Army*, 217; Matthews, *149th Pennsylvania*, 73.

17. Ernest L. Waitt, *History of the Nineteenth Regiment Massachusetts Volunteer Infantry* (Salem, Mass.: Salem Press Company, 1906), 215; Thomas Keppler, *History of the Three Months and Three Years' Service: Fourth Regiment Ohio* (Cleveland: Leader Printing Company, 1886), 122; Muffly, ed. *Story of Our Regiment*, 458; Holcombe, *First Minnesota*, 314–15.

18. Ward, *History of the 106th Pennsylvania*, 174–75, 176; J. Favill, *Diary of a Young Officer* (Chicago: R. R. Donnelly & Sons, 1909), 240; Holcombe, *First Minnesota*, 317; Wayne Mahood, *Written in Blood* (Hightstown, N.J.: Longstreet House, 1997), 109; Cowtan, *Services of the Tenth New York* , 202–3.

19. Mattocks, *Unspoiled Heart*, 42; Sulliken, *Rebel Yell and Yankee Hurrah*, 96; Haynes, *History of the Second New Hampshire*, 134–35; Marbaker, *History of the Eleventh New Jersey*, 87; The Civil War Diary of Wyman S. White, copy in Brake Collection, USAMHI; Bardeen, *Little Fifer's War Diary*, 211; Asa W. Bartlett, *History of the Twelfth Regiment, New Hampshire Volunteers in the War of the Rebellion* (Concord, N.H.: Ira C. Evans, Printer, 1897), 116; P. Regis de Trobriand, *Four Years With the Army of the Potomac* (Boston: Ticknor and Company, 1889), 521.

    Charles Bardeen of Carr's brigade considered this to be one of the hardest marches made in the campaign (the other two were on June 12 and 15).

20. George Ervay Diary; Samuel Keene Diary; Alfred Apted Diary; William Crennell Diary.

21. Nesbitt, *35 Days to Gettysburg*, 113; Adoniram J. Warner Account, Pennsylvania Save the Flags Collection, USAMHI.

22. Rosenblatt, *Hard Marching Every Day*, 112.

23. Pula, *The Sigel Regiment*, 154; Wallace Diary; Priest, *John McMahon's Diary*, 51.

24. OR, vol. 27, pt. 1, 798; Spencer Jansen Diary, Copy in 137th New York folder, GNMP.

JUNE 26

1. Nye, *Here Come the Rebels*, 301.

    The close relationship between Generals Lee and Longstreet continued. They usually camped near each other and conferred on a regular basis. Lt. Col. Arthur Fremantle wrote, "Longstreet is never far from General Lee, who relies very much upon his judgment. The relationship between him and Longstreet is quite touching—they are almost always together" (Jeffry Wert, *Longstreet*, 252; Walter L. Lord, ed. *The Fremantle Diary* (New York: Little, Brown and Company, 1954), 190, 198.

2. OR, vol. 27, pt. 2, 693.

3. OR, vol 27, pt. 2, 307; Hoke, *The Great Invasion*, 172–73; Schildt, *Roads to Gettysburg*, 233.

4. Lippitt journal; Thomas Pollack letter, Southern Historical Collection, University of North Carolina; Dooley, *John Dooley*, 96.

5. Silver, *A Life for the Confederacy*, 152; Ware journal; Calvin L. Collier, *They'll Do To Tie To!—The Story of the Third Regiment Arkansas Infantry* (Little Rock, Ark.: Civil War Roundtable Associates, 1988), 127; Augustus Dickert, *History of Kershaw's Brigade* (Newberry, S.C.: Elbert H. Hull Company, 1899), 230; Coles, *Fourth Alabama*, 102; OR, vol. 27, pt. 2, 371.

6. Gary J. Laine and Morris M. Penny, *Law's Brigade in the War Between the Union and the Confederacy* (Shippensburg, Pa.: White Mane Publishing Co., Inc., 1996), 71; Miles V. Smith, "Reminiscences of the Civil War," Civil War Miscellaneous Collection, USAMHI, 34–35; Jno. W. Stevens, *Reminiscences of the Civil War* (Hillsboro, Tex.: Hillsboro Mirror Print, 1902), 106.

7. Smith, "Reminiscences," 34–35; Simpson, *Hood's Brigade*, 251.

8. Ware journal; Coles, *Fourth Alabama*, 102; Smith, "Reminiscences," 35.

9. OR, vol. 27, pt. 2, 366; Silver, *A Life for the Confederacy*, 152.

10. Monroe, "The Road To Gettysburg," p. 512; Samuel Pickens Diary; OR, vol. 27, pt. 2, 566; Schildt, *Roads to Gettysburg*, 223.

11. Anonymous 1st Maryland journal; Firebaugh journal; McKim, *A Soldier's Recollections*, 163, 165.

12. OR, vol. 27, pt. 2, 465; Malone, *Whipt 'Em*, 84.

13. OR, vol. 27, pt. 2, 465; Coddington, *The Gettysburg Campaign*, 166; Hoke, *The Great Invasion*, 170–71; Charles C. Osborne, *Jubal—The Life and Times of General Jubal A. Early, CSA* (Chapel Hill, N.C.: Algonquin Books, 1992), 181; Early, *Autobiographical Sketch*, 256.

Eminent modern historian Edwin Coddington called this act "rank insubordination" of Lee's General Orders No. 72. Riding past the smoldering ruins somewhat later, General Lee was visibly upset. He told an aide to distribute supplies to the now unemployed workers. Charles Osborne, Early's modern biographer, found no evidence that General Lee ever rebuked his subordinate.

14. OR, vol. 27, pt. 2, 465, 491; White, *History of the Thirty-first Georgia*, 85; Bradwell, "Crossing the Potomac," *Confederate Veteran Magazine*, vol. 30 (1922), 371.

The 26th Pennsylvania Militia had been mustering into service a few days before and was no match for these Southern veterans.

15. Nye, *Here Come the Rebels*, 277.

16. Paul M. Angle and Earl S. Miers, *Tragic Years, 1860–1865; A Documentary History of the American Civil War* (New York: Simon and Schuster, 1960), 630–31; Bradwell, "Crossing the Potomac," 371.

17. OR, vol. 27, pt. 2, 465–66; Early, *Autobiographical Sketch*, 258.

According to Jacob Hoke, Early asked for the following supplies: 60 barrels of flour, 7,000 pounds of bacon or pork, 1,200 pounds of sugar, 100 pounds of coffee, 1,000 pounds of salt, 40 bushels of onions, 1,000 pairs of shoes, 500 hats, or $10,000 in greenbacks (*The Great Invasion*, 171).

18. Hale and Phillips, *Forty-ninth Virginia*, 74.

19. Foote, "Marching In Clover"; OR, vol. 27, pt. 2, 613.

20. George Hall Diary; James McElvany Diary; Davis, *Boy Colonel*, 282–83.

21. OR, vol. 27, pt. 3, 314, 335, 336.

Unlike Hooker's two closely situated pontoon bridges, Lee's crossing points were miles apart at Williamsport and Shepherdstown, although his men did need to ford the stream. Another difference was that Hooker's men were not as enthusiastic as Lee's when crossing the river. They had been beaten again by their old adversary, who was again taking the war into their own homeland. This created a strong sense of concern among the men (Coddington, *Gettysburg Campaign*, 125–26).

22. OR, vol. 27, pt. 3, 333, 335.

23. OR, vol. 27, pt. 3, 344, 345; Nye, *Here Come the Rebels*, 272–73, 276; M. Jacobs, *Notes on the Rebel Invasion of Maryland and Pennsylvania and the Battle of Gettysburg* (Philadelphia: J. B. Lippincott & Company, 1864), 15.

24. Schildt, *Roads to Gettysburg*, 195.

25. OR, vol. 27, pt. 3, 344, 345.

26. OR, vol. 27, pt. 3, 347.

27. Davis, *Three Years in the Army*, 219; Nolan, *The Iron Brigade*, 229; Small, *16th Maine*, 114; Matthews, *149th Pennsylvania*, 73.

28. Charles A. Fuller, *Personal Recollections of the War of 1861: In the 61st New York Volunteer Infantry* (Sherburne, N.Y.: News Job Printing House, 1906), 91; Favill, *Diary of a Young Officer,* 240; William A. Child, *A History of the Fifth Regiment, New Hampshire Volunteers in the American Civil War* (Bristol, N.H.: R. W. Musgrove, Printer, 1893), 203.

29. Mattocks, *Unspoiled Heart,* 42; Sulliken, *Rebel Yell and Yankee Hurrah,* 97; OR, vol. 27, pt. 1, 542, 547; Bardeen, *Little Fifer's War Diary,* 211; Rauscher, *Music on the March,* 80; Jordan, *Red Diamond Regiment,* 65.

30. Alfred Apted Diary; George Ervay Diary; Pettit, *Diary of a Dead Man,* 148; William Read Diary, copy in the 118th Pennsylvania folder, GNMP; Samuel Keene Diary.

31. Nesbitt, *35 Days to Gettysburg,* 115; Hardin, *History of the Twelfth Pennsylvania Volunteers,*141; Bradley M. Gottfried, "Fisher's Brigade at Gettysburg: The Big Round Top Controversy," *Gettysburg Magazine,* number 19, 85–87.

    Because the division had been scattered around Washington, it was only now that the men realized that merely McCandless's First Brigade and Fisher's Third Brigade had joined the Army of the Potomac. Sickel's Second Brigade had been left behind because the military governor of Alexandria felt that he needed additional troops. The men were not happy about this turn of events.

32. Rosenblatt, *Hard Marching Every Day,* 112.

33. Newell, *Ours,* 219–20; Haines, *The Fifteenth New Jersey,* 75; Roe, *Tenth Massachusetts,* 203.

34. OR, vol. 27, pt. 3, 336; Simmers, *The Volunteer's Manual,* 27.

35. Wallace Diary; Smith, *107th Ohio,* 84; Henny Diary; Priest, *John McMahon's Diary,* 51; Andrew J. Boies, *Record of the Thirty-third Massachusetts Volunteer Infantry, from Aug. 1862 to Aug. 1865* (Fitchburg, Mass.: Sentinel Printing Company, 1880), 33; Pula, *The Sigel Regiment,* 155.

36. Wilson, *Seventh Ohio,* 252; OR, vol. 27, pt. 1, 798; John Storrs, *The Twentieth Connecticut* (Ansonia, Conn.: Press of the Naugatuck Valley Sentinel, 1886), 72; Brown, *History of the Twenty-Seventh Indiana,* 359–60; Charles L. English, "The Gettysburg Campaign of the 137th New York," copy in the Brake Collection, USAMHI.

JUNE 27

1. Samuel P. Bates, *History of Cumberland and Adams Counties* (Chicago, n.p., 1886), 119–22; Nye, *Here Come the Rebels,* 303–6.

2. OR, vol. 27, pt. 2, 307; OR, vol. 27, pt. 3, 943; Nye, *Here Come the Rebels,* 307–8.

3. Isaac Trimble, "The Campaign and Battle of Gettysburg," *Confederate Veteran Magazine,* vol. 25 (1917), 209–13.

4. OR, vol. 27, pt. 3, 942–43.

    John Schildt ranked the behavior of the Confederates, from best to worst as: Georgians, North Carolinians, Alabamians, South Carolinians, Texans, Louisianians, and Virginians. Schildt believed that Virginians were the worst because the hardships they had seen, or their families had experienced, in their home state (Schildt, *Roads to Gettysburg,* 397).

    Filching of hats was an ongoing problem. According to Jacob Hoke, the Confederate soldiers continually grabbed hats from civilians and crushed them into a unrecognizable condition before donning them. Hoke could not complain about the violence of the enemy. He knew of only one civilian who was killed during the invasion (Hoke, *The Great Invasion,* 176–77).

5. Charles Bachelor letter, copy in Brake Collection, USAHMI.

6. H. B. McClellan, *I Rode with Jeb Stuart: The Life and Campaigns of Major General J.E.B. Stuart* (Bloomington, Ind.: Indiana University Press, 1958), 323.

7. OR, vol. 27, pt. 3, 941–42.

8. Lippitt journal; Loving journal.

9. Henry L. Figures letter, copy in Brake Collection, USAMHI; Ware journal; Everson and Simpson, *Far, Far From Home,* 251; Coles, *Fourth Alabama,* 102.

10. Ware journal; Powell, "With Hood at Gettysburg"; Lord, *Fremantle Diary,* 191; W. C. Ward, "Incidents and Personal Experiences," *Confederate Veteran,* vol. 8 (1900), 345–46; West, *A Texan In Search of a Fight,* 90–92.

11. Mitchell journal; OR, vol. 27, pt. 2, 366, 371; "Some Incidents on the March to Gettysburg," copy in the 10th Georgia folder, GNMP.

12. Ware journal; Lord, *Fremantle Diary,* 189.

13. Monroe, "The Road To Gettysburg," 512; Manly W. Wellman, *Rebel Boast* (New York: Henry Holt and Co., 1956), 118; Samuel Pickens Diary; Schildt, *Roads to Gettysburg,* 265.

14. Pfanz, *Ewell,* 299.

15. Sheeran, *Confederate Chaplain,* 47–48; Thomas W. Brooks and Michael D. Jones, *Lee's Foreign Legion: A History of the 10th Louisiana Infantry* (Gravenhurst, Ont., Watts Printing, 1995), 46; Anonymous 1st Maryland journal; Firebaugh journal.

16. OR, vol. 27, pt. 2, 466; Malone, *Whipt 'Em,* 84; Hale and Phillips, *Forty-ninth Virginia,* 74.

17. Moore, *Rebellion Record,* vol. 7, 321.

18. Foote, "Marching in Clover"; Lightsey, *The Veteran's Story,* 34; OR, vol. 27, pt. 2, 613; Riley, *Grandfather's Journal,* 147–48; Francis P. Fleming, "Letters from Francis P. Fleming to His Brother," *The Florida Historical Quarterly,* vol. 27 (October 1949), 146; OR, vol. 27, pt. 2, 613.

19. Mills, *History of the 16th North Carolina,* 35; George Hall Diary; Samuel W. Hankins, *Simple Story of a Soldier* (Nashville: Confederate Veteran, n.d), 43; William D. Pender, *The General to his Lady* (Chapel Hill, N.C.: University of North Carolina Press, 1965), 254–55; A. J. Dula, "Civil War Incidents," Duke University Library.

20. Hoke, *The Great Invasion,* 238.

21. OR, vol. 27, pt. 3, 355–58.

22. OR, vol. 27, pt. 1, 59.

23. OR, vol. 27, pt. 1, 59, 60.

24. OR, vol. 27, pt. 1, 60.

25. OR, vol. 27, pt. 3, 358, 361, 363, 364.

26. OR, vol. 27, pt. 3, 353; Nye, *Here Come the Rebels,* 303–6.

    General Knipe, with his two regiments, briefly rallied about two miles south of Carlisle and decided to make a stand here. However, when he learned that two powerful Confederate divisions were approaching, he wisely pulled his men back to safety (Hoke, *The Great Invasion,* 173).

27. Small, *16th Maine,* 114; Davis, *Three Years in the Army,* 219; Matthews, *149th Pennsylvania,* 75; Tervis, *Fighting Fourteenth,* 78; Rufus R. Dawes, *Service with the Sixth Wisconsin Volunteers* (Marietta, Ohio: E. R. Alderman and Sons, 1890), 156–57.

28. Ward, *One Hundred and Sixth Pennsylvania,* 175–77; Fuller, *Personal Recollections of the War,* 91; Holcombe, *First Minnesota,* 318; Favill, *Diary of a Young Officer,* 241.

29. Sulliken, *Rebel Yell and Yankee Hurrah,* 97; Rauscher, *Music on the March,* 80; Marbaker, *Eleventh New Jersey,* 88; Mattocks, *Unspoiled Heart,* 43.

30. Samuel Keene Diary; George Ervay Diary.

31. Nesbitt, *35 Days to Gettysburg,* 121.

32. Rosenblatt, *Hard Marching Every Day,* 113; Haines, *The Fifteenth New Jersey,* 75; Britton and Reed, *To My Beloved Wife,* 106; Newell, *Ours,* 220.

33. Osborn, *Trials and Triumphs,* 89; Priest, *John McMahon's Diary,* 51; Heller Diary; Wallace Diary.

34. Edwin E. Marvin, *The Fifth Regiment, Connecticut Volunteers* (Hartford, Conn.: Wiley, Waterman & Eaton, 1899), 274; Storrs, *The Twentieth Connecticut,* 73; Cruickshank Diary; English, "Gettysburg Campaign of the 137th New York"; Morhous, *Reminiscences of the 123rd New York,* 45.

JUNE 28

1. Hoke, *The Great Invasion,* 207–8, 210, 213.

2. OR, vol. 27, pt. 2, 694; Nye, *Here Come the Rebels,* 318–19.

3. Hoke, *The Great Invasion,* 182–83; Nye, *Here Come the Rebels,* 331–32, 340–42.

   Some of Jenkins's men demanded the Federal flag flying over the public square, and one subsequently sat on top of it as he rode away (Hoke, *The Great Invasion,* 183).

4. Charles Marshall, "Events Leading Up to the Battle of Gettysburg," *SHSP,* vol. 23 (1895), 226–27; Longstreet, "Lee's Invasion of Pennsylvania," *Battles and Leaders of the Civil War,* vol. 3, 249–50.

   Edwin Coddington could not believe that Lee was surprised by Harrison's news as he knew on June 23 of pontoon bridges being built across the Potomac River. He did agree that General Robertson, who commanded two cavalry brigades, did not provide Lee with a continuous stream of information, as he should have. In response to Meade's leadership, Lee answered, "General Meade will commit no blunder in my front, and if I make one he will make haste to take advantage of it" (Coddington, *Gettysburg Campaign,* 182, 184; George Cary Eggleston, *A Rebel's Recollections* [New York: G. P. Putnam's Sons, 1905], 145–46).

5. William F. Shine Journal, N.C. Dept. of Archives and History; Everson and Simpson, *Far, Far From Home,* 252.

   Jacob Hoke took issue with some of the Confederate veterans who wrote that the U.S. flag floated from every building. Many were squirreled away so they would not be captured and desecrated by the enemy. Hoke indicated that many women wore miniature flags pinned to their chests (Hoke, *The Great Invasion,* 215).

6. OR, vol. 27, pt. 2, 366; Ware journal; OR, vol. 27, pt. 2, 358.

7. Lippitt journal; Gregory, *Thirty-eighth Virginia,* 36; David E. Johnston, *Four Years a Soldier* (Princeton, W.Va., n.p., 1887), 240.

8. OR, vol. 27, pt. 2, 551; Schildt, *Roads to Gettysburg,* 312; J. D. Hufham, "Gettysburg," *The Wake Forest Student,* vol. 16 (April 1897), 452; Clark, *N.C. Regiments,* vol. 2, 233.

   The Confederate troops apparently conducted these searches in a courteous manner (Schildt, *Roads to Gettysburg,* 312).

9. Glenn Tucker, *High Tide at Gettysburg: The Campaign in Pennsylvania* (Indianapolis: Bobbs-Merrill Company, 1968), 63.

10. Firebaugh journal; McKim, *A Soldier's Recollections,* 166; Anonymous 1st Maryland journal.

11. OR, vol. 27, pt. 2, 466, 491; Moore, *Rebellion Record,* vol. 7, 321; Gordon, *Reminiscences of the Civil War,* 143.

    General Gordon later insisted that as he rode through the town, a 12-year-old girl ran up to him with a bouquet of roses that contained a note with a full description of the enemy forces at Wrightsville.

12. Robert Stiles, *Four Years under Marse Robert* (New York: The Neale Publishing Company, 1903), 202–5; Driver, *Fifty-Second Virginia,* 39.

13. Clark, *N.C. Regiments,* 412; OR, vol. 27, pt. 2, 466; Malone, *Whipt 'Em,* 84.

14. OR, vol. 27, pt. 2, 466; Osborne, *Jubal,* 178.

15. OR, vol. 27, pt. 2, 466–67, 492.

The bridge, owned by the Columbia Bank, was 5,620 feet long, and cost $157,300 to build (Hoke, *The Great Invasion,* 189).

Helping to put out the blaze in Wrightsville must have been difficult for some of the Georgians, as Darien, Georgia, had recently been torched by Federal troops (Schildt, *Roads to Gettysburg,* 301).

16. OR, vol. 27, pt. 2, 467.

17. OR, vol. 27, pt. 2, 467; Early, *Autobiographical Sketch,* 261.

18. OR, vol. 27, pt. 2, 613; George Hall Diary.

19. OR, vol. 27, pt. 2, 613; George Hall Diary; McDaid, *Four Years of Arduous Service,* 204.

20. Welch, *A Confederate Surgeon's Letters,* 57–58.

21. OR, vol. 27, pt. 1, 61.

Hardie's experiences in Frederick were harrowing. Arriving about midnight, he found many of the soldiers drunk, and no one seemed to know Meade's location. Using money to loosen tongues, Hardie was finally able to locate Meade's camp (Schildt, *Roads to Gettysburg,* 288).

22. George Gordon Meade, *The Life and Letters of George Gordon Meade: Major-General United States* (New York: Charles Scribner's Sons, 1913), vol. 2, 1–13.

Meade, who had often despaired to his wife about not being elevated to army command, wrote to her, "it has pleased Almighty God to place me in the trying position that we have been talking about." Meade was not the first corps commander to be approached about taking over the army. General John Reynolds had been informally asked earlier in June, but he declined because of the lack of autonomy he would have.

Meade later testified, "my predecessor...left camp in a very few hours after I relieved him. I received from him no intimation of any plan, or any views that he may have had up to that moment, and I am not aware that he had any, but was waiting for the exigencies of the occasion to govern him, just as I had to do subsequently" (Hoke, *The Great Invasion,* 247–48).

23. OR, vol. 27, pt. 1, 61.

24. OR, vol. 27, pt. 3, 373–74.

25. OR, vol. 27, pt. 3, 374.

26. OR, vol. 27, pt. 1, 64.

27. OR, vol. 27, pt. 3, 384, 389; Nye, *Here Come the Rebels,* 282–93.

The militia numbered about 1,400 men; Gordon's about 1,800 (Busey and Martin, *Regimental Strengths and Losses,* 158).

28. George Soult Diary; Matthews, *149th Pennsylvania,* 75; Tervis, *Fighting Fourteenth,* 80; Chamberlin, *150th Pennsylvania,* 114, 115; Dawes, *Service with the Sixth Wisconsin,* 157–58.

29. H. P. Clare letter.

30. Ward, *One Hundred and Sixth Pennsylvania,* 175–77; OR, vol. 27, pt. 1, 367; Bradley M. Gottfried, *Stopping Pickett—The History of the Philadelphia Brigade* (Shippensburg, Pa.: White Mane Publishing Co., Inc., 1999), 151.

31. Mattocks, *Unspoiled Heart,* 44–45; Marbaker, *Eleventh New Jersey,* 89; Cornelius Van Santvood, *The One Hundred and Twentieth N.Y.S. Volunteers* (Rondout, N.Y.: Regimental Association & Kingston Freeman Press, 1894), 66; de Trobriand, *Four Years in the Army of the Potomac,* 521; Bardeen, *Little Fifer's War Diary,* 211.

During their march through these towns, the men were arranged in "column by companies."

32. Samuel Keene Diary; Alfred Apted Diary; William Read Diary; Joshua Wilbur Letter, copy in Brake Collection, USAHMI; Reese, *Sykes' Regular Infantry,* 234–35.

33. Nesbitt, *35 Days to Gettysburg*, 129.

34. Haines, *The Fifteenth New Jersey*, 79; Bowen, *The Thirty-Seventh Masachusetts*, 167; Britton and Reed, *To My Beloved Wife*, 106.

35. Rosenblatt, *Hard Marching Every Day*, 112; Bowen, *The Thirty-Seventh Masachusetts*, 167.

36. Priest, *John McMahon's Diary*, 51; Smith, *107th Ohio*, 84.

37. Simmers, *Volunteer Manual*, 28; Heller Diary; Wallace Diary.

38. Marvin, *The Fifth Connecticut*, 274; Alonzo H. Quint, *The Record of the Second Massachusetts Infantry* (Boston: James P. Walker, 1867), 177; *The 28th and 147th Pennsylvania at Gettysburg*, 4; Brown, *History of the Twenty-Seventh Indiana*, 361; Cruickshank Diary; Morhous, *Reminiscences of the 123rd New York*, 46.

39. Brown, *History of the Twenty-Seventh Indiana*, 360–61; Williams, *From the Cannon's Mouth*, 221; George K. Collins, *Memories of the 149th Regiment, New York Volunteer Infantry* (Syracuse, N.Y.: Author Published, 1891), 129.

JUNE 29

1. OR, vol. 27, pt. 3, 943, 944.

   Lee explained that the reason for the change in marching orders was to keep the corps on the east side of the mountains. Edwin Coddington believed that Lee also saw the wisdom of not marching his army along the same road toward Cashtown/Gettysburg (Coddington, *Gettysburg Campaign*, 189).

2. OR, vol. 27, pt. 2, 307.

3. OR, vol. 27, pt. 2, 201–3, 695.

4. OR, vol. 27, pt. 3, 947; Hoke, *The Great Invasion*, 199, 200–203.

5. Loving journal; Lippitt journal; John E. Divine, *Eighth Virginia* (Lynchburg, Va.: H. E. Howard, Inc., 1983), 20.

6. Ware journal; Silver, *A Life for the Confederacy*, 152.

7. Pfanz, *Ewell*, 301.

8. Samuel Pickens Diary; Chapala, *Forty-eighth Virginia*, 57; McKim, *A Soldier's Recollections*, 167.

9. OR, vol. 27, pt. 2, 467; Hale and Phillips, *Forty-ninth Virginia*, 72.

   Early was right, and before long the total-war policies against civilians would only worsen.

10. OR, vol. 27, pt. 2, 467; Pfanz, *Ewell*, 303.

11. "James McElvany Diary"; McDaid, *Four Years of Arduous Service*, 205.

12. OR, vol. 27, pt. 2, 613; Riley, *Grandfather's Journal*, 147.

13. Caldwell, *Brigade of South Carolinians*, 93–94.

14. OR, vol. 27, pt. 1, 67; OR, vol. 27, pt. 3, 375.

    Meade found time to write his wife on June 29. Colonel Hardie apparently told Meade prior to giving him the written order that he had come "to give me trouble." He also wrote, "it appears to be God's will for some good purpose" (Schildt, *Roads to Gettysburg*, 370–71).

15. OR, vol. 27, pt. 3, 398, 399.

16. Nye, *Here Come the Rebels*, 322.

    Stahel was ordered to report for duty to General Couch (OR, vol. 27, pt. 3, 373). General Buford was disgusted to learn that he missed an opportunity to attack two detached Confederate infantry regiments because the local citizens were too afraid to tell him that they were nearby (O.R. vol. 27, pt. 1, 926).

17. OR, vol. 27, pt. 3, 407–8, 409.

18. OR, vol. 27, pt. 3, 408, 409.

19. Coddington, *Gettysburg Campaign,* 173–74.

20. OR, vol. 27, pt. 3, 412.

21. Matthews, *149th Pennsylvania,* 75; Chamberlin, *150th Pennsylvania,* 1115; Davis, *Three Years in the Army,* 221; Smith, *The 76th New York,* 232.

22. OR, vol. 27, pt. 1, 367; OR, vol. 27, pt. 3, 396; Jacob H. Cole, *Under Five Commanders* (Patterson, N.J.: News Printing Company, 1906), 188; Fuller, *Personal Recollections of the War,* 91; Benjamin W. Thompson, "Recollections of War Times," Civil War Times Illustrated Collection, USAMHI; William Lochren, "The First Minnesota at Gettysburg," Minnesota MOLLUS, vol. 3, 45.

23. Frederick, *The Story of a Regiment,* 164; Baxter, *The Gallant Fourteenth,* 148–49; Wilson Paxton Diary, Civil War Miscellaneous Collection, USAMHI; Cowtan, *Services of the Tenth New York,* 203.

    General Alexander Hays, who commanded a newly arrived brigade, assumed command of the Third Division. Colonel George Willard took over Hays's brigade (Cowtan, *Services of the Tenth New York Volunteers,* 202).

24. Sulliken, *Rebel Yell and Yankee Hurrah,* 98; Mattocks, *Unspoiled Heart,* 45; Jordan, *Red Diamond Regiment,* 67; Hays, *Under the Red Patch,* 191; Haynes, *History of the Second New Hampshire,* 165; Marbaker, *Eleventh New Jersey,* 90.

25. Jordan, *Red Diamond Regiment,* 68.

26. George Ervay Diary; Samuel Keene Diary; Alfred Apted Diary; Anonymous 1st Michigan Diary, copy in 1st Michigan folder, GNMP.

    According to John Schildt, the V Corps could not begin the march at an earlier hour because of the late start of the II Corps, which it was to follow (Schildt, *Roads to Gettysburg,* 414).

27. OR, vol. 17, pt. 1, 595; Nesbitt, *35 Days to Gettysburg,* 135; Hardin, *History of the Twelfth Pennsylvania Volunteers,* 143.

28. Roe, *Tenth Massachusetts,* 204; Haines, *Fifteenth New Jersey,* 79; Newell, *Ours,* 220.

29. Bowen, *The Thirty-Seventh Masachusetts,* 169–70; Rosenblatt, *Hard Marching Every Day,* 113.

30. Smith, *107th Ohio,* 85; Heller Diary; Priest, *John McMahon's Diary,* 53; Wallace Diary.

31. Wilson, *Seventh Ohio,* 253; Collins, *Memories of the 149th New York,* 130–31; Spencer Jansen Diary; Cruickshank Diary; Brown, *History of the Twenty-Seventh Indiana,* 362–63.

JUNE 30

1. Lee suspected that a battle would be fought at Cashtown or Gettysburg, so his order for Rodes's and Early's divisions (II Corps) to march to Heidlersburg was a good one, for it was equidistant between the two towns (Coddington, *Gettysburg Campaign,* 191).

2. OR, vol. 27, pt. 2, 695–96.

    This was the period when Lee sorely missed his cavalry. While he did have the services of Imboden's, Jenkins's, and Robertson's brigades, they were not effective in ascertaining the enemy's location.

3. Nye, *Here Come the Rebels,* 324–25.

    Stuart took time at Jefferson to parole many of the prisoners.

4. OR, vol. 27, pt. 3, 951.

5. Mitchell journal; Ware journal; OR, vol. 27, pt. 2, 358; Silver, *A Life for the Confederacy,* 152; Thomas L. McCarty, "Battle of Gettysburg July 1st 2 & 3 1863," copy in Brake Collection, USAMHI.

    According to Jacob Hoke, these two divisions were in such a hurry to get to Fayetteville that they often left the roads and traveled cross-country (Hoke, *The Great Invasion,* 204).

6. OR, vol. 27, pt. 2, 358; Coles, *Fourth Alabama*, 103.

7. Ralph W. Gunn, *Twenty-fourth Virginia* (Lynchburg, Va.: H. E. Howard, Inc., 1987), 43; Robertson, *Eighteenth Virginia*, 20.

Not everyone believed that the Confederates should treat the Northern civilians with such respect. According to Randolph Shotwell, "we cannot hope to whip the Yankees until we touch their pockets seriously, and this cannot be done by merely killing their men, who are chiefly hirelings—but by destroying their property" (Hamilton, *Shotwell Papers,* vol. 1, 496).

8. Anonymous 1st Maryland journal; Firebaugh journal; John Garibaldi letter, VMI Library.

9. Monroe, "The Road To Gettysburg," 513; William Calder letter, copy in Brake Collection, USAMHI; Clark, *N.C. Regiments,* vol. 2, 234; J. M. Thompson, "Reminiscences of the Autauga Rifles," copy in 12th Alabama folder, GNMP; Col. Risden T. Bennett Recollections, copy in 14th North Carolina folder, GNMP.

Some of the men with relatives in Carlisle were tempted to remain behind, but there is no record that any succumbed.

10. OR, vol. 27, pt. 2, 467; Nye, *Here Come the Rebels,* 360–61.

11. Clark, *N.C. Regiments,* vol. 2, 342–43; Jacobs, *Notes on the Rebel Invasion,* 21; Henry Heth, *The Memoirs of Henry Heth* (Westport, Conn.: Greenwood Press, 1974), 173; David Martin, *Gettysburg—July 1* (Conshohocken, Pa.: Combined Books, 1996), 25–27.

12. Henry Heth, "Letter From Major General Henry Heth of A. P. Hill's Corps, A.N.V." *Southern Historical Society Papers,* vol. 4 (1877), p. 157; Heth, *Memoirs,* 173; Clark, *N.C. Regiments,* vol. 5, 116.

13. Riley, *Grandfather's Journal,* 148; Fleming, "Letters From Francis P. Fleming to His Brother," 145.

14. OR, vol. 27, pt. 1, 68–69; Coddington, *Gettysburg Campaign,* 237.

Meade indicated in this dispatch that two units new to the army, the Pennsylvania Reserve division and Lockwood's brigade (XII Corps), could not keep up with the veterans. Meade moved his headquarters from the Middleburg area to Taneytown.

15. OR, vol. 27, pt. 3, 415.

16. OR, vol. 27, pt. 3, 414–15.

17. Nye, *Here Come the Rebels,* 322–23.

18. Ibid., 348–56.

19. OR, vol. 27, pt. 3, 429, 432, 437–38.

20. Matthews, *149th Pennsylvania,* 76; Smith, *The 76th New York,* 233; John Irvin Diary; Davis, *Three Years in the Army,* 223; Edwin F. Palmer, *The Second Brigade or Camp Life* (Montpelier, Vt.: Printed by E. P. Walton, 1864), 175; Schildt, *Roads to Gettysburg,* 405.

21. Cole, *Under Five Commanders,* 189.

22. Sulliken, *Rebel Yell and Yankee Hurrah,* 99; Mattocks, *Unspoiled Heart,* 46; Wyman White Diary; Marbaker, *Eleventh New Jersey,* 90.

23. OR, vol. 27, pt. 3, 420.

24. Charles Bowen Diary; Jonathan B. Hager, "Civil War Memoirs," University of Virginia; Porter, *Under the Maltese Cross,* 153; Chilion Lukens letter, Duke University Library; Alfred Apted Diary; OR, vol. 27, pt. 1, 1065; Reese, *Sykes' Regular Infantry,* 237–38; Hoadley Horford Diary, copy in 44th New York folder, GNMP; Brian A. Bennett, *Sons of Old Monroe: A Regimental History of Patrick O'Rorke's 140th New York Volunteer* (Dayton, Ohio: Morningside House, Inc., 1992), 198.

25. Nesbitt, *35 Days to Gettysburg,* 139; Hardin, *History of the Twelfth Pennsylvania,* 144.

26. Rosenblatt, *Hard Marching Every Day*, 113; Britton and Reed, *To My Beloved Wife*, 106; Roe, *Tenth Massachusetts*, 204; Bowen, *The Thirty-Seventh Masachusetts*, 170–71.

27. Smith, *107th Ohio*, 85, 86; Heller Diary; Pula, *The Sigel Regiment*, 157.

28. Warren W. Packer Diary, Connecticut State Library; Samuel Toombs, *Reminiscences of the War* (Orange, N.J.: Printed at the Journal Office, 1878), 71–72; English, "Gettysburg Campaign of the 137th New York"; Morhous, *Reminiscences of the 123rd New York*, 46–47; Cruickshank Diary; Storrs, *The Twentieth Connecticut*, 76–77.

JULY 1

1. OR, vol. 27, pt. 2, 696; Nye, *Here Come the Rebels*, 325–26.

2. OR, vol. 27, pt. 2, 366; Ware journal; William J. Fluker, "An Account of the Battle of Little Round Top Hill at Gettysburg," copy in 15th Georgia folder, GNMP.

3. Johnson, *Four Years a Soldier*, 243; Norbonne Berkeley, "Gettysburg," copy in 8th Virginia folder, GNMP.

   According to Jacob Hoke, Pickett's men did not set the shops on fire because they were afraid that nearby buildings would also burn (Hoke, *The Great Invasion*, 204–5).

4. Coddington, *Gettysburg Campaign*, 193–94.

5. Samuel Pickens Diary; Leon, *Diary of a Tar Heel*, 34; Diary of James E. Green, copy in Brake Collection, USAMHI.

6. OR, vol. 27, pt. 2, 467.

7. Goldsborough, "With Lee at Gettysburg," *Philadelphia Record*, July 8, 1900; Stone letter; Firebaugh journal; Anonymous 1st Maryland journal.

8. James McElvany Diary; OR, vol. 27, pt. 2, 613; Foote, "Marching in Clover."

9. OR, vol. 27, pt. 3, 458–59.

10. OR, vol. 27, pt. 3, 461–67.

11. Small, *The 16th Maine*, 116; Smith, *The 76th New York*, 235; Matthews, *149th Pennsylvania*, 78.

12. John W. Plummer Letter, *The Minnesota State Atlas*, August 26, 1863; Cowtan, *Services of the Tenth New York*, 205.

13. John W. Plummer Letter.

14. OR, vol. 27, pt. 1, 502; Bardeen, *Little Fifer's War Diary*, 216; Mattocks, *Unspoiled Heart*, 46; Sulliken, *Rebel Yell and Yankee Hurrah*, 100.

    deTrobriand deployed his men around St. Joseph's Catholic School for girls.

15. OR, vol. 27, pt. 1, 482; Charles H. Weygant, *History of the One Hundred and Twenty-Fourth Regiment, N.Y.S.V.* (Newburgh, N.Y.: Journal Printing House, 1877), 172; Wyman White Diary; OR, vol. 27, pt. 1, 497, 500, 531; Ladd and Ladd, Clark Baldwin Account, *Bachelder Papers*, vol. 1, 191; Bradley M. Gottfried, *Brigades of Gettysburg*, vol. 1, (ms).

16. Pettit, *Diary of a Dead Man*, 150; Survivor's Association, *History of the One Hundred and Eighteenth Pennsylvania*, 233.

17. James Houghton Journal, Bentley Library, University of Michigan; Chilion Lukens Letter; MacNamara, *History of the Ninth Massachusetts Volunteers*, 314.

18. Porter, *Under the Maltese Cross*, 155, 156; Samuel Keene Diary; George Ervay Diary; Theodore Gerrish, *Army Life; A Private's Reminiscences of the Civil War* (Portland, Maine: Hoyt, Fogg & Donham, 1882), 101; Chilion Lukens Letter; Joshua Wilbur letter; Barrett *Reminiscences, Incidents, and Battles of the Old Fourth Michigan*, 21–22.

19. Bowen, *The Thirty-Seventh Massachusetts*, 171–72; Newell, *Ours*, 221; Penrose G. Mark, *Red: White: and Blue Badge: A History of the 93rd Regiment* (Harrisburg, Pa.: The Aughinbaugh Press, 1911), 213; Britton and Reed, *To My Beloved Wife*, p. 106.

20. Bowen, *The Thirty-Seventh Masachusetts,* 172; Britton and Reed, *To My Beloved Wife,* 107; Elisha Hunt Rhodes, *All for the Union* (Lincoln, R.I.: A. Mowbray, 1985), 115; Morse, *Personal Experiences,* 34.

21. Pula, *The Sigel Regiment,* 160; OR, vol. 27, pt. 1, 700; Smith, *107th Ohio,* 86, 87. Barlow's trek was a slow one as the roads were rutted and rocky and partially blocked by the I Corps wagons.

22. OR, vol. 27, pt. 1, 825; Morhous, *Reminiscences of the 123rd New York,* 47; Wilson, *Seventh Ohio,* 253; *Pennsylvania at Gettysburg,* vol. 1; vol. 2, 568; William Henry Tallman Recollections, copy in Brake Collection, USAMHI.

JULY 2

1. OR, vol. 27, pt. 2, 366.

2. Coles, *Fourth Alabama,* 103; James Longstreet, *From Manassas to Appomattox* (Philadelphia, J. B. Lippincott, 1903), 365.

3. Lippitt journal; Loving journal; Gunn, *Twenty-fourth Virginia,* 43; Wallace, *First Virginia,* 42.

4. Galway, *The Valiant Hours,* 101.

5. Sulliken, *Rebel Yell and Yankee Hurrah,* 100–101; Jordan, *Red Diamond Regiment,* 70; Theodore, Garrish, *Army Life,* 99.

6. Samuel Keene Diary; Charles Bowen Diary; Reese, *Sykes' Regular Infantry,* 239; MacNamara, *History of the Ninth Massachusetts,* 318.

7. Woodbury, *Second Rhode Island,* 194; Bowen, *The Thirty-Seventh Masachusetts,* 172–73.

8. Bowen, *The Thirty-Seventh Massachusetts,* 173; Britton and Reed, *To My Beloved Wife,* 107.

9. Ibid., 174.

10. Ibid., 174.

11. Ibid., 174–75; Haines, *The Fifteenth New Jersey,* 79.

Bibliography

Angle, Paul McClelland, and Earl Schenck Miers. *Tragic Years, 1860–1865; A Documentary History of the American Civil War.* New York: Simon and Schuster, 1960.

Armstrong, Richard L. *Twenty-fifth Virginia Infantry and Ninth Virginia Infantry.* Lynchburg, Va.: H. E. Howard, Inc., 1990.

Barclay, Ted. *Ted Barclay, Liberty Hall Volunteers: Letters from the Stonewall Brigade (1861–1864).* Natural Bridge Station, Va.: Rockbridge Publishing Co., 1992.

Bardeen, Charles W. *A Little Fifer's War Diary.* Syracuse: C. W. Bardeen, Publisher, 1910.

Barrett, O. S. *Reminiscences, Incidents, and Battles of the Old Fourth Michigan Infantry in the War of the Rebellion, 1861–1864.* Detroit: W. S. Ostler, 1888.

Bartlett, Asa W. *History of the Twelfth Regiment, New Hampshire Volunteers in the War of the Rebellion.* Concord, N.H.: Ira C. Evans, Printer, 1897.

Bates, Samuel P. *History of Cumberland and Adams Counties.* Chicago, n.p., 1886.

———. *History of Pennsylvania Volunteers, 1861–5.* Wilmington, N.C.: Broadfoot Publishing Co., 1993.

Baxter, Nancy Niblack. *Gallant Fourteenth: The Story of an Indiana Civil War Regiment.* Traverse City, Mich.: Pioneer Study Center Press, 1980.

274

Bennett, Brian A. *Sons of Old Monroe: A Regimental History of Patrick O'Rorke's 140th New York Volunteers.* Dayton, Ohio: Morningside House, Inc., 1992.

Bilby, Joseph G. *Remember Fontenoy! The 69th New York and the Irish Brigade in the Civil War.* Hightstown, N.J.: Longstreet House, 1995.

Blake, Henry N. *Three Years in the Army of the Potomac.* Boston: Lee and Shepard, 1865.

Blue, True. "From the 140th Interesting Particulars of the Late Fight." *Rochester Evening Express,* July 11, 1963.

Boies, Andrew J. *Record of the Thirty-third Massachusetts Volunteer Infantry, from Aug. 1862 to Aug. 1865.* Fitchburg, Mass.: Sentinel Printing Company, 1880.

Bowen, George A. "The Diary of Captain George A. Bowen, 12th New Jersey Volunteers." *The Valley Forge Journal,* vol. 2 (June, 1984).

Bowen, James L. *History of the Thirty-Seventh Regiment, Mass., Volunteers, in the Civil War of 1861–1865.* Holyoke, Mass.: C. W. Bryan & Company, 1884.

Bradwell, Isaac. "Crossing the Potomac, *Confederate Veteran Magazine,* vol. 30 (1922): 371.

Britton, Ann H., and Thomas Reed. *To My Beloved Wife and Boy at Home.* Madison, N.J.: Fairleigh Dickinson University Press, 1997.

Brooks, Thomas W., and Michael D. Jones. *Lee's Foreign Legion: A History of the 10th Louisiana Infantry.* Gravenhurst, Ont.: Watts Printing, 1995.

Brown, Edmund R. *The Twenty-Seventh Indiana Volunteer Infantry in the War of the Rebellion.* Monticello, Ind.: n.p., 1899.

Busey, John W., and David G. Martin. *Regimental Strengths and Losses at Gettysburg.* Hightstown, N.J.: Longstreet House, 1994.

Caldwell, J. F. J. *The History of a Brigade of South Carolinians.* Marietta, Ga.: Continental Book Company, 1951.

Casler, John O. *Four Years in the Stonewall Brigade.* Marietta, Ga.: Continental Book Co., 1951.

Chapla, John D. *The Forty-Second Virginia Infantry.* Lynchburg, Va.: H. E. Howard, Inc., 1983.

Chapla, John. *The Forty-Eighth Virginia Infantry.* Lynchburg, Va.: H. E. Howard, Inc., 1989.

Chamberlin, Thomas. *History of the One Hundred and Fiftieth Regiment Pennsylvania Volunteers, Second Regiment, Bucktail Brigade.* Philadelphia: J. B. Lippincott Co., 1895.

Child, William A. *A History of the Fifth Regiment, New Hampshire Volunteers in the American Civil War.* Bristol, N.H.: R. W. Musgrove, Printer, 1893.

Clark, Walter, ed. *Histories of the Several Regiments and Battalions from North Carolina, in the Great War, 1861–'65.* 5 vols. Raleigh, N.C.: E. M. Uzzell, Printer, 1901.

Coddington, Edwin B. *The Gettysburg Campaign: A Study in Command.* New York: Charles Scribner's Sons, 1968.

Cole, Jacob H. *Under Five Commanders.* Patterson, N.J.: News Printing Company, 1906.

Coles, R. T. *From Huntsville to Appomattox: R.T. Coles's History of 4th Regiment, Alabama Volunteer Infantry, C.S.A., Army of Northern Virginia.* Knoxville, Tenn.: University of Tennessee Press, 1996.

Collier, Calvin L. *"They'll Do To Tie To!"—The Story of the Third Regiment Arkansas Infantry, C.S.A.* Little Rock, Ark.: Civil War Roundtable Associates, 1988.

Collins, George K. *Memories of the 149th Regiment, New York Volunteer Infantry.* Syracuse: Author Published, 1891.

Cooke, John Esten. *Wearing of the Gray; Being Personal Portraits, Scenes and Adventures of the War.* New York: E. B. Treat & Co. 1867.

Cowtan, Charles W. *Services of the Tenth New York Volunteers (National Zouaves) in the War of the Rebellion.* New York: C. H. Ludwig, 1882.

Craft, David. *One Hundred and Forty-First Regiment Pennsylvania Volunteers.* Towanda, Pa.: Reporter-Journal Printing Company, 1885.

Cudsworth, William H. *History of the First Regiment Massachusetts Infantry.* Boston: Walker, Fuller and Company, 1866.

Curtis, O. B. *History of the Twenty-Fourth Michigan of the Iron Brigade, Known as the Detroit and Wayne County Regiment.* Detroit: Winn and Hammond, 1891.

Davis, Archie K. *The Boy Colonel: The Life and Times of Henry King Burgwyn, Jr.* Chapel Hill, N.C.: University of North Carolina Press, 1985.

Davis, Charles E. *Three Years in the Army: The Story of the Thirteenth Massachusetts Volunteers from July 16, 1861 to August 1, 1864.* Boston: Estes & Lownat, 1864.

Davis, Oliver Wilson. *Life of David Bell Birney, Major General United States Volunteers.* Philadelphia: King & Baird, 1867.

Dawes, Rufus R. *Service with the Sixth Wisconsin Volunteers.* Marietta, Ohio: E. R. Alderman and Sons, 1890.

de Trobriand, P. Regis. *Four Years with the Army of the Potomac.* Boston: Ticknor and Company, 1889.

Dickert, August. *History of Kershaw's Brigade.* Newberry, S.C.: Elbert H. Hull Company, 1899.

Divine, John E. *Eighth Virginia.* Lynchburg, Va.: H. E. Howard, Inc., 1983.

Dooley, John Edward. *John Dooley, Confederate Soldier, His War Journal.* Washington, D.C.: Georgetown University Press, 1945.

Douglas, Henry Kyd. *I Rode with Stonewall.* Chapel Hill, N.C.: University of North Carolina Press, 1940.

Dowdey, Clifford, and Louis H. Manarin. *The Wartime Papers of R. E. Lee.* New York: Bramhall House, 1961.

Downey, James W. *A Lethal Tour of Duty: A History of the 142nd Pennsylvania Volunteer Infantry, 1862–1865.* M. A. Thesis—Indiana University of Pennsylvania, 1995.

Driver, Robert J. *52nd Virginia Infantry.* Lynchburg, Va.: H. E. Howard, Inc., 1986.

Dunkelman, Mark H., and Michael J. Winey. *The Hardtack Regiment: An Illustrated History of the 154th Regiment, New York State Infantry Volunteers.* East Brunswick, N.J.: Fairleigh Dickinson University Press, 1981.

Dunn, Craig L. *Iron Men, Iron Will.* Indianapolis: Guild Press, 1995.

Early, Jubal A. *Autobiographical Sketch and Narrative of the War Between the States.* Philadelphia: J. B. Lippincott Company, 1912.

Eggleston, George Cary. *A Rebel's Recollections.* New York: G. P. Putnam's Sons, 1905.

Everson, Guy R., and Edward W. Simpson, Jr. *Far, Far from Home.* New York: Oxford University Press, 1994.

Favill, J. *Diary of a Young Officer.* Chicago: R. R. Donnelly & Sons, 1909.

Fields, Frank E. *Twenty-eighth Virginia.* Lynchburg, Va.: H. E. Howard, Inc., 1985.

Fleming, Francis P. "Francis P. Fleming in the War for Southern Independence." *The Florida Historical Quarterly,* vol. 27 (1949): 143–55.

Floyd, Frederick C. *History of the Fortieth (Mozart) Regiment, New York Volunteers.* Boston: F. H. Gilson Company, 1909.

Foote, Frank. "Marching in Clover." *Philadelphia Weekly Times,* October 8, 1881.

Ford, Andrew. *Story of the Fifteenth Regiment Massachusetts Volunteers Infantry.* Clinton, Mass.: Press of W. J. Coulter, 1898.

Frederick, Gilbert. *The Story of a Regiment—The Fifty-Seventh New York Volunteer Infantry in the War of the Rebellion.* Chicago: C. H. Morgan Company, 1895.

Freeman, Douglas S. *R. E. Lee.* New York: Scribners, 1935.

———. *Lee's Lieutenants.* 3 vols. New York: Charles Scribner's Sons, 1949–51.

Frye, Dennis. *Second Virginia Infantry.* Lynchburg, Va.: H. E. Howard, Inc., 1984.

Fuller, Charles A. *Personal Recollections of the War of 1861: In the 61st New York Volunteer Infantry.* Sherburne, N.Y.: News Job Printing House, 1906.

Fulton, W. F. *The War Reminiscences of William Frierson Fulton II, 5th Alabama Battalion, Archer's Brigade.* Gaithersville, Md.: Butternut Press, 1986.

Galway, Thomas F. *The Valiant Hours: Narrative of "Captain Brevet," An Irish-American in the Army of the Potomac.* Harrisburg, Pa.: Stackpole, 1961.

Gerrish, Theodore, *Army Life; A Private's Reminiscences of the Civil War.* Portland, Maine: Hoyt, Fogg & Donham, 1882.

Gibbon, John. *Personal Recollections of the War.* New York: G. P. Putnam's Sons, 1928.

Gilmor, Harry. *Four Years in the Saddle.* New York: Harper & Brothers, 1866.

Goldsborough, William W. *The Maryland Line.* Port Washington, N.Y.: Kennikat Press, 1972.

Gordon, John B. *Reminiscences of the Civil War.* New York: Charles Scribner's Sons, 1903.

Gottfried, Bradley M. "Fisher's Brigade at Gettysburg: The Big Round Top Controversy." *Gettysburg Magazine,* number 19: 84–93.

———. *Stopping Pickett—The History of the Philadelphia Brigade.* Shippensburg, Pa.: White Mane Publishing Co., Inc., 1999.

Gragg, Rod. *Covered with Glory.* New York: HarperCollins, 2000.

Gregory, G. Howard. *Thirty-eighth Virginia.* Lynchburg, Va.: H. E. Howard, Inc., 1988.

Grunder, Charles S., and Brandon H. Beck. *The Second Battle of Winchester,* Lynchburg, Va.: H. E. Howard, Inc., 1989.

Gunn, Ralph W. *Twenty-fourth Virginia.* Lynchburg, Va.: H. E. Howard, Inc., 1987.

Haines, Alanson A. *History of the Fifteenth Regiment New Jersey Volunteers.* New York: Jenkins & Thomas, Printers, 1883.

Hale, Laura V., and Stanley S. Phillips. *History of the Forty-Ninth Virginia Infantry, C.S.A.: "Extra Billy Smith's Boys."* Lanham, Md.: S. S. Phillips, 1981.

Hamilton, J. G. de Roulhac. *The Shotwell Papers, Volume I.* Raleigh, N.C.: North Carolina Historical Commission, 1929–31.

Hamlin, Percy Gatling. *Old Bald Head—The Portrait of a Soldier.* Strasburg, Va: Shenandoah Publishing House, 1940.

Hankins, Samuel W. *Simple Story of a Soldier.* Nashville: Confederate Veteran, n.d.

Hardin, M. D. *History of the Twelfth Regiment, Pennsylvania Reserve Volunteer Corps.* New York: M. D. Hardin, 1890.

Harris, James S. *Historical Sketches: Seventh Regiment, North Carolina Troops.* Ann Arbor, Mich.: University Microfilms, 1972.

Haskell, Monroe. "The Road to Gettysburg—The Diary and Letters of Leonidas Torrence of the Gaston Guards," *North Carolina Historical Review* (October 1959): 512.

Haynes, Martin A. *History of the Second New Hampshire Regiment: Its Camps, Marches, and Battles.* Manchester, N.H.: Charles F. Livingston Printer, 1865.

Hays, Gilbert A. *Under the Red Patch—The Story of the Sixty-Third Regiment, Pennsylvania Volunteers, 1861–1864.* Pittsburgh, Pa: Sixty-Third Pennsylvania Volunteers Regimental Association, 1908.

Heth, Henry. "Letter from Major General Henry Heth of A. P. Hill's Corps, A.N.V." *Southern Historical Society Papers,* vol. 4 (1877): 151–60.

———. *The Memoirs of Henry Heth.* Westport, Conn.: Greenwood Press, 1974.

Hitz, Louise W., ed. *The Letters of Frederick C. Winkler.* Privately printed, 1963.

Hoke, Jacob. *The Great Invasion.* New York: Thomas Yoseloff, 1959.

Holcombe, R. I. *History of the First Regiment Minnesota Volunteer Infantry, 1861–1864.* Gaithersburg, Md.: VanSickle, 1987.

Holt, David. *A Mississippi Rebel in the Army of Northern Virginia: The Civil War Memoirs of Private David Holt.* Baton Rouge, La.: Louisiana State University Press, 1995.

Houghton, Edwin B. *Campaigns of the Seventeenth Maine.* Portland, Maine: Short and Loring, 1866.

Howard, Oliver O. *Autobiography of Oliver Otis Howard.* 2 vols. New York: Baker and Taylor Company, 1907.

Hufham, J. D., Jr. "Gettysburg." *The Wake Forest Student,* vol. 16 (1897): 452–54.

Hussey, George A. *History of the Ninth Regiment N.Y.S.M. (Eighty-third N.Y. Volunteers).* New York: J. S. Ogilvie, 1889.

Irby, Richard. *Historical Sketch of the Nottoway Grays.* Richmond: J. W. Ferguson and Son, 1878.

Jacobs, M. *Notes on the Rebel Invasion of Maryland and Pennsylvania and the Battle of Gettysburg.* Philadelphia: J. B. Lippincott & Company, 1864.

Jones, Terry L. *Lee's Tigers.* Baton Rouge, La.: Louisiana State University Press, 1987.

Johnston, David E. *Four Years a Soldier.* Princeton, W.Va.: n.p., 1887.

Jordan, William B. *Red Diamond Regiment: The 17th Maine Infantry, 1862–1865.* Shippensburg, Pa.: White Mane Publishing Co., Inc., 1996.

Judson, Amos M. *History of the Eighty-Third Regiment, Pennsylvania Volunteers.* Erie, Pa.: B. F. H. Lynn, 1865.

Kepler, Thomas. *History of the Three Months' and Three Years' Service from April 16, 1861, to June, 1864, of the Fourth Regiment Ohio Volunteer Infantry in the War for the Union.* Cleveland: Leader Printing Company, 1886.

Ladd, David L., and Audrey J. Ladd. *The Bachelder Papers.* 3 vols. Dayton, Ohio: Morningside Press, 1994.

Laine, Gary J., and Morris M. Penny. *Law's Alabama Brigade in the War Between the Union and the Confederacy*. Shippensburg, Pa.: White Mane Publishing Co., Inc., 1996.

Leon, Louis. *Diary of a Tar Heel*. Charlotte, N.C.: Stone Publishing Company, 1913.

Loehr, Charles T. *War History of the Old First Virginia Infantry Regiment, Army of Northern Virginia*. Richmond: William Ellis Jones, Printer, 1884.

Lochren, William. "The First Minnesota at Gettysburg." Minnesota MOLLUS, vol. 3: 41–56.

Longacre, Edward. *To Gettysburg and Beyond: The Twelfth New Jersey Volunteer Infantry, II Corps, Army of the Potomac, 1862–1865*. Hightstown, N.J.: Longstreet House, 1988.

Longstreet, James. "Lee's Invasion of Pennsylvania." *Battles and Leaders of the Civil War*, vol. 3: 244–51.

———. *From Manassas to Appomattox*. Philadelphia: J. B. Lippincott, 1903.

Lord, Walter L., ed. *The Fremantle Diary*. New York: Little, Brown and Company, 1954.

Lynch, John W. *The Dorman-Masbourne Letters*. Senoia, Ga.: Down South Publishing Company, 1995.

MacNamara, Daniel G. *The History of the Ninth Regiment, Massachusetts Volunteer Infantry, Second Brigade, First Division, Fifth Army Corps, Army of the Potomac, June, 1861–June, 1864*. Boston: E. B. Stillings, 1899.

McClellan, H. B. *I Rode with Jeb Stuart: The Life and Campaigns of Major General J.E.B. Stuart*. Bloomington, Ind.: Indiana University Press, 1958.

McDaid, William K. *Four Years of Arduous Service*. Ph.D. Dissertation, Michigan State University, 1987.

McKim, Randolph. *A Soldier's Recollections*. New York: Longmans Green, 1911.

Mahood, Wayne. *Written in Blood*. Hightstown, N.J.: Longstreet House, 1997.

Malone, Bartlett Y. *Whipt 'Em Everytime; The Diary of Bartlett Yancey Malone.* Jackson, Tenn.: McCowat-Mercer Press, 1960.

Marbaker, Thomas B. *History of the Eleventh New Jersey Volunteers.* Hightstown, N.J.: Longstreet House, 1990.

Mark, Penrose G. *Red: White: and Blue Badge, Pennsylvania Veteran Volunteers. A History of the 93rd Regiment.* Harrisburg, Pa.: The Aughinbaugh Press, 1911.

Marshall, Charles. "Events Leading Up to the Battle of Gettysburg," *SHSP,* vol. 23 (1895): 205–29.

Martin, David. *Gettysburg—July 1.* Conshohocken, Pa.: Combined Books, 1996.

Marvin, Edwin E. *The Fifth Regiment, Connecticut Volunteers: A History Compiled from Diaries and Official Reports.* Hartford, Conn.: Wiley, Waterman & Eaton, 1899.

Matthews, Richard E. *The 149th Pennsylvania Volunteer Infantry Unit in the Civil War.* Jefferson, N.C.: McFarland & Company, 1994.

Mattocks, Charles. *Unspoiled Heart, The Journal of Charles Mattocks of the 17th Maine.* Knoxville, Tenn.: University of Tennessee Press, 1994.

Maury, Dabney Herndon. *Recollections of a Virginian in the Mexican, Indian, and Civil Wars.* New York: C. Scribner's Sons, 1894.

Meade, George Gordon. *The Life and Letters of George Gordon Meade: Major-General United States.* New York: Charles Scribner's Sons, 1913.

Mills, George Henry. *History of the 16th North Carolina Regiment (originally 6th N.C. Regiment) in the Civil War.* Hamilton, N.Y: Edmonston Pubishers, 1992.

Moore, Frank, ed. *Rebellion Record: A Diary of American Events with Documents and Narratives, Illustrative Incidents, Poetry, etc.* Vol. 7. New York, 1864.

Moore, Robert Augustus. *A Life for the Confederacy.* Jackson, Tenn.: McCowat-Mercer Press, 1959.

Morhous, Henry C. *Reminiscences of the 123rd Regiment, New York State Volunteers.* Greenwich, N.Y.: People's Journal Book and Job Office, 1879.

Morse, F. W. *Personal Experiences in the War of the Rebellion, from December, 1862, to July, 1865.* Albany, N.Y.: Munsell Printer, 1866.

Muffly, Joseph W., ed. *The Story of Our Regiment: A History of the 148th Pennsyvlania Volunteers.* Des Moines, Iowa: Kenyon Printing and Manufacturing Company, 1904.

Nash, Eugene A. *A History of the 44th New York Volunteer Infantry.* Chicago: R. R. Donnelley & Sons Company, 1911.

Nesbitt, Mark. *35 Days to Gettysburg.* Harrisburg, Pa.: Stackpole Books, 1992.

Newell, Joseph. *"Ours" Annals of the Tenth Regiment Massachusetts Volunteers.* Springfield, Mass.: C. A. Nichols & Co., 1875.

Nolan, Allen T. *The Iron Brigade.* New York: McMillan Company, 1961.

Nye, Wilbur Sturtevant. *Here Come the Rebels!* Baton Rouge, La.: Louisiana State University Press, 1965.

Oates, William C. *The War Between the Union and Confederacy and its Lost Opportunities.* New York: Neale Publishing Co., 1905.

Osborn, Hartwell. *Trials and Triumphs: The Record of the Fifty-fifth Ohio Volunteer Infantry.* Chicago: A. C. McClurg, 1904.

Osborne, Charles C. *Jubal—The Life and Times of General Jubal A. Early, CSA.* Chapel Hill, N.C.: Algonquin Books, 1992.

Page, Charles D. *History of the Fourteenth Regiment, Connecticut Vol. Infantry.* Gaithersburg, Md.: Van Sickle, 1987.

Palmer, Edwin F. *The Second Brigade or Camp Life.* Montpelier, Vt.: Printed by E. P. Walton, 1864.

Parker, Francis J. *The Story of the Thirty-Second Massachusetts Infantry.* Boston: C. W. Calkins & Company, 1880.

Parker, John L. *Henry Wilson's Regiment: History of the Twenty-second Regiment, Massachusetts Infantry.* Boston: Press of Rand Avery Company, 1887.

Parsons, George W. *Put the Vermonters Ahead: The First Vermont Brigade in the Civil War.* Shippensburg, Pa.: White Mane Publishing Co., Inc., 1996.

Pender, William D. *The General to his Lady.* Chapel Hill, N.C.: University of North Carolina Press, 1965.

Pendleton, Constance. *Confederate Memoirs.* Bryn Athyn, Pa.: n.p., 1958.

Pennsylvania at Gettysburg—Ceremonies at the Dedication of the Monuments, Harrisburg, Pa.: Wm. Stanley Ray, State Printer, 1904.

Pettit, Ira S. *Diary of a Dead Man.* New York: Eastern Acorn Press, 1976.

Pfanz, Donald C. *Richard S. Ewell—A Soldier's Life.* Chapel Hill, N.C.: University of North Carolina Press, 1998.

Polley, Joseph B. *Hood's Texas Brigade.* New York: Neale Publishing Company, 1910.

Poriss, Gerry H., and Ralph G. Poriss. *While My Country is in Danger: The Life and Letters of Lieutenant Colonel Richard S. Thompson.* Hamilton, N.Y.: Edmonston Publishing 1994.

Porter, John T. *Under the Maltese Cross: Campaigns of the 155th Pennsylvania Regiment.* Pittsburgh, Pa.:155th Regimental Association, 1910.

Powell, R. M. "With Hood at Gettysburg." *Philadelphia Weekly Times,* December 13, 1884.

Priest, John M. *John T. McMahon's Diary of the 136th New York.* Shippensburg, Pa.: White Mane Publishing Co., Inc., 1993.

Pula, James S. *The Sigel Regiment: A History of the Twenty-sixth Wisconsin Volunteer Infantry, 1862–1865.* Campbell, Calif.: Savas Publishing Company, 1998.

Quint, Alonzo H. *The Record of the Second Massachusetts Infantry, 1861–1865.* Boston: James P. Walker, 1867.

Rauscher, Frank. *Music on the March: 1861–'65 with the Army of the Potomac, 114th R egiment P.V., Collis' Zouaves.* Philadelphia: Press of W. F. Fell and Company, 1892.

Rankin, Thomas. *Twenty-Third Virginia.* Lynchburg, Va.: H. E. Howard, Inc., 1985.

Reese, Timothy. *Sykes' Regular Infantry Division, 1861–1864: A History of Regular United States Infantry Operations in the Civil War's Eastern Theater.* Jefferson, N.C.: McFarland, 1990.

Reidenbaugh, Lowell. *Thirty-Third Virginia.* Lynchburg, Va.: H. E. Howard, Inc., 1987.

———. *Twenty-Seventh Virginia.* Lynchburg, Va.: H. E. Howard, Inc., 1993.

Rhodes, Elisha Hunt. *All for the Union: A History of the 2nd Rhode Island Volunteer Infantry in the War of the Great Rebellion.* Lincoln, R.I.: A. Mowbray, 1985.

Riggs, David F. *Seventh Virginia Infantry.* Lynchburg, Va.: H. E. Howard, Inc., 1982.

Riley, Franklin L. *Grandfather's Journal.* Dayton, Ohio: Morningside, 1988.

Robertson, James Irwin. *Eighteenth Virginia Infantry.* Lynchburg, Va.: H. E. Howard, Inc., 1984.

Roe, Alfred S. *The Tenth Regiment, Massachusetts Volunteer Infantry, 1861–1864.* Springfield, Mass.: Tenth Regiment Veteran Association, 1909.

Rosenblatt, Emil, and Ruth Rosenblatt. *Hard Marching Every Day.* Lawrence, Kans.: University Press of Kansas, 1992.

Schildt, John W. *Roads to Gettysburg.* Parsons, W.Va.: McClain Printing Co., 1978.

Sheeran, James B. *Confederate Chaplain.* Milwaukee, Wisc.: Bruce Publishing Company, 1960.

Silliken, Ruth L., ed. *The Rebel Yell & Yankee Hurrah.* Camden, Maine: Down East Books, 1985.

Silver, James W., ed. *A Life for the Confederacy.* Wilmington, N.C.: Broadfoot Publishing Company, 1991.

Simmers, William. *The Volunteers' Manual, or Ten Months with the One Hundred and Fifty-third Pennsylvania Volunteers.* Easton, Pa.: D. H. Neiman, 1863.

Simpson, Harold B. *Hood's Texas Brigade: Lee's Grenadier Guard.* Waco, Tex.: Texian Press, 1970.

Small, A. R. *The Sixteenth Maine Regiment in the War of the Rebellion 1861–1865.* Portland, Maine: Thurston & Co., 1886.

Smith, A. P. *The Seventy-Sixth Regiment, New York Volunteers.* Cortland, N.Y.: Truair, Smith and Miles, Printers, 1867.

Smith, Jacob. *Camps and Campaigns of the 107th Regiment Ohio Volunteer Infantry.* N.p., n.d.

Spear, Ellis. *The Civil War Recollections of General Ellis Spear.* Orono, Maine: University of Maine Press, 1997.

Stevens, Jno. W. *Reminiscences of the Civil War.* Hillsboro, Tex.: Hillsboro Mirror Print, 1902.

Stiles, Robert. *Four Years under Marse Robert.* New York: The Neale Publishing Company, 1903.

Storrs, John. *The Twentieth Connecticut.* Ansonia, Conn.: Press of the Naugatuck Valley Sentinel, 1886.

Tervis, C. V. *The History of the Fighting Fourteenth: Published in Commemoration of the Fiftieth Anniversary of the Muster of the Regiment into the United States Service.* Brooklyn: Brooklyn Eagle Press, 1911.

Toombs, Samuel. *Reminiscences of the War.* Orange, N.J.: Printed at the Journal Office, 1878.

Trimble, Isaac. "The Campaign and Battle of Gettysburg." *Confederate Veteran Magazine,* vol. 25 (1917): 209–13.

Tucker, Glenn. *High Tide at Gettysburg: The Campaign in Pennsylvania.* Indianapolis, Ind.: Bobbs-Merrill Company, 1968.

Uhler, George H. *Camps and Campaigns of the 93d Regiment, Penna. Vols.* N.p., n.d., 1898.

United States War Department. *The War of the Rebellion: A Compilation of the Official Records of the Union and Confederate Armies.* 128 vols. Washington: U.S. Government Printing Office, 1880–1901.

Van Santvood, Cornelius. *The One Hundred and Twentieth N.Y.S. Volunteers. A Narrative of its Services in the War for the Union.* Rondout, N.Y.: Regimental Association & Kingston Freeman Press, 1894.

Vautier, John D. *History of the Eighty-Eighth Pennsylvania Volunteers in the War for the Union, 1861–1865.* Philadelphia: J. B. Lippincott Company, 1894.

Waitt, Ernest L. *History of the Nineteenth Regiment Massachusetts Volunteer Infantry.* Salem, Mass.: Salem Press Company, 1906.

Wallace, Lee A. *First Virginia Infantry.* Lynchburg, Va.: H. E. Howard, Inc., 1985.

Ward, Joseph. *History of the One Hundred and Sixth Pennsylvania Volunteers, 2d Brigade, 2d Division, 2d Corps, 1861–1865.* Philadelphia: Grant, Faires & Rodgers, 1883.

Ward, W. C. "Incidents and Personal Experiences on the Battlefield at Gettysburg," *Confederate Veteran,* vol. 8 (1900): 345–49.

Welch, Spencer Glasgow. *A Confederate Surgeon's Letters to His Wife.* New York: Neale Publishing Co., 1911.

Welles, Gideon. *Diary of Gideon Welles.* Boston: Houghton Mifflin Company, 1911.

Wellman, Manly W. *Rebel Boast.* New York: Henry Holt and Co., 1956.

Wert, Jeffry D. *General James Longstreet: The Confederacy's Most Controversial Soldier.* New York: Simon & Schuster, 1993.

West, John C. *A Texan in Search of a Fight.* Waco, Tex.: Press of J. S. Hill and Company, 1901.

Weygant, Charles H. *History of the One Hundred and Twenty-Fourth Regiment, N.Y.S.V.* Newburgh, N.Y.: Journal Printing House, 1877.

White, Gregory C. *A History of the 31st Georgia Volunteer Infantry: Lawton-Gordon-Evans Brigade Army of Northern Virginia Confederate States of America 1861–1865.* Baltimore: Butternut and Blue, 1997.

Williams, Alpheus. *From the Cannon's Mouth.* Detroit: Wayne State University Press, 1959.

Wilson, Lawrence. *Itinerary of the Seventh Ohio Volunteer Infantry, 1861–1864, With Roster, Portraits, and Biographies.* New York: Neale Publishing Company, 1907.

Wood, William N. *Reminiscences of Big I.* Charlottesville, Va.: Michie Company, 1909.

Woodbury, Augustus. *The Second Rhode Island Regiment: A Narrative of Military Operations.* Providence, R.I.: Valpey, Angell, and Company, 1875.

Woodward, Evan M. *Our Campaigns—The Second Regiment, Pennsylvania Reserve Volunteers.* Philadelphia: J. E. Potter, 1865.

Wyckoff, Mac. *A History of the Third South Carolina Infantry, 1861–1865.* Fredericksburg, Va.: Sergeant Kirkland's Museum and Historical Society, 1995.

Young, William A. *56th Virginia Infantry.* Lynchburg, Va.: H. E. Howard, Inc., 1990.

Index

First names were added where known.